Surviving Deployment

A guide for military families

Karen M. Pavlicin

Elva Resa Publishing   Saint Paul, Minnesota

Surviving Deployment: A guide for military families

Front cover photo by Chris Taraschke. Back cover photo by Karen Pavlicin.
Cover design by Steve Swenson.
All personal stories used with permission. Some names have been changed.
Referenced articles, surveys, and book passages used with permission.
Information in this book is intended to provide ideas and suggestions to military families
for positively coping with separations. Each situation is unique and you should seek
professional or medical advice as appropriate.

Library of Congress Catalog Card Number 2002095570

ISBN-13: 978-0-9657483-6-0
ISBN-10: 0-9657483-6-7

Printed in the United States of America.
                    10

Fonts: Minion Pro, Lucida Sans, Minion Condensed, Switzerland Condensed.

http://www.elvaresa.com/
http://www.survivingdeployment.com/

To the service members of the United States Armed Forces.

*To their loved ones who watch them leave home
to fight wars, keep peace, and help the less fortunate.*

To my husband, Fightin' Bob.

Semper fi

de • ploy (de ploi´) *v. to spread out so as to form a wider front*

de • ploy´ ment *n. 1. the assignment of military personnel to temporary, unaccompanied tours of duty 2. a fact of military life*

Contents

Acknowledgments

Although I cannot list everyone by name, I would like to first acknowledge the hundreds of military spouses, service members, and children, who willingly shared their stories in the hopes of making a deployment easier for a fellow military family. This book is as much their story as it is mine, and now yours. Thank you, especially, to Kristin Smith who was brave enough to share her personal journals.

Thanks to Joan Lorenz from Camp Pendleton's Family Service Center for her dedication to the Key Volunteer Training program and to Pat Millish from Camp Lejeune's Family Service Center for her leadership and support of the Bride's School.

To the many volunteers who serve military families in all branches, you rarely see the awesome impact of your kind words and caring deeds. My appreciation to the many Marine Corps families who helped me to see the positive side of deployments, especially to Carol Scheferman, a key volunteer who truly cared.

Thanks to Gene Peters, Jodi Parker Seidner, Paula Price, Chris Taraschke, Kelly Vandiver, Crystal Marsden, Deb Quinn Foley, Julie LaBelle, Linda Greene, Jen Juckes, Judy Hissong, Donna Gamble, Gwen Gerdes, and Jake simply for being there. To the band of brothers who kept Bob safe and sane, you know who you are; I owe you more than care package chocolate chip cookies.

A special thank you to my parents, David and Alma Price, for their unending support of all my endeavors. For their guidance to live each day for today. They and my siblings Dave, Tammy, and Lori, have always strengthened my faith.

Thanks also to my mother-in-law. Mary Pavlicin's kind words during my husband's deployments showed an understanding and empathy that emerged from the many long nights she waited for her husband, Major George Pavlicin, USMC (Ret), to return from lengthy deployments to post-WWII China and the Korean War. Thank you for your wonderful example.

My editor, Major H-C. "Pete" Peterson, USMC (Ret), deserves a medal for his patience, candor, tact, and insight. Thank you, Pete, for your constant encouragement.

Many dear friends and colleagues took on all sorts of jobs to make sure I completed this project; thanks especially to Christy Lyon, Michelle Judd, Steve Swenson, and Beth Hjort.

Lt Colonel Kevin Foley, USMC, held me up. Thanks Kevin, Gene, Kurt, Jim, Tom, Dave, Andy, Russ, and Captain Peyton Berg, USMC, and the team at Ft Snelling, for helping me and Alexander send Bob on his final deployment.

Finally, and most importantly, to my loving and much loved husband: Thank you, Bob, for loving me from the ends of the earth, literally. Our survival through your many deployments enriched our life together, deepened our respect and appreciation for each other, and made our love grow stronger. Thank you for learning with me what is important in life. Welcome home.

A Personal Introduction

It was a warm and windy autumn afternoon. Orange leaves blew across the lawn. As my husband and I walked under the Arch of Swords and down the church steps, many onlookers thought of it as just another special part of our wedding ceremony. Our Best Man slapped my behind with his sword and shouted, "Welcome to the Marine Corps, Mrs. Pavlicin."

Two years earlier, my then boyfriend, Bob Pavlicin, had set off on a six-month "cruise." I was in graduate school intent on becoming a teacher. And though it was difficult to be apart, we both found his Mediterranean deployment to be a good learning experience. Bob was able to visit several port cities in a relatively peaceful time of history and I was able to concentrate on my studies. We learned how to communicate through letters and discovered something we hadn't necessarily realized in our prior three years of dating: we truly loved one another.

As homecomings usually are, the "six-month embrace" was better than any chocolate sundae I'd ever tasted. We were engaged and began the lifelong planning of a marriage. Nine months later, just as we were about to blow out the candles on Bob's birthday cake, the TV screen threw out flames of its own. The Coalition had bombed Baghdad and Operation Desert Storm was underway. The following week Bob deployed with the 24th Marine Expeditionary Unit (MEU).

As I watched the buses leave through my rear view mirror, I understood this deployment would be different. Several things were against me on this one: we were planning a wedding in New York, while I lived in Bob's townhouse outside the base in North Carolina and he lived on a ship off the coast of Iraq. I didn't know very many people in town because I hadn't lived there long, and had done almost everything with just Bob. Since I was not yet a *military wife* it was difficult to get involved with the spouse support groups. I didn't even have an ID to get on base.

It was my first experience with *imminent danger pay*. Somehow the fact he was getting paid *more* worried me! "Imminent" seemed such an ominous word, not to mention "danger." In a short while, the 24th MEU moved ashore into Northern Iraq to set up a security zone for the Kurds. I became glued to CNN, searching for any news about Operation Provide Comfort. I spent many nights just sitting by the phone.

The ship was delayed a month but we did finally have a grand homecoming at the beach exactly two months before our wedding day.

Which brings us back to "Welcome to the Marine Corps, Mrs. Pavlicin." By marrying a Marine, I became a Marine Corps Wife. I remember thinking it would be *easier*! (At least I would have an ID card!) In reality, I had no idea how all-encompassing that welcome would be. For however distinctly civilian and independent I tried to be, with my husband ordered half way around the world, I could not escape being an intimate and integral part of this way of life.

You have to know a bit about my personality. I am not quite as forgiving, patient, or assenting as most of the other faithful spouses I've met. In fact, as far as independence goes, I'm downright stubborn and I'm my own boss. I quickly learned that in the military, my opinion didn't count. I didn't mind giving up my first teaching offer to move to Virginia. It didn't matter that we were only going to be there four months. We were together. That mattered. Moving across country to California was exciting and I truly looked forward to it, even though my teaching credentials wouldn't transfer. We were together...for two months anyway.

That summer Bob joined a busy outfit. We discovered that a Marine division does a lot of *field exercises*. We counted once. During his 19-month tour there, the longest period of time Bob had a "normal" routine (which in this case means coming home to sleep at night) was five weeks. He spent our first wedding anniversary in the California high desert at Twenty-Nine Palms. He came home for a week in November during which we attended the Marine Corps Birthday Ball. The total number of days he didn't have to report to work (including weekends) was four between September and December. Two of those included Thanksgiving Day and the day after. Talk about needing a vacation together. All we could think about was how peaceful Christmas in the mountains was going to be. True to form, it wasn't long before I could hear gunfire in the background on a scratchy phone line from half way around the world: in December, Bob flew to Somalia for yet another military operation, Restore Hope.

It was after the second canceled homecoming from Somalia that I decided to write this book.

And now that I've complained as much as we spouses are allowed to (after all, I *did* marry a Marine!), allow me to brag. The fact that we made it through so much separation at such a crucial time in our relationship is a tribute to our love, commitment and friendship. The fact is, thousands of couples and families do it all the time. It is never easy for anyone.

During our initiation into the Corps (this all happened within four years), we had many military friends who did not deploy. This is no longer the case. Every active duty service member we know personally has deployed more than once. And we know reservists and national guardsmen who have been called as well. It shows no signs of slowing down.

My hope in writing this book is that what I have learned, as well as the experiences other spouses and families have shared in this book, will help someone else — *you* — to survive your spouse's military deployment.

I've tried to make this book as practical as possible, so you'll find lots of checklists and examples. I've also relied on the practical wisdom passed on by the many people I interviewed, so you'll find heartfelt, touching, and often familiar personal stories.

I hope you will come to see your separation as a positive challenge: a time in which to mature individually, grow closer together, appreciate and discover more about yourselves, your relationship, and life.

And always, thank God for homecomings.

—kmp

The Way It Is

It's when you're safe at home that you wish you were having an adventure. When you're having an adventure you wish you were safe at home.

—Thornton Wilder

Duty in a Changing World

"Eleven years with no deployments, and she gets sent in her last eight months."

> — Tony, in a letter to family announcing his wife Linda's short-notice 6-month deployment to Guantanamo Bay, Cuba, shortly after announcing her plans to resign from her post as Navy family doctor.

"There is no longer any doubt in my mind that my Reserves work is more than a weekend hobby."

> — Michael, an Army Reserve Military Policeman in Georgia. As one of more than 80,000 Guard and reserve members mobilized for the war on terrorism, he helped rig humanitarian loads of food and cold weather materials for airdrops in Afghanistan.

"I'm so happy this is over, now we can get back to normal life!"

> — Sabrina, to her fiancé, Raymond, an Air Force Major, upon his return from Operation Provide Relief in Mombasa, Kenya. He flew back to Somalia three months later to assist the United Nations with Operation Restore Hope.

"My husband is a computer expert in a communications unit. Only grunts deploy."

> — Ginger, whose husband Peter, a Marine Corporal, later deployed for six months to Desert Storm in the Persian Gulf, stopping in Bangladesh on his way home to help flood victims in Operation Sea Angel. Much to Ginger's surprise, he even got his hands dirty.

Everyone in the military—or married to someone in the Armed Forces (Army, Navy, Air Force, Marines, the seven Reserve components, and the Coast Guard)—knows about deployments. Yet even the most experienced feel unprepared when we find out our loved one is deploying. On top of the very personal concerns we have, we ask: Why does my spouse have to deploy? Why is the United States involved? Why is the world like this? Before you read this book on how to deal positively with your spouse's deployment, it may help to first understand that deployments are a reality for everyone in the military and understand why deployments are necessary.

Ten years after the end of the Cold War, at the beginning of 2001, there were about 1.4 million people on active duty in the US military. At any given time, almost 200,000 were stationed overseas, and almost 20,000 afloat. Some were stationed in foreign countries, but many were deployed: Army units rotated in and out of Bosnia and Kuwait, Navy ships steamed the seven seas for months at a time, Marine expeditionary units provided "forward presence," Air Force units deployed to Saudi Arabia and Europe, and Coast Guard ships went off on extended anti-drug missions.

And deployments aren't only for those on active duty. The Armed Forces also include Reserves, and in early 2001 there were just about as many Reserves (members of units, as well as individual and standby) as active duty members. On any given day, about 5,000 were deployed, some for active duty training aboard ships and at warfare centers, others providing logistics and other expertise in Central America, the Middle East, Asia, Africa, and around the globe—even in Antarctica. Some Reserve and National Guard units—like the 49th Armored Division from Texas—were even on multi-month deployments as units, serving next to and indistinguishable from the "regular" military.

Deployments are part of the duty assumed by anyone in the military. Whether for training, exercises, contingencies, operations, or combat, since we live in a world of threats, our military needs to be ready to respond. And that means leaving home.

The Defense Department considers you deployed if you are: "performing duties in a training exercise or operation at a location or under circumstances that make it impossible or infeasible for the member to spend off-duty time in the housing at the member's permanent duty station or home port."

What these words translate to in the everyday lives of service members, spouses, and families is separation, excitement, loneliness, worry, and challenge!

The World Is Ever-Changing. But Duty Remains.

When she was preparing this book, Karen told me about when she was in high school in the 1980s. She attended a "Critical Issues Seminar," where a group of high school juniors gathered to conduct research on the major problems facing our nation and to prepare recommendations to the President for action. Her group studied the Nuclear Arms Race. She remembers discussions about nuclear war and what kind of people the Russians might be that they would pose such a threat to us.

In her research, she found that our military strategic goals had been the same for over 40 years: to deter nuclear attack and contain communism. Back in high school, she thought that if we got rid of the Soviet threat, if there were no Cold War, we would no longer have this great need for a trained and ready Armed Forces. She now realizes this isn't true. Critical issues continue, they just take on different faces. Our enemies have changed, but there still are enemies.

I remember when I was in Navy ROTC, preparing for a commission in the Marines. The Vietnam war was ending, and I commented to Burl Wright, a tough old Marine Master Sergeant who had fought at the Chosin Reservoir in Korea as well as Vietnam: "Hey, Top, I guess peace is here and they won't need us military types any more!" He answered my cocky college smartness with the wisdom of one who has seen too much war and knows its firm place in the human experience: "You know, Mr. Peterson, this country has never seen a decade without American troops shooting and getting shot at somewhere in the world, and it ain't gonna change now; you stay in for twenty, you'll see a war." How right he was.

Not everyone realized this, however. In the early 1990s it looked like a period of sustained peace might be at hand. The Cold War was over, and its great symbol, the Berlin Wall, had been torn down. The Soviet Union was no more. Arms control agreements eliminated entire classes of nuclear weapons. In January 1993, the Chemical Weapons Convention was signed in Paris, renouncing the use of chemical weapons. Desert Storm showed that aggression "will not stand." And the number of armed conflicts in the world was actually starting to decrease. President George H. W. Bush even spoke about a "new world order."

Thinking that the threat had been greatly reduced, our active duty force was downsized by more than eight hundred thousand during the 1990s, the Reserve force by almost two hundred thousand. Army divisions and Air Force wings were eliminated. The US Navy went from almost 600 ships in 1987 to just over 300 ships in 2002—the lowest number since before World War II. Military bases across the country were closed and turned into parks, housing, and commercial enterprises. Echoing the words of the Old Testament prophet Isaiah, we were truly turning our swords into plowshares.

Despite this optimism, violent conflict continued in virtually every continent, including narco-armies in Columbia, armed gangs in Somalia, Balkan rebels in Europe, nationalist and separatist fighters in Indonesia, and continued aggression in Iraq. And America responded. In addition to numerous active duty deployments, Reserves were called to duty for Operations Desert Storm and Restore Democracy (in Haiti). And for the first time in American history, under three simultaneous Presidential Reserve Call-Ups, our "weekend warriors" deployed to Bosnia, Kosovo, and Southwest Asia. American military forces were—and still are— involved in many of these conflicts as fighters, humanitarians, advisors, and peacekeepers. They also confront asymmetrical warfare: forces armed not with tanks, but with powerful anti-tank weapons; not with mighty warships, but with small, fast coastal patrol boats firing long-range missiles; not with fighter-bombers, but with suicide bombers; not the Red Army, but Al-Qa'ida. Though the threats are different, they are just as dangerous, and deadly. The 1999 book, and 2002 movie, *Black Hawk Down*, about asymmetrical war in Somalia, was prophetically subtitled "A Story of Modern War."

The attack on America on September 11, 2001 added new dimensions to this duty, and new requirements for deployment. Homeland security and anti-terrorism became much more than catch-phrases for speech writers and budget makers. Despite the supposed gains of arms control agreements, chemical and biological warfare is more real than ever, and even the threat of nuclear attack within our borders is credible. Defending our homes, our way of life, and our very lives has taken on new meaning and urgency.

America's role in the world has changed. The US doesn't just promote peace, sustain freedom, and encourage prosperity. American military men and women now actively protect us at home and go overseas to seek out and counter those who mean America harm. The war on terrorism makes duty more immediate and will take Americans on deployments to the farthest places on earth—and to our own neighborhoods. Operational deployments to the rugged mountains of Afghanistan, the steamy jungles of the Philippines, the baking sands of Yemen, the gorges of Georgia, and flying combat air patrols over American cities are no longer just planning scenarios, but new realities for American service men and women—and their families. These deployments may be boring (guarding airports) or terrifying (looking for nuclear weapons), but they will be in the utmost national interest. And they will take loved ones away from home, again.

The emerging world order is really a tremendous global power shift, seeing the rise in national, religious, ethnic, tribal, and factional conflict worldwide. Author Robert D. Kaplan wrote about this shift as *The Coming Anarchy*, and Harvard political scientist Samuel P. Huntington as *The Clash of Civilizations*. While they may be overly pessimistic, both give us insight into an increasingly chaotic and dangerous world. As a result, there are increasing demands on our forces for rapid, short-notice deployments not just in support of humanitarian, peacemaking, and peacekeeping efforts, but to conduct actual combat operations, and be prepared to engage in major regional conflicts (North Korea and Iraq still demand our daily attention). Some of these missions may be protracted: American and NATO peacekeepers have been in the Balkans since 1995, we have conducted combat flight operations over Iraq since the end of Desert Storm in 1991, and in 2002 the Army set up six-month rotation cycles for duty in Afghanistan.

Just consider some Operations in the decade after Desert Storm:

- Sea Angel (flood relief in Bangladesh)
- Fiery Vigil (assistance after Mount Pinatubo erupted in the Philippines)
- Provide Comfort (for the Kurds in Turkey and Northern Iraq)
- IFOR, SFOR, and KFOR (peacemaking and peacekeeping forces in the Balkans)
- Restore Hope and Sustain Hope (dealing with anarchy in Somalia)
- Support, Restore, and Uphold Democracy (in Haiti)
- Joint Endeavor, Joint Guard, Deny Flight and Sharp Guard (operations in the Balkans)
- Garden Plot (riots in Los Angeles)
- Stabilize (peacekeeping in East Timor)
- Non-combat evacuations in Rwanda, Albania, Cambodia, Liberia

- Avid Response (earthquake relief in Turkey)
- Focus Relief (peacekeeping in Sierra Leone)
- Atlas Response (flood relief in Mozambique)
- Northern and Southern Watch (enforcing no-fly zones in Iraq)
- Desert Strike and Desert Fox (deterrence in the Gulf region)
- Deliberate Force, Joint Endeavor, Joint Guardian, Joint Forge (more in the Balkans)
- Enduring Freedom (the war against terrorism, conducted overseas)
- Noble Eagle (the war against terrorism, conducted within the US)
- Joint Task Force 160 (running Camp X-Ray in Guantanamo, Cuba)
- Joint Task Force Olympics (providing security for the Winter Olympics in Utah)

And the list certainly shows no sign of slowing down. Indeed, our times now seem more in accord with yet another Old Testament prophet, Joel, who wrote about beating plowshares back into swords!

Deployments—The Other Side

Since Operation Enduring Freedom began in October 2001, units and service men and women from all branches have been deployed to an increasing number of regions in the world. Three days after September 11th, President Bush authorized a Reserve Call-Up, and in less than six months, more than 80,000 Reserve and National Guard members, from all 50 states, were brought on active duty. Some units were given missions that were to last at least a year.

Duty calls and men and women deploy. As necessary and important as these deployments are, they have a human cost.

Then-Major General Charles E. Wilhelm, commanding the First Marine Division at Camp Pendleton in California, noted about his infantry Marines, that "If we add the time that he is in the field or deployed within CONUS, we find that he sleeps in a place other than his quarters for 60% of his FMF [Fleet Marine Force] tour." He added, "...the lifestyle...strains even mature marriages..."

Change the uniforms, the units, the home bases, and the story is pretty much the same in much of the Armed Services. The tempo at which our service members live is increasing. The Defense Department, which has special terms for just about everything, measures the speed of military life like the tempo in an orchestra. Personnel tempo ("perstempo") looks at how much time is spent away from home. Operational tempo ("optempo") considers how much equipment is used, such as flying hours, or ship steaming days. "Worktempo" is the pace of work back at home base. And deployment tempo ("deptempo") is how many days a unit is deployed. Each service measures these tempos slightly differently, but the effect is the same: more time away from home, even if the service member is stationed "at home."

The quickening tempos of military life are indeed one of the most worrisome factors for our military leadership, and since 2000 Congress told all the services to keep track of every service member's deployment time. But even keeping track of deployment doesn't mean there won't be more of it: In 2002 Secretary of Defense Donald Rumsfeld made the point that the best defense against terrorism is a persistent offense, and that "we need to be leaning forward and not leaning back." Tempo will not lessen, deployments will not diminish.

In July 1994, just barely two weeks after the 24th Marine Expeditionary Unit (MEU) returned home to Camp Lejeune, North Carolina from a six-month Mediterranean and Indian Ocean deployment, Marines and sailors were called back from vacation with friends and family to reboard their ships and sail to Haiti. And in December 2001, the 13th MEU found itself deploying six weeks earlier than expected (and missing the Christmas holidays at home) because of the war on terrorism.

Why Me?

These rapid-response deployments raise two important issues. First is the validity of our country's involvement. The second is the fact that the same service members and families are experiencing deployment over and over again.

During the 1990s there was lots of controversy over America's role in foreign affairs. Our government clearly wanted to protect our national interests and gain political leverage, but other countries were suspicious of our efforts. We thought of ourselves as the world's "911 force"; others saw the US as an arrogant superpower (a French Foreign Minister even called the US a "hyperpower"!). Some people said emphatically that we were not the world's police and that we should not try to resolve the conflicts of so many other countries.

The reason for our involvement, however, was a fear of what might happen if we did not play police officer and get involved in emerging threats. In a February 1993 report, General Colin Powell, then Chairman of the Joint Chiefs of Staff, explained the need for our involvement: to prevent a full scale war now, rather than have to fight one later. As he put it:

> World War I was "the war to end wars," and when it was "over over there," we brought the troops home and settled into isolation. Throughout the Roaring Twenties and the Great Depression that followed, maintaining a strong military was never a national priority. And we paid for it. We paid when totalitarian governments began their expansionist aggression, aggression that might have been deterred by the existence of strong US forces. We paid at Pearl Harbor, and at Kasserine Pass in North Africa.
>
> When World War II ended in victory, we repeated our mistake. Again we failed to keep our forces ready, and we

again paid the price in Korea, in the awful retreat to the Pusan perimeter. This time we are determined to get it right.

Consider these words eight years later in October 2001 by Colin Powell, now the Secretary of State, and a senior member of an administration that would have to cope with the consequences of having downsized our Armed Forces and reduced investment in the military:

The events of September 11 brought home to us in tragic fashion the global reach of terrorists in today's world. The lesson is clear: To defeat terrorists, we must identify them, we must find them, and we must seize them wherever they are in the world doing their evil deeds or plotting new evil deeds.

And now, of course, there is a new meaning to American being a "911 force," as our military forces respond to the 2001 attack on our nation on 9/11.

After September 11, there is much less questioning of the validity of our country's involvement in world politics. We know we must be engaged. This "green light" to more deployments is closely connected to the second major issue: the same service members experiencing deployment over and over.

This is due to many factors, but especially to recurring requirements for the relatively few "ready" combat units, such as the Navy's Carrier Battle Groups and Amphibious Ready Groups, the Army's 82nd and 101st Airborne Divisions, the Marine Corps' Expeditionary units, and the relatively new Air Force's Aerospace Expeditionary Force.

As the Air Force Chief of Staff said in February 2002, "the combination of multiple crises operations and our ongoing steady state commitments has placed extraordinary stress on our expeditionary air force."

And this stress is not just on combat units, but also on logistics and medical experts, intelligence specialists, military police, air traffic controllers, transport crews, those trained to support special operations, and innumerable others in uniform. The military calls these "High Demand/Low Density" units for good reason: they are essential for any operation, but there are very few of them. They get "the call" all the time, and part of their Standard Operating Procedure is saying goodbye to family.

Another factor is that American fighting forces are learning to fight better by fighting together. To maintain high readiness for rapid deployment, our smaller military relies on increasing teamwork among the Armed Forces. Each branch has, in the past, been specially trained to perform very different tasks. Today's military strategy combines all services into joint task forces that train together so they are better equipped to deploy and operate together.

One example of successful joint combat operations was in the Persian Gulf War when the Tiger Brigade of the Army's Second Armored Division was attached to the Second Marine Division. The Marine division gained a great deal of maneuverability and firepower from the Army's extra tanks and self-propelled artillery. The Army gained a much stronger right flank. And General Schwarzkopf gained a much more powerful ground force.

In Operation Restore Democracy in Haiti, Army helicopters flew off Navy aircraft carriers, and despite concerns that this would establish a "bad" precedent, such innovative joint thinking proved itself in combat less than a decade later in Operation Enduring Freedom, when Air Force special forces helicopters carrying Army and Navy special forces soldiers used a Navy aircraft carrier as an operating base for initial operations against Taliban and Al-Qa'ida forces in Afghanistan. Seeing American special forces on horseback using state-of-the-art Global Positioning Systems and hi-tech communications gear to call in lethal air strikes from lumbering 50-year old B-52s, sleek B-1 and stealthy B-2 bombers, Navy F-14 and Marine F-18 attack fighters, Air Force AC-130 gunships, and Army Apache attack helicopters certainly shows the power of joint operations. Today it is unthinkable that any major operation would be done by just one service.

This teamwork helps keep our forces "ready," and makes for much more effective fighting units, but it does not relieve the stress of matching increasing missions for joint task forces with limited numbers of people and equipment. To make joint operations work, everyone needs to do what they always have—master their own specialties—and train, deploy, and operate together. The simple fact is: more people will deploy, more frequently. And that means more families will experience more separation.

Family Support is Readiness Support

During the Persian Gulf War and the busy decade that followed, the military opened its eyes to the tremendous impact of family readiness on military readiness. The services developed many Quality of Life plans, opened numerous Family Service Centers, tried to make deployments more predictable, and implemented many support programs for the families of deployed personnel.

The senior military leadership also supported these developments, since they understood taking care of families wasn't a distraction from preparing for war, but an important contribution to readiness. A service member who is confident his or her family is prepared for and supported during deployment is a much stronger team member. This is especially important as the front lines now can be found at home. Any mission can and will impose strain on all our personal lives. And that strain has a direct impact on military readiness. The lesson: reduce the strain, increase readiness.

Duty

The actions of our Armed Forces service men and women, be they active duty, reserve, or National Guard, ultimately will protect the great freedom we enjoy in our lives. Whatever our feelings about the purposes, timing, and location of the missions assigned, it is the job—and duty—of service members to follow orders in good faith.

Spouses of those military personnel also have a duty: to support them and, throughout the changes in our world and daily lives, to send them off to do their duty with love, prayers, and the confidence that we will be here waiting when they return.

But following orders, accepting deployments, and providing support isn't enough. Attitudes, skills, and knowledge are also required. Military members, their spouses, and family members need to know what deployment will mean to their lives in specific ways; they need to understand what stresses they will encounter, and they need to know what they can do.

This wonderful book Karen has written brings exactly this information to every service member and family facing deployment—in other words, every service family. Karen has gone through an enormous amount of material and used her years of personal experience to put together in one easy-to-read, easy-to-use book exactly what you need to know and where to find out about deployments. I wish this book had been around when I was deploying, or sending and supporting units to distant lands. I know it will be of great help to all who face and endure deployments, especially as new and challenging ones loom on America's strategic horizon. Making use of Karen's sound advice, numerous resources, and poignant perspectives, every service family should discover that they are indeed *Surviving Deployment*.

—H-C. Peterson, Jr., Ph.D.
Major, USMC (Ret.) and Navy Spouse

Chapter 1
The Deployment Cycle

Separation is one of the most heart-wrenching facts of military life. Field training exercises, temporary duty, unaccompanied tours, remote assignments, and overseas deployments all force couples and families to be separated. It can be a stressful, lonely experience that non-military friends and family just don't understand. New and added responsibilities can be overwhelming, yet they also develop new skills and uncover hidden talents. Separation can also be a positive opportunity for personal growth that will change your outlook on life forever.

Separation makes or breaks families, marriages, and friendships, and that is why I have titled this book "*Surviving* Deployment."

The first step in surviving *anything* is preparation. You wouldn't trek off in the woods without water and a first aid kit. Before you cook a meal, you'd first look in the cupboard and make sure you have the correct ingredients. You wouldn't begin to build a cabinet without first measuring the space it's going to go in. And you certainly wouldn't marry someone without first sharing feelings and getting to know your partner.

For any project to be successful, a certain amount of planning and preparation is essential. In the same way, you don't want to face a deployment without first gathering tools, checking ingredients, taking measurements, and communicating your feelings.

In the military, there are anticipated and unanticipated separations. Many couples ask, "How can we prepare for something we aren't sure will ever happen to us, or when?" As any veteran deployment survivor will tell you: expect it to happen at any time. Your spouse could come home from work today and say he's deploying tomorrow. And in military life's version of Murphy's Law, deployment virtually guarantees one of the kids will get sick, a major appliance will break, the car will start leaking oil, and the dog will run away. You'll crawl into a lonely bed, hear creaks in the house you've never heard before, and wonder what could possibly go wrong the next day.

As my husband, Bob, and I have discovered, right after one deployment, you must start preparing for the next one. Indeed, that is why it is called the deployment *cycle*: prepare—deploy—return—prepare again.

Types of Deployments

Three main factors categorize deployments:

- the deployment mission
- how long the deployment is scheduled to last
- the time between official notification and actual departure

Deployment Mission

Training. Humanitarian efforts and emergency relief. Peacemaking and peacekeeping. Deterrence. War. All are common deployment missions. With the dramatic increase in the number and duration of military missions, and the special requirements of the war on terrorism, any type or size military unit is liable to deploy, as is any individual service member. It isn't just the infantry soldier or fighter pilot or warship sailor who gets the call. And it isn't just the active duty forces who get deployment orders; reserves and National Guard members also get the call.

There will be days when you'll ask why *your* spouse is the one to go, instead of one of the thousands of *other* available military members. And sometimes the only reason is simply: *your loved one is in the military*.

Whatever the reason for the deployment, you must support each other. Questioning the mission or why your loved one got the call won't help either of you survive the deployment. Remember that *your* duty is just as important to the success of the mission as the duty of the deployed spouse.

There are also separations that may result from situations other than formal deployment orders, such as extended temporary duty, being attached to a deploying unit, and specialized individual duties. Sometimes separation is caused by PCS (Permanent Change of Station) orders. A service member may get orders overseas that are designated as remote or unaccompanied. Reserves and National Guard service may be activated or called up to active duty. And more families are staying behind when a service member is called to duty or transferred, even within the United States. Common reasons include children in school, a spouse's career, financial benefits, or inability to sell a home in a depressed real estate market. In this case, the service member becomes a *geographical bachelor*.

Dual-service couples also experience separation in the course of regular duty. Although the services try to keep them stationed in the same geographical area, these couples often end up serving on different coasts or even in different countries. In 2000, there were almost 80,000 dual-service couples, and almost ten percent of all married active duty service members were in dual-service marriages.

The strategies for surviving deployment presented in this book, though centered on traditional deployments, will work for any extended separation.

Length of Deployment

Field assignments range from a few days to several months for regular training exercises. These exercises usually take place close to the home military base, although some may involve traveling to a larger base or more specialized area or even overseas. The Marines, for example, send battalions from east and west coast bases to the Mountain Warfare Training Center in Bridgeport, California, for month-long training. Another common Marine deployment is the six to eight weeks of Combined Arms Exercise (CAX) at Twentynine Palms, California. The Army sends units to its National Training Center at Fort Irwin, California, for combat training; other deployments for training may include Fort Drum, New York, or Fort Greely, Alaska, for cold weather training, and to the Mountain Warfare School in Vermont. Forces also travel to Joint Task Force Bravo, in Central America, for training and international assistance.

Many joint training exercises take place each year around the world, ranging from small specialized ones involving less than a hundred people, to much larger exercises involving dozens of units and thousands of men and women. Training often is done with armed forces from other nations. Exercises with intriguing names such as Shark Hunt, Iron Magic, Infinite Shadow, Cobra Gold, Rim of the Pacific, Ulchi Focus Lens, Bright Star, Team Spirit, Display Determination, give units and individuals opportunities to hone their mission skills and learn how to work with each other. But they all involve extensive time deployed away from home.

Most services also send units on regular deployments. The Army has a rotation plan for its forces assigned to the Balkans and the Persian Gulf, for example. The Air Force also rotates units for selected overseas assignments. Navy and Marine Corps fleet units from both coasts have regularly scheduled six-month deployments. Accordingly, when your spouse is stationed in a Fleet Marine Force (FMF) unit or assigned to a Navy ship, he or she will most likely be scheduled for one or more of these deployments. Examples are the Carrier Battle Groups, Amphibious Ready Groups, and Marine Expeditionary Units (MEUs) from Navy Fleets and Marine Forces in the Pacific and Atlantic. These units typically do two six-month deployments, six to nine months apart, during a tour. The Navy ships associated with these deployments homeport mainly in Norfolk, Virginia, and San Diego, California, along with smaller bases on each coast. The Marines deploy from

Camp Lejeune, North Carolina, and Camp Pendleton, California, as well as from the associated Marine Corps air stations. Unit Deployment Program (UDP) is also a common deployment for Marines: battalion and squadron units deploy from a multitude of air and ground bases on both coasts to Japan for six months of training and forward deployed "presence."

> In a survey released in 1994 by the Pentagon, 46 percent of military spouses said separations are a "chronic source of high stress."

Air Force service members assigned to units of the Aerospace Expeditionary Force (AEF) participate in 15-month AEF Cycles, usually involving a three-month rotation followed by a year before the next rotation, although some rotations can extend up to six months.

Examples of longer assignments for some services include unaccompanied tours to Japan or Korea for 12 to 18 months or to various Task Forces in the Persian Gulf region. To get an idea of where U.S. armed forces are deployed, visit *DeploymentLINK*, an official military Web site at http://deploymentlink.osd.mil/.

Amount of Preparation Time

It's imperative for families and service members to be as ready as possible for *any* separation, but particularly for short-notice, rapid deployments. Notice of deployment can be as little as a few hours in an emergency situation! Some troops barely said goodbye to families as they hurried off to the Gulf War in 1990-1991, to Somalia in 1992-1993, and to Afghanistan and Central Asia in 2001. Some units deployed to the Los Angeles riots in 1992 with less than six hours' notice. Combat missions and humanitarian emergencies remain the most common reasons for these rapid deployments.

For scheduled deployments, you may have as much as two years' notice, though nine to twelve months is usual. Under normal circumstances, you'll know the departure date and the return date and ships and units will operate as close to that as possible.

The combination of type of mission, duration, and notification time, as well as special circumstances, and even the size of the family and ages of family members at the time, makes each deployment unique. Separation is never easy, but it does run much smoother if you know what to expect...*and expect it.* It helps to look at the whole picture.

Phases and Stages of Deployment

Though there are many types of deployments, all share three basic time phases:

Phase I	Pre-deployment	Preparation
Phase II	Deployment	Separation
Phase III	Post-deployment	Homecoming/Reunion

Each individual, couple, and family reacts differently to the challenges of a deployment, but most go through a cycle of eight basic emotional and psychological stages:

Phase I Pre-deployment/Preparation

Stage 1	Shock/denial/anger
Stage 2	Anticipation of loss
Stage 3	Emotional detachment

Phase II Deployment/Separation

Stage 4	Disorientation/depression
Stage 5	Adaptation
Stage 6	Anticipation of homecoming
Stage 6 ½ (sometimes) Deployment extension	

Phase III Post-deployment/Homecoming/Reunion

Stage 7	Honeymoon
Stage 8	Reintegration

You'll find that throughout each phase and stage of the deployment there are a variety of issues everyone has to deal with:

❑ *logistical* (preparing a will, getting the car fixed, paying bills and balancing the checkbook, making an emergency contact list, keeping the house in order, etc.)

❏ *relational* (developing a plan for communicating with each other, discussing how to cope with conflict and misunderstandings, deciding how to handle upcoming birthdays, etc.)

❏ *emotional* (dealing with feelings of loneliness, anger, and frustration; coping with the deployed spouse missing out on the children growing up; helping children handle their emotions, etc.)

How well you handle these issues often depends on what phase and which stage of the deployment you are in. Some matters are easier to handle at certain times—and very difficult to deal with during other stages. Knowing the deployment cycle, the challenges it presents, and your own strengths and weaknesses, will help you manage the deployment experience well.

Phase I. Pre-deployment/Preparation

What you do in this preparation phase can positively set the stage for the deployment. To your credit, by reading this book you have already taken the first step in preparing for deployment. You are learning more about it. Some military couples prepare for deployment *before* they receive the orders. Take time to prepare, even if you have only a few hours.

Sometimes, with scheduled deployments, you'll have months to prepare and plan. Often, however, especially in cases of war or other emergency, deployment orders can come only a few weeks, days, or even hours before the departure. In any case, you should begin planning as soon as you think a deployment may be imminent. With all the logistical items out of the way early, you can focus on the emotional and relational issues, and relax and enjoy your last few days together with less stress.

Receiving news of a pending deployment several months before the departure date *should* be a blessing in terms of preparation. In reality, many couples confess to waiting until the last minute to prepare, regardless of how soon they find out, because it's hard to face the reality of separation. Thus the cycle begins.

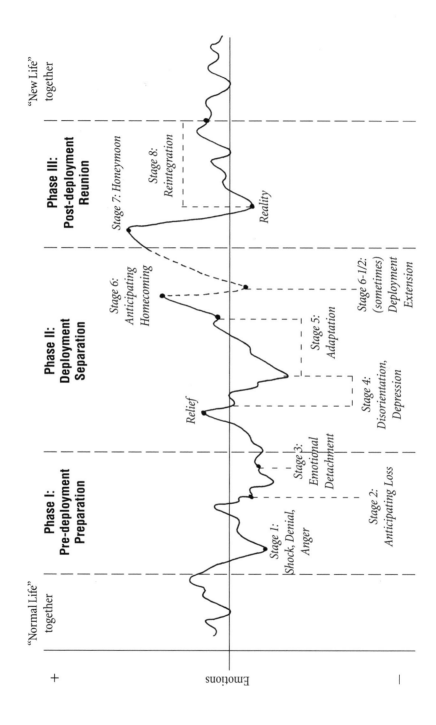

Stage One: Shock, Denial, Anger

Many couples have difficulty accepting the reality of leaving or separating.

No matter how much time you're given, the first reaction to the news of a deployment is usually shock. "You're WHAT?" will be the first words out of your mouth as you fight the lump in your throat and the dizziness from the rush of confused emotions whirling through you.

Then there is the denial. "No, we're still going to be able to go on our vacation." "You WILL be home for Christmas!" "I thought we agreed to have this baby TOGETHER?"

The next feeling in this early stage is anger or resentment. "Why us?" "Let the Somalis take care of themselves!" "I hate the Army!" "Why can't the Marines do it?" Just remember not to take your anger out on your spouse. Sometimes an entire unit deploys, other times individuals are selected, and often—because it is their profession—individuals volunteer to deploy. Even if your spouse did have a say in the orders, you have to believe that no one *wants* to be away from his family. The decisions of whom to deploy and when are never easy ones to make. Trust that someone put thought and experience into the decision. Even though you may feel that your spouse was chosen out of pure luck, it is his duty (and job!) to go. The quicker you accept this and get down to the business of real preparation, the less you'll have to worry about as the departure date nears.

Stage Two: Anticipation of Loss

Eventually, you both come to realize that the deployment really will happen. The anticipation of "loss" and of losing the daily contact of your loved one is often intermingled with the shock, denial, and anger from stage one.

You may find yourself crying at silly or seemingly insignificant things. Family members each try to adjust in different ways, causing increased tension. Couples may argue. Children may misbehave or become withdrawn. It's common for spouses to cram in a month's worth of projects (fixing things, making things...the "Honey-Do" list) into a few days. Other couples put off doing chores or procrastinate finishing projects because they think it will somehow delay the departure. It's common in this stage for couples to have difficulty being intimate or having loving sexual relations because of the added tension. Restlessness, concern about the future, irritability, anxiety, or panic (even though plans are going well) can lead to a difficult stage of emotional detachment just before the physical departure.

Stage Three: Emotional Detachment

This is an especially difficult stage. It is also very important because it can set the emotional tone—for better or worse—for the rest of the deployment cycle. Sometimes couples misread the signals given during this stage of preparation and adjustment. Remember that you're reacting to the deployment *situation*, not rejecting each other *personally*.

Couples and families experience withdrawal and detachment in varying degrees. Some experience a sense of despair, along with an overwhelming urge to run away and dissociate themselves from the pain of separating. Others experience feelings of ambivalence toward each other, making physical intimacy difficult.

At this point, there is often a sense of "nothing left to say." Difficulty making decisions, a lack of energy, and feelings of depression are also common. Many couples facing their first deployment are alarmed to find how easily they become irritated with each other, even arguing or fighting at a time when they feel they should be closer than ever. This is unfortunately quite common. But it is normal. Even though you are physically together, mentally and emotionally you are preparing for separation. Reaffirm your love. Hug a lot. And smile.

These first three stages may last a few days or a few weeks. Try not to focus on negative emotions. *Talk* to and *listen* to your spouse. Encourage and help your children to express their feelings. Spend time as a family, and as a couple, without distractions, developing positive ways to continue to grow individually and to love one another during the deployment. Accept the orders and move on.

Working through these emotional and relational adjustments is a critical step in this pre-deployment phase. Equally crucial are the logistical preparations necessary for a successful deployment. The next chapter discusses many of these preparations in detail including preparing important papers such as wills and powers of attorney, establishing networks or support groups, creating emergency

> Stress before and at the beginning of a deployment often increases if the deployment is rapid, dangerous, unplanned, or prohibits rapid and reliable communication.
>
> Life events that add to this stress include parenting difficulties, marital problems, pregnancy, confusion over pay and benefits, and concern about car and household repairs.

and panic lists, and deciding the best way to manage your family and home while apart. Although we can never fully prepare for the future, this phase of preparation will set the tone for your survival of the deployment. Don't take it lightly.

Phase II. Deployment/Separation

The sequence of events in the deployment phase vary as greatly as the families being separated. This phase always begins, however, with the departure itself.

Kelly Hannan watched her single-parent dad get on a plane for Saudi Arabia when she was 12. "That was a confusing time of life for me," she explained. "I had to live with my grandmother and change schools. I thought I would never see my dad again. To this day, I cry if I see a green sea bag."

Husbands, wives, and children all react differently to the actual "goodbye." There is a great sense of loss but also of hope. Fear and excitement. The unknown. "Are we prepared for this?" Kisses and hugs and tears. It's very important that *each* member of the family say goodbye to the deploying member. Young children especially need to have that physical separation in order to understand that the parent is leaving. As hard as it is, there needs to be a break before there can be a reunion.

Once the deployment is finally underway, life will never again be the same. As family routines change, there is often discouragement, and a sense of disorientation and depression can set in. This is the "I miss you too much" stage.

Stage Four: Disorientation/Depression

After the goodbyes are said and the plane or ship has gone, many spouses feel relieved. One painful step is finally over. Along with that relief often comes guilt and second-guessing. "Why am I glad he's gone?" "Why didn't I plan for this better?" "Why was I so irritable last week?" "I should have told her I loved her more."

At first it can be overwhelming to think about your new responsibilities or going it alone. You'll remember little things you forgot to do or say before the departure, leaving you feeling like your preparation was inadequate. Some spouses find themselves feeling aimless for a few days.

Anger at the military for taking your spouse when you need him can resurface throughout the deployment. Jealousy, triggered by friends or neighbors whose spouses are at home with them, can cause you to want to withdraw from those contacts. Disruptions in your daily routine due to your partner's absence can cause a tendency to sleep or eat too much or too little, further stressing your life. All this can lead you into a state of depression.

The overwhelming sense of responsibility seems to weigh more heavily on your shoulders every day. It's not easy to have to handle everything physically and emotionally. Depression can linger due to these changes. Have a small, private pity party and then stop the depression while it's in the healthy stage. Don't let it begin to rule your life. Think positive. Now. Remember, even though you feel you have the worse end of the deal, getting stuck alone or at home with the kids, the deployed person has little or no contact with people other than his professional peers. He is missing out on all the things he loves about home and being with you. He needs your support and encouragement, too.

Stage Five: Adaptation

After a few weeks routines become familiar and, as e-mail is permitted and the regular mail system catches up, communication between spouses becomes more regular. A new sense of organization, independence, and control over life lifts your spirits. This is the "I can make it" stage. You have adapted. That doesn't mean you *like* being separated, it just means you are making the best of it, and hopefully enjoying life somewhat. At the very least, most spouses come to a point of tolerating if not accepting the situation.

During this stage, most people establish workable family patterns and interactions. They become more comfortable with the situation and with themselves, and they begin to show increased self-confidence.

This is also a volatile stage, however. Spouses may experience more sickness due to the stress of their increased responsibilities. Healthy habits are essential. Some spouses will appear more mature and independent, developing new activities or talents. Others may be uncertain of their ability to cope, experiencing increasing feelings of despair, and wanting simply to give up until it's over.

Pay attention to your personal appearance. It's easy to fall into the trap of not caring for yourself because your spouse isn't around to "look good for." Reassure yourself that you are still attractive. While many spouses develop an asexual attitude, feeling they no longer need sexual attention, others may have thoughts of cheating on their spouses because of forced suppression of their needs and desires. Remember that sex is only one element of marriage. Being celibate during this separation is a sacrifice that will keep the relationship strong and trustworthy.

Once you enter this adaptation stage, you should rely on your support system (extended family, friends, key volunteer network, fellowship group, clergy, etc.) to help you stay there. Minor crises can temporarily set you back to the disorientation stage. Keep the faith. You can make it. Some key points:

- ❑ Take care of yourself throughout the deployment. Stay healthy. Eat right, exercise, and take time for yourself each day to do something you enjoy.

- ❑ Take care of your children. They also need proper rest, nutrition, exercise, and time with friends. Spend time with each child individually as well as with the family as a group.

- ❑ Teach children how to stay safe. Use peepholes and locks. Keep emergency numbers handy. Discuss what to say on the phone or to strangers who might ask about the deployment. Have a male's voice on the answering machine.

- ❑ Keep the communication lines open between you and your children, you and your spouse, and your children and your spouse. Letters, phone calls, pictures, e-mail, video and audio tapes are a few ways to send your love.

- ❑ Share the work load. Be realistic in your expectations of yourself, your spouse, and your children.

- ❑ Work through everyone's emotions. Try to understand your doubts or fears, don't ignore them. Seek help at the first sign you may need it. Don't be afraid to get professional help if you feel overwhelmed.

Looking back at the illustration on page 8, you can see that no deployment is going to be free of emotional rollercoaster rides. In fact, the deployment separation is *going* to be an emotional rollercoaster! Rumors, incorrect news reports, too many things breaking down for your hammer and nail to keep up with, are all part of the normal ups and downs. You may question yourself, your sanity, and the dog's loyalty, but always believe that the downs will go up.

Stage Six: Anticipation of Homecoming

About a month before the redeployment date, it dawns on you. Wow, your spouse is finally coming home! That long awaited day. Joy and excitement run rampant. This is a time when many spouses become hyperactive busybodies. So many things to be done. The house needs to be cleaned. What about that hair cut and new outfit? Finding it hard to sleep or eat again? Seems like you just went through this, right?

Unfortunately, along with the warm and fuzzies you have about being together again come the anxieties of more changes and relationship adjustments. You may think, "Will he like what I've done to the house?" "Will she still find me attractive?" "Will I have to give up my independence?" "Will sex be awkward or romantic?" Your spouse is wondering, "Will the kids like or even remember me?" And your children may think, "I wonder if mom and dad will go off by themselves and forget about me." Everyone has feelings of uncertainty, wondering what will come with the homecoming besides the "Welcome Home" sign. It helps to communicate your expectations of homecoming and post-reunion adjustments. Plan the actual homecoming event as a family so that everyone feels involved and loved.

Stage Six and a Half: Deployment Extension (sometimes)

One stage I'll throw in here that you won't find in most brochures from your family center or in a pre-deployment briefing is the deployment extension stage. There are many circumstances under which the homecoming can be delayed. My husband, Bob, was deployed to Northern Iraq while we were engaged. He warned me not to put a date on our wedding invitations. Though he was delayed one month, he still made it back in time for the ceremony. Later, during his deployment to Somalia, his scheduled homecoming changed four times. One time I knew the flight he was supposed to come in on and had already filled the refrigerator with groceries. Unfortunately, a co-worker became sick and had to be medevaced back to the United States. Bob stayed five more weeks in his place.

As hard as it is not to get your hopes up, don't listen to home-coming rumors—and there will be many of them—of early arrivals. Wait for official word from your command or key volunteer. Then stay in close contact so you are aware of any last minute changes in arrival plans. Expect plane delays or even changes in arrival airfields. Marines and sailors returning to Camp Pendleton, California, from Desert Storm flew to four different airports, dozens of miles apart, and changes often were made within hours of arrival. Be flexible, be alert, and make sure your phone network is working!

Phase III. Post-deployment/Homecoming-Reunion
Stage Seven: The Honeymoon

When you see the whites of his eyes, it's honeymoon time! All fears and anxieties subside for a few brief moments when the family does the hug and huddle. Enjoy these blissful seconds. Try to save a little extra money for your honeymoon to treat your spouse to all those favorite things he's missed over the months. Be careful to stick to your plan, though. There will be temptations to buy gifts and splurge on fancy vacations. After all, you deserve it, right? Your budget may not have changed, however, and there are less expensive activities you can do that will keep from causing more stress later.

The homecoming is never as perfect as you want it to be—other than that your loved one is home. The elation can last from the hug to the car or for weeks. Then the reality of how much you've all changed creeps in. Don't let it spoil the soup.

Stage Eight: Renegotiation/Reintegration

Though your life together will not be the same as it was before the deployment (so don't try to make it the same), with patience, love, and reassurance, it can be even better.

Plan for a reintegration period, refocusing on your relationship. Expect questions. Try not to find these questions threatening. Understand that you should be curious about each other and your experiences but not judgmental. Share your needs and feelings without forcing each other to talk. Sometimes we need time to just be around each other and gradually tell about our experiences. Spend time talking as a couple and a family, rather than watching TV. Plan special activities to get reacquainted. It can take weeks to get to know each other and the children again. Be sensitive to each other's need for individual alone time as well. Too much togetherness after so much separation can cause unwanted friction. Court each other and reestablish intimacy.

As your emotional and physical adjustment to being together becomes more comfortable, you'll begin to make decisions together again. New routines, that include everyone, must be set up again. You may feel a loss of freedom or control. Your returning spouse may at first feel isolated, unwanted, unneeded, or left out. When you renegotiate roles and responsibilities—and you *do* need to renegotiate them—be sure to consider each other's input. Rebuild your family *team*. Children tend to follow your lead. This is a great chance to establish or revive trusting and understanding relationships between each member of the family.

Support each other, especially as friends. Family members may miss the friendships that developed with those who helped them through the separation. Returning spouses may miss the camaraderie of those who served with them during the deployment.

Keep a sense of humor. Try not to hog the bed, and just ignore those hairs on the sink. You adjusted to pet peeves once, you can do it again.

A New Life

When a couple or family goes through a deployment, their lives will change forever. Most of the time, the changes are for the better. Most couples and families find they've gained more knowledge of the important things in life. At the end of the deployment cycle, life is back to normal, although *normal* is not what it used to be!

You are with each other every day. You can talk with each other any time. You are relaxed and comfortable with each other.

You can enjoy being close to each other and your children. You dream of never having to go through this separation again—which brings you back to the denial stage. Oh, no. This is a deployment *cycle* and we should all be prepared for it to begin again at any time! Remember that you and your spouse are best friends. And for now, are together again.

Preparation

*One does not discover new lands without
consenting to lose sight of the shore
for a very long time.*

—André Gide

Chapter 2
The Call:
A Checklist Response

My journal entry, January 16, 1991 (Bob's 26th birthday):

> *Bob is still at home, but with the Gulf War looming, it's only a matter of time until he deploys.*
>
> *At 3:50 AM we received a phone call. I answered the request to speak with Lt. Robert W. Pavlicin and sat wide-eyed with anticipation at what news might await the next dial tone.*
>
> *It wasn't a call to war. One of the troops shot himself. He was UA [unauthorized absence] in Atlanta, Georgia.*
>
> *...[Later that night,] we sat down in front of the newly broken-in Sony Trinitron with our taco salad and, in what has become a habit lately, watched the usual ABC news. Peter Jennings made a routine call to Baghdad and Gary Shepard made a routine "all's well" response. Less than a minute later Gary was on the line describing tracer fire across the sky. At 7 PM EST UN forces attacked Iraq.*
>
> *We watched four hours of Peter Jennings... marveled at how calm he seemed, speculated about how pumped he must be to have gotten this first scoop, and wondered how he could go so long without "taking a leak."*

> *Amidst TV talk of weapons, battle plans, and Presidential briefs, we sang Happy Birthday and ate chocolate cake with banana cream pudding.*
>
> *We didn't talk really. Basic commentary.*
>
> *Bob wrote on a bottle of expensive French champagne... "chilled 2130 16 Jan 91 - to be opened when Bob returns," and put it in the frig.*
>
> *There's much to be said. Much to be left unsaid.*
>
> *I still pray for Peace.*

Bob deployed one week later.

The decision to deploy is made for many different reasons by many different people. For example, each branch of service requires of each member a certain amount of overseas, remote, or offshore duty. Sometimes this involves deploying with a unit, other times it means being assigned to a base or unit in a foreign land. Many times the orders just happen to come along, and away you go.

Occasionally, the decision to deploy can be made voluntarily. In some cases, spouses are able to discuss the choices together, just as any civilian couple would decide to change jobs or move to a new location. Sergeant Bill Smith and his wife Kristin thought it would be better for Bill to get his overseas time done while their two boys were very young. Together they decided he should volunteer for a six-month unit deployment from the West Coast. The fact that both Bill and Kristin, together, had a say in that decision made it much easier for them to plan.

Other times the decision is a voluntary one, made by the military member without family input, and then the spouse is not so understanding. It's difficult to understand why a spouse *wants* to deploy. Lieutenant John Shapiro volunteered to go to Somalia. He said it took weeks to convince his wife Karla that he did not want to be *apart* from his family but he did want to be *a part* of the action. "That's why I joined. It's my job," he explained.

More often, though, the decision to deploy is not made by either spouse. The service member simply receives orders to go.

After almost two years of separation due to her husband's deployments and assignments, Barbara Mathews was looking forward to being with Tim again soon. She had maintained their house in Hawaii while he served as a geographical bachelor at Camp Pendleton, California. When she arrived in San Diego, Tim was at the airport to pick her up. In the same moment Barbara was elated to be with Tim again, he reluctantly gave her the news he'd just received the day before: he was deploying to Somalia that week. Suddenly, Barbara was in a new place with a shipment of household goods on the way, and her husband was going far away again.

From watching the news and knowing her husband's job, Nancy McKenzie assumed her husband would go to Somalia. She casually asked him, "Are you going to be home for Christmas? Do I need to get your present early?" And when he didn't answer right away, she asked, "When do you leave?" The McKenzie family had 1½ weeks to prepare for Mac's departure.

For Julie LaBelle, the news that her husband Ed, a Gunnery Sergeant, had received orders for a one-year unaccompanied tour to Saudi Arabia came as a complete surprise. Ed's squadron had been deactivated due to budget cutbacks. Julie knew they would be receiving some kind of orders. But when Ed was moved to another squadron, he was given two months notice of his orders to the Gulf. "You could've knocked me over with a feather," Julie recalled. "I was absolutely stunned. I kind of expected something like Okinawa or a boat. But Saudi—that was the last thing on my mind. And a year..."

Reservists and those stationed overseas or at a new duty station have an especially difficult time accepting orders to deploy. Sara Johnson came home from teaching school one day to find her husband Gary going through his Army uniforms. There was a sea bag on the bed and piles of underwear, T-shirts, and toiletries. She stood frozen in the bedroom doorway, crying. Gary was not even an active reservist as a "weekend warrior." He was in the Individual Ready Reserves, a state in which most former military members try to forget about their military duty and get on with their new lives. He had a full-time job in marketing. But he also had an inactive reserve obligation of seven months. He flew to California to join a support unit whose active personnel had deployed to the Persian Gulf War.

Salvadoria "Sally" Gates had lived in the Philippines her entire life, until she met and married Major John Gates and moved with him to Camp Lejeune, North Carolina. They were in the Hostess House (or as Sally relates it, the "Hostage House") their third day on base when John received his orders to go overseas with his new unit. They had not yet found a place to live. Sally had never been to the United States before and had no family or friends here. In fact, she had only met two people in the whole country so far, John's parents, who lived in Pennsylvania. John left one week later.

Intense shock and anger can also surface when separations are too close together. When your spouse gets that call to go again, you may think: "It's not fair, it's someone else's turn. We've only been together two months, nine months...seems like a few weeks." When Bill and Kristin Smith made what they thought was the best decision for Bill to go on that six-month assignment, they had no way of knowing that one month after his return he would be sent to Somalia.

Sometimes just the thought that it *might* happen to your spouse when so many people around you are experiencing it is enough to send you into a tizzy.

I remember my mental agony over the call that wasn't even "The Call." Bob had just spent six months in Somalia and we expected him to leave again. After all, he had been back in the United States for three whole months! The quotas came down and someone with prior service in Somalia had to go from his section. At the time, Bob was the obvious candidate, as he was the correct rank, and he had already served in Somalia.

I found myself trying to think of anything but the possibilities of his leaving, and yet I was on the verge of tears every time the phone rang. I was so sure. I was angry. I was scared. I was convinced he would deploy.

I constantly planned for his imminent departure. I nagged him when something broke—I was afraid he would leave before he had time to fix it! I cut out coupons for deodorant and told him he should pick up two or three just to have on hand. Whenever the phone rang and someone asked for him, I figured if he didn't pull out his worn, folded up list of sea bag essentials, that was a good sign. Then I thought, maybe he's in denial, he doesn't want to go back.

With the possibility right in front of me that he might be leaving again, my mind tried to think of all the reasons *he* should *not* be the one to go. It's someone *else's* turn! I felt guilty wishing it on someone else. Of course, I wish no one had to go. I kept reminding myself that I am supposed to be supportive of his job. I am proud of him. I shouldn't be so selfish. Some guys even volunteer to go.

When we found out Bob wasn't chosen to go back to Somalia, my heart went out to the family facing the deployment with only two days notice. The decision was made Sunday. The orders were drawn up Monday morning and TJ was on a plane Tuesday headed for Somalia. TJ is married with two children, one born just a month before his deployment.

This is the reality military families must deal with every day.

No matter what our differences, male-female, enlisted-officer, married-single-engaged, with or without children, from many geographical and financial backgrounds, in the military we all share a common unspoken bond—the fear, frustration, stress, exhaustion, and pride that comes from dealing with the realities, challenges, and life or death promises of the military way of life. It begins with the call.

"The Call"—that dreadful news that our spouse is being deployed—as we've seen, comes in many ways. None of us are ever truly prepared to hear it, even when we have a good idea that it's imminent. Reactions of shock, denial, and anger are common. (Remember? Stage one of the predeployment phase!) It's hard to stay calm when the signs that your spouse will be leaving are all around you. The TV has stories about a looming crisis. Your family calls and asks questions. Neighbors stop and ask if your spouse will be involved. There are late hours at work. Some, like Corporal Tim Gerdes, pull out their folded up list and make a run to the exchange for supplies. Tim's wife Gwen says, "That's when I know. Before he even tells me, he's going through the closet looking for his gear." It's hard not to be bitter or upset. You want to help him get ready but you're also angry and wish it were all just a bad dream. As we learned in Chapter 1, the sooner we get down to the business of preparing ourselves for the real thing, the better.

Julie LaBelle did not waste any time getting prepared. Since Ed was in limbo for two months at a new squadron with only a few responsibilities, he had the flexibility to leave work early occasionally. Julie started a panic list. "I took one page just to jot down things that had to be done before he left," Julie said. "Some of them were really stupid, which is why I called it a panic list. Things like pulling out the refrigerator so we can vacuum behind it because it won't be done for a year."

In addition to the panic list, she had little yellow Post-It notes all over the counter with things for him to do every day. She included "everything I could possibly think of that I couldn't do alone...there were heavy things, lifting things, repairing things, things that weren't even a concern before. I would wake up at two in the morning and write notes—you have to get this done, you have to get that done. And then in addition to all that, he panicked too. He likes to do woodworking. He decided that he was going to do all the woodworking projects that he wanted to do in the next five years... in one month. So he was running night and day."

Some of the items on the lists included:

> —*repair fence, make sure dog can't get out*
> —*clean out garage*
> —*pull out stereo so we can clean behind it*
> —*we should shampoo rugs while you're here*
> —*get blinds washed*
> —*plan a trip to Seattle*

"A million things. I saved the list so I could look back at it and laugh at how panicked I was," Julie said.

Jane and Ensign David Henson only had a few days to prepare for his latest deployment. "I thought to myself, we've been through this before during ship duty," Jane said. "I didn't want him to do anything. I felt *guilty* asking him to do anything. I just wanted him all to myself, to spend as much time as I could with him. 'To do' lists seemed useless on such short notice. I didn't know what I would need done the most."

I think it's our human nature to want to know everything that's going to happen to us before it happens. We plan and prepare. We agonize over decisions. And sometimes, no matter how much we plan, prepare, or complain, we still have no control over what will happen next.

"There's always the car," Nancy McKenzie noted. "That will always go on you. Little things will happen [to your Quarters] that Base Maintenance will not take care of. [During my husband's last deployment] the garage door wouldn't open because it was waterlogged, making it too heavy. I needed someone with the strength to open the door so I could get the car out. Some things you can prepare for but there are things that will happen that you can't prepare for."

Nevertheless, preparation that *can* be done should begin the day you or your spouse enters the military. Most spouses report trouble with emotions more than any other aspect of deployment.

Preparation helps with this, because when you actively prepare, you gain more confidence and develop a greater sense of control over the situation.

In Chapter 1, we saw that there are three types of preparation issues in this critical predeployment phase: logistical, relational, and emotional.

Logistical Preparation

Logistics means all things pertaining to the "procurement, maintenance, and transportation of materiel, facilities, and personnel"—which is to say, *everything* having to do with running a household! When your spouse is deployed, how good a logistician you become has a direct impact on how well you handle the separation.

Logistics is, as any military member (except a logistician!) will tell you, boring, unglamorous, and tedious. But without it, neither the military nor your household will run very well.

Successful logistics planning sets the groundwork for the operational issues of separation, such as communicating with each other, dealing with the emotional ups and downs, family issues, and planning for reunion time.

Living Arrangements

One of the first and maybe the biggest decision for many families or couples is where family members will live during the deployment. Some spouses prefer to "go home" to be with parents or family during the separation. Many others have full-time jobs or children in school that prevent them from moving. If orders are due for a new duty station at the end of the deployment, some families prefer to move to the new station before or during the deployment, while others wait for the return of the deployed spouse at the current station.

Personally, I always preferred to stay near the base from which Bob was deployed. At the very least, the fact that I could get information or news about him sooner and have other spouses nearby who knew what I was going through far outweighed any advantages to leaving. During Bob's first deployment I moved to attend graduate school in Cincinnati, Ohio, which was quite a different world from Camp Lejeune, North Carolina. Though I learned a great deal where I was, I also missed out on the military support and friendships I've found during subsequent separations.

On the other hand, a few young mothers I talked with greatly benefited from going home. They gained the support and freedom they needed when parents offered to help with child rearing responsibilities.

In 1990, the 13th COSCOM at Fort Hood, Texas, conducted a family care survey of spouses whose partners deployed to Operation Desert Shield/Storm. Among spouses under age 22, 44% wanted to return to their home of origin and 28% actually planned to go. Of those 22 years or older, only 14% wanted to go home and 4% planned to do so. In addition to spouse age, spouse employment and not having school-aged children weighed heavily in this decision.

Your situation is unique. Write down the pros and cons of the choices you have for where to live, and *decide together.*

Contact Information/Networks

Give your spouse's deployed mailing address to family and friends. Some units require you to include a social security number and rank. *Your unit should provide the exact deployment address.* Let family and friends know how to get in touch with both of you in case of emergency.

Find the number of the local American Red Cross, who can contact the service member in an emergency. Give this number to both parents in case something happens to you at home.

Get the name and work phone number of your unit's Family Contact person, or someone in your spouse's unit who works in

To make it easy for family and friends to contact you, e-mail your contact information or print it on 3x5 cards, such as this:

Joe is deployed from March 2003 to September 2003

SGT Joseph F. Billings, USMC   Sally Billings

123-45-6789   654 North St.

24th MEU, Det. H   Swansboro, NC 28584

MSSG-24, HQ. PLT.   (123) 555-1234

FPO New York, NY 09502-8533   *sally@isp.com*

joe.billings@24meu.marines.mil

      over the holidays, reach Sally at her mom's:

Mrs. Edna Millay

123 Washington Rd.

Cityville, MD 21050

(321) 555-4321

sallysmom@isp.com

the office and is not being deployed. In general, your contact with the command will be through your key volunteer/ombudsman. In certain circumstances, it's appropriate to contact the unit directly. Check your unit's policies.

Give a neighbor or close-by friend a list of parents'/relatives' names and phone numbers in case of emergency.

Give school/work a nearby friend's phone number in place of your spouse's work number as your backup emergency contact.

Get a list of other spouses in the deploying unit. If you have time, introduce yourself to some other couples/families before your spouse leaves. Having this support network of other spouses "in the same boat" can alleviate anxiety and frustration later.

Become familiar with the many military and community resources that are available to you. (See Chapter 8.)

Keep a handy list of phone numbers for:

- ❑ Chaplain/pastor/rabbi
- ❑ Key volunteer/ombudsman/family coordinator/Family Readiness Officer
- ❑ American Red Cross representative
- ❑ Relief Society
- ❑ Legal officer
- ❑ Doctor/dentist/pediatrician/veterinarian
- ❑ TRICARE
- ❑ Housing/landlord
- ❑ Community Services, Morale, Welfare and Recreation (MWR)
- ❑ Exchange (BX, MCX, NEX, PX)
- ❑ Child care/babysitter service
- ❑ Family Service Center, Fleet & Family Support Center
- ❑ Nearby neighbors
- ❑ Reliable handyman (If you don't know one, check with a local real estate property manager for recommendations; they have lots of little "fix-its" all the time.)
- ❑ Emergency numbers (see below)
- ❑ A great pizza delivery place
- ❑ Other _____

Emergency Plans/Safety

Put up a list of emergency numbers by each phone. Include:

- ❑ Police/base security/PMO
- ❑ Fire department
- ❑ Ambulance/hospital/emergency room
- ❑ Poison control (national number: 800-222-1222; check for your state or county as well)
- ❑ Local utility emergency number

Give a duplicate set of home and car keys to someone you trust.

Consider getting a security system for your home. This can include an electric/laser/monitored system, a dog, or at the very least good locks on all windows and doors. Install a peephole in the front door. Your local police department or base security may provide security advice as a community service. In some communities, they may even do an evaluation of your house and make recommendations.

Check smoke, heat, and carbon monoxide detectors and alarms. Inspect fire extinguishers. Plan and rehearse escape routes from your home in case of fire or burglary. Practice safety rules, especially with children, for example:

- ❑ Do not open the door unless you know the person. Ask repair people to show ID. Ask delivery people to leave parcels at the door. If someone wants to use your phone to make an emergency call, get the number and call for them.
- ❑ Do not give information over the phone to someone you don't know.
- ❑ When chatting on the Internet, do not give out personal information, including the school you attend, your address, where a parent works, or the fact that someone in your family is deployed.
- ❑ Do not bring home friends of a friend unless you know them.

Are you in an area with a high risk of natural disasters? Especially if you've recently moved to a new area, knowing the basics will help you sleep better. My neighbor Julie said to me that the worst disasters always happen when your husband is away. Her husband was deployed to Saudi Arabia and Bob was on an extended exercise at Twentynine Palms when we made plans for an evacuation if the California wildfires got too close. I thought about taping the news of the fires, to go along with last year's tape of the

Do you know what to do in a natural disaster?

Earthquakes:

Indoors: Take cover under a sturdy table, desk, bench, or doorway of an inside wall. Stay away from outside walls and windows.

Outdoors: Get to an open area or field away from the range of falling debris.

In a vehicle: Drive away from any structure (including wires and poles) that could fall on or near your vehicle.

Tips: Store heavy objects on the floor or lower shelves. Fasten bookshelves and cabinets to the wall. Keep a supply of nonperishable foods and bottled water. Learn how to shut off gas and electricity to prevent fires after a quake. Prepare an emergency kit to include a first aid kit, battery powered radio, flashlight, and batteries.

Tornados:

Usually a "watch" means weather conditions are favorable for a tornado to develop. "Warning" means a tornado has been sighted or indicated by weather radar; seek shelter.

Shelter: The best protection is an underground shelter or cave or a steel-framed or reinforced concrete building. If you can't get to a shelter, go to the basement. If you have no basement, take cover under heavy furniture on the ground floor in the center of the house or in a small room (e.g., bathroom/ tub) away from outside walls and windows. Keep windows closed. Get out of trailers and mobile homes.

Outdoors: Drive away from the tornado at a right angle to its path or take cover and lie flat in the nearest ditch or ravine.

floods. Poor Bob misses everything! Does he plan that? Here's what you can plan:

❑ How do you get warnings (sirens, broadcast announce-ments, phone number with recorded warning messages,

Weather Channel alerts)?

❑ Where are shelters located? When are they used (tornados, hurricanes, etc.)?

❑ What are your emergency plans? Rehearse them with the entire family.

❑ Be prepared to leave home quickly. Think ahead of time what you'll take: irreplaceables (pets, photos, critical medical prescriptions, key computer disks), and facilitating things (checkbooks, ATM and credit cards, wallet, ID cards). Know what *not* to waste valuable time worrying about, especially things you can easily buy, such as food, clothing, and bedding.

Finances

Develop a family deployment budget and rules for spending. (See Chapter 3.)

Make sure direct deposit and allotments are in order and that you can easily access the account to which the money is being deposited. Talk about checking accounts. Do you need separate accounts? Do you have overdraft protection? Discuss how the deployed spouse will pay for expenses and how much and often that might be. You don't want to accidentally overdraw an account.

Set up an emergency fund and have a plan for accessing it. You need emergency funds for situations like paying for an unplanned airline ticket for a family emergency.

Discuss policies, debts, and payment due dates. This discussion is especially important if the person deploying usually takes care of paying the bills. It's also important if the spouse/family will be traveling to see relatives or moving to a new duty station, where routines are upset or mail is forwarded. Include:

❑ Rent/mortgage

❑ Insurance (life, vehicle, etc)

❑ Taxes (property, estimated income, etc)

❑ Student/business/other loans

- ❑ Utility bills (phone, gas, electric, water, cable)
- ❑ Credit card bills
- ❑ Savings plans/investments
- ❑ Groceries, toiletries
- ❑ Vehicle loan
- ❑ Subscriptions, memberships
- ❑ Gas and vehicle maintenance
- ❑ Other _____

Review your vehicle insurance. In high cost areas it may be financially beneficial to "garage" a car. You may have to take the plates off and de-register the car. Check with both your insurance company and your motor vehicle department. In any case, you'll definitely want to keep theft insurance.

Do taxes early or at least have everything in order, such as documentation for itemized deductions. File an extension or get a special power of attorney for filing without the deployed spouse's signature.

Paperwork

Check expiration/renewal dates for driver's licenses, vehicle registration, vehicle license plates, vehicle safety inspection sticker, and military base decal/registration.

Register to vote. Arrange absentee voting if your spouse will be deployed during elections.

Periodically review and update all important documents, such as wills, powers of attorney, and tax withholding (W-4) forms. Do this at least annually for most records and always ensure they are updated before a deployment.

Keep original records in a place where they are protected from fire, flood, and other damage. If you choose to store records in a safe deposit box, check with your bank or trust company about policies for sealing the box upon an owner's death. Keep one set of photocopies at home for reference and another set with parents or relatives in another city.

Complete and sign a will.

Telling your family how you would like your affairs handled if you die is not the same as putting it in writing. If you die without a will, your estate will be handled by your state of residence according to its inheritance laws. It may take quite some time to settle.

You and your spouse should each have a will. In most cases, a basic will can be prepared at your spouse's unit by a legal officer or adjutant coordinator prior to deployment. Ask.

If any of the following apply to you, you should consider hiring a lawyer to do a more personalized will. The military legal services officer can advise you on this, and in some cases, a military lawyer can write a personalized will.

❑ your net worth (including property and life insurance) exceeds $600,000

❑ you are divorced or planning a divorce

❑ you have one or more children

❑ your parents are divorced and you don't want to leave equal shares to them

❑ you have a nontraditional family or want to leave a portion of your property to a person or institution outside the inheritance schedule set by law (usually spouse, then children, parents, siblings)

❑ you're not married but have a significant relationship, such as a longtime live-in companion, and you want all or a portion of your estate to go to this person

Before you meet with your lawyer or legal assistance attorney to prepare a will, decide on:

❑ what assets, such as family heirlooms, should be expressly included

❑ primary and alternate beneficiaries, and if and how assets will be divided

❑ an executor who will carry out the wishes expressed in the will

- ❏ a guardian for your children in the event you die as a single parent, or if you and your spouse both die
- ❏ any special instructions you want included (such as trust funds or living wills)

Along with your will, prepare a letter of instruction. A letter of instruction:

- ❏ provides a current inventory of your assets, which your will does not do
- ❏ describes your desired funeral and burial arrangements
- ❏ tells where to find important papers and assets so that nothing will be overlooked in the settling of your estate
- ❏ lists people to call and documents to retrieve
- ❏ outlines any other wishes you want to pass along.

A letter of instruction does not take the place of your will and is not legally binding; it makes the settling of your estate easier for your survivors. Don't just write it; discuss it with your family. Answer questions about burial instructions and death benefits. Since this should be the first document used in the event of a death, make it easy to get to. You should completely review a letter of instruction each year.

Complete and sign a power of attorney.

A *general power of attorney* authorizes a person you designate to sign any legal document in your name. For example, this person could sell your home, close out your savings account, register your car, pay or collect your taxes, or enroll your child in school. The power is broad; give it with caution.

A *special/limited power of attorney* gives a person you designate specific and limited authority, with an expiration date, to act on your behalf. For example, many active duty members give their spouses a special power of attorney to handle everything related to a household move (housing, household goods, transportation, closing and opening accounts). You may get another special power of attorney, for example, to grant a sibling the authority to sell your car on your behalf, and yet another to authorize someone to take care of your child during your absence.

A *medical power of attorney* is a type of special/limited authority that allows the designated person to give consent for medical treatment, often for minor children. You might consider such authority for a caregiver to make everyday or emergency medical decisions while caring for your child in your absence.

Ask your lawyer or legal assistance specialist to help you decide if you or a caregiver needs a power of attorney. Also ask your bank, child-care agency, medical provider, real estate agent, and so on, under what circumstances they might not accept powers of attorney.

Each spouse should also prepare a *living will* (stating your medical-care wishes in case you are incapacitated) and a *durable power of attorney for health care* (giving someone the right to act as your health care proxy). California combines these in one document, the California Advanced Health Care Directive, but each state has its own requirements. Check.

Update DD Form 93 (Record of Emergency Data).

DD Form 93 is used to record information on the service member's next of kin, whom to notify in the case of death, the recipient of any unpaid pay and allowances, the location of the service member's will, insurance policies, and the beneficiary of a death gratuity. If this is not updated, the wrong person might be notified and provided benefits. The original goes in the service member's personnel file; you should keep a copy.

Place a Family Care Plan on file with the unit.

A Family Care Plan is critical—and mandatory—for service members such as single parents, or dual-service couples who might deploy with no one to take care of their dependents. The plan designates a civilian caregiver/guardian for your family while you are deployed and in the event of your death or the death of both parents/service members. Each service has a standard form for this certificate; keep a copy with your important papers.

Complete the Family Care Plan Certificate, designating caregiver(s) for:

- ❏ while on duty (e.g., normal duty hours, alert, recalls, extended duty hours)
- ❏ short-term absences (30 days or less, e.g., temporary duty for school or training)
- ❏ long-term absences (more than 30 days, e.g., operational deployment, PCS to dependent-restricted area)
- ❏ in the event of service member's death or incapacity

A caregiver is defined by the Department of Defense as "an individual who is not a member of the Armed Forces or a member of a Reserve component, is at least 21 years of age and is capable of self-care and care of children or other dependent family members. This individual must agree in writing to care for one or more family members during the [service] member's absence for indefinite periods to ensure the member is available for worldwide duties."

Prepare the caregiver(s).

- ❏ Make financial and legal arrangements to support children during your absence, such as a bank account, dependent support allotment, special powers of attorney.
- ❏ Determine logistics for transporting or relocating family members when necessary, including travel arrangements, money, and an escort in case you aren't available.
- ❏ Have the caregiver sign the Family Care Plan Certificate.
- ❏ At least three weeks before deploying, have the child stay with the caregiver for a test period.
- ❏ Give the caregiver important names and addresses/ phone numbers, including the unit contact person and key volunteer/ombudsman.
- ❏ Inform the caregiver of each child's sports activities, favorite foods, appropriate toys, interests, fears, and habits.

❑ Discuss rules with both the caregiver and your children. Make sure everyone understands your expectations. If you involve children in the decision-making, they're more likely to feel ownership of and responsibility for honoring the rules.

❑ Leave self-addressed, stamped envelopes for the caregiver and school teacher(s), to provide you with reports on the child.

❑ Get a full medical exam for each child before leaving. Give the caregiver information on each child's medical benefits, record locations, and the name and phone number of the child's dentist and doctor.

❑ Military children who are at least 10 years old must have a military dependent ID, but *all* children staying with a civilian caregiver should have an ID, no matter what age. Before you or your spouse deploy, make sure all your children have military dependent ID cards.

❑ Provide any supporting documentation the caregiver might need such as a special power of attorney (definitely one for authorizing medical care), sealed copy of your will, copy of each child's birth certificate, copies of military dependent IDs, copy of the active duty parent's military ID, financial access information, and a list and description of military benefits and facilities.

Review, update, and understand insurance policies.

Having insurance policies only helps you if they cover your current needs and you know how to access the policies and receive due benefits.

❑ Medical and dental
Know your benefits and options. Keep records of all your claims.

❑ Property/rental
Make sure your homeowners or rental insurance reflects the current value of your property and belongings.

If you rent, the landlord's insurance does not cover your possessions, so you must have your own renter's insurance. Keep a list of all personal property, including serial numbers for electronics and major appliances, and photographs or a video inventory of home furnishings and other valuables. Don't forget valuable rugs, artwork, computers, vehicles, camera equipment, musical instruments, recreational equipment, and your house. There are several good home inventory computer programs that can help you keep an accurate list. If you use these, be sure to keep a copy on disk in a safe place with other important documents. Update your personal property insurance whenever you significantly change your personal inventory.

❏ Vehicle

Vehicle insurance requirements change from state to state. The requirements apply to where you store or use your vehicle. Don't confuse insurance with registration requirements. Update your policy or you may forfeit some benefits.

❏ Life

A will does not designate the beneficiary of life insurance. Locate, inventory, and review all life insurance policies. Designate a beneficiary by name on the Servicemen's Group Life Insurance (SGLI) form and on private life insurance records. If you have private life insurance, make sure it doesn't contain a "war" or "combat" exclusion clause that would prohibit coverage if the service member were killed in combat or a war zone. Keep a copy of your SGLI election form with your insurance records.

Other important papers

Make a list of other important papers to update and keep safe, with copies accessible, such as:

- ❑ Rental lease or mortgage papers/deed
- ❑ Copies of military IDs, Social Security cards
- ❑ Birth certificates
- ❑ Passports
- ❑ Marriage certificate
- ❑ Religious certificates (e.g., baptismal)
- ❑ Divorce papers
- ❑ Adoption papers, custody papers
- ❑ Naturalization papers
- ❑ Vehicle titles, copies of registration
- ❑ Copy of driver's license(s), proof of auto insurance
- ❑ Appraisals of jewelry or other valuables
- ❑ Current Leave and Earnings Statement (LES)
- ❑ Military records, including copy of current orders
- ❑ Family medical and dental histories, including shot records for family members and pets
- ❑ Most recent tax return
- ❑ List of credit card numbers and phone numbers to call if they are lost or stolen
- ❑ Loan agreements
- ❑ Information about current investments, including bond serial numbers
- ❑ Bills of sale on major items/guarantees/warranties

Health Check-ups

Double check that all dependents have current ID cards, are enrolled in DEERS, and that TRICARE benefits (medical and dental) are properly set up. Bring records to and become familiar with the hospital/clinic/medical treatment facility before the service member's departure.

Visit your family physician and talk about what you and your family will be going through. This is especially important for children who will be cared for by someone other than a parent. The stress of deployment can cause increased illness. It's good to have a normal record to refer to.

Brush up on your CPR. Learn or review basic first aid, especially for cuts, bruises, blisters, bites, and burns.

If you have a new baby or you're pregnant, ask your doctor about common illnesses for infants and pregnant women and learn the remedies. Sometimes when we're sick and alone, we worry more about an illness being serious. Having more information can help alleviate some of that worry.

Review health and safety factors with your family. For example, make sure harmful cleaners are locked away from children, plan healthy snacks together, and enforce rules for safety equipment such as wearing helmets when bicycling, skating, skateboarding.

Maintenance/Tune-ups

Follow recommended maintenance schedules for all vehicles. Budget for repairs, and select a repair shop ahead of time for inevitable breakdowns.

Consider joining AAA or an equivalent auto club that has a no-fee towing service. Also check with your insurance company or your vehicle warranty for towing service and rental-during-repair options.

Check with your local dealer for the best way to store a vehicle that will not be in use. For example, our motorcycle dealer suggested the following: The gas tank should be full but the gas turned off to the carburetor. Add a gasoline stabilizer. Drain the float bowls. Do not start up the bike to "keep it warmed up"; only run it if you'll actually be riding it (and then you wouldn't take storage precautions). Many motorcycle dealers will prep and store a cycle for a modest fee. If you store a vehicle, check references and the Better Business Bureau to assure you're leaving it with a reputable company. Also tell your insurance company your plans.

Complete all major repairs and seasonal home maintenance:

- ❑ check furnace/air conditioner (often utility companies will perform safety checks)

- ❏ replace or clean furnace filters
- ❏ test smoke, heat, and carbon monoxide detectors; install new batteries if necessary
- ❏ sweep chimney
- ❏ fertilize lawn
- ❏ make sure winter preparations are in order (e.g., storm windows, snow tires)
- ❏ other _____

If You're Waiting for On-Base Housing

Notify the Family Housing Office of the deployment. Confirm a number where they can reach you. Tell them your plans:

- ❏ If you want to move into housing and it becomes available during your spouse's absence, get a special power of attorney and any other needed paperwork from the housing office that gives you the authority to move household goods.
- ❏ If you don't want to move during your spouse's absence, tell the housing office before the departure and ask to retain your place on the housing list.

Preparation for the Deploying Spouse: Personal Packing

The personal gear the service member will pack depends, of course, on the unit mission, deployment location, and duration. Find out as much as possible about the conditions you'll move into. A year-long deployment to Okinawa or Korea, for example, may require only a scaled down version of the daily toiletries, uniforms and casual clothes you use and wear now, since there are good military exchanges. However, a six-month MEU deployment or an open-ended journey to Central Asia, the Horn of Africa, or the Persian Gulf will require more thought.

No generic pack list will be complete, given these diverse parameters. But then again, when you go home for the holidays or on a family vacation, you always bring one too many shirts and not enough bug repellent. You may find yourself restricted to a certain number of bags, often one pack and a duffel/sea bag, parachute bag, or foot locker. Usually the command will issue a recommended personal gear list for the specific deployment, along with any luggage restrictions.

Add to your gear list a non-military, personal list of items such as:

- ❑ photos of spouse, children, parents, good friends
- ❑ special occasion cards (anniversaries, birthdays, religious holidays, etc.). Make a list and mail the cards early so loved ones back home don't feel forgotten. Put waxed paper over the envelope seals to keep them from sticking until you want to send them.
- ❑ vitamins
- ❑ a few interesting paperback books
- ❑ CD or cassette player and favorite CDs or tapes. Consider bringing a player that uses media your family can record and send to you with their personal messages.

Relational Preparation

Now that all the *things* are check-listed and the logistics are taken care of, you can move on to the *people* side of separation. This includes *relations* and *emotions*. You are not ready to part from your family until you have developed a plan for dealing with the personal and family issues related to separation. Preparing your relationship with your spouse is something you must do just as carefully as you prepared logistics: deliberately, together, and with a checklist.

First of all, stay informed, and keep each other informed. The military command means well. The military tells its members to pack the duffle bag, get shots up-to-date, and take home to spouses a list of contacts and a deployment package. This package contains useful information on many of the things discussed in this book. Most likely, there is some notice of a pre-deployment briefing for families. I think I saw one of these packages once in all the times Bob deployed. I borrowed it from a wife whose husband had left it on the back seat of his car! Everyone has busy minds during this time and may forget a few details! Use your support network and be inquisitive. There are some very good pre-deployment as well as during-deployment programs that are helpful for those who find out about them and actually attend.

Many of the following issues are addressed in detail in later chapters as part of the deployment phase. However, it is important to discuss them as much as possible in the preparation phase to allow for a smoother transition at the time of departure and to set the stage for an easier separation.

Commitment

Reaffirm your love and commitment to each other. Set ground rules. Discuss relationship expectations. It's *very important* to put your marriage and friendship with a significant other above all else in this stage. Remember, absence can make hearts grow fonder...or farther apart. Say you'll think of each other every day.

If you have a strong relationship, wonderful! Keep up the open, positive communication about your feelings for each other. Unstable marriages are often characterized by poor communication between partners and this can result in a lack of relational preparation before the deployment. In abusive relationships, the abused partner often looks forward to the separation and thinks everything will be better after the return; often it's worse. Before the deployment is the time to really commit to building stronger bonds with your partner, especially in an underdeveloped or unhealthy relationship. If this is you, get help (see Chapter 8), and begin a new commitment to a better future together.

Communication

Spend time creating a comfortable base of communication. Direct communication comes easier for some than others. If it does for you, great—communicate! If it doesn't come easily, work on it. Some family centers have excellent workshops on partner communications. It's an investment that will help both of you in everything else you do.

Openly discuss your fears. Families often avoid discussing things that worry them. They're afraid that talking about unpleasant issues will make matters worse. In reality, open discussion provides the opportunity to clarify potential misunderstandings and to know better what to expect.

For example, none of us like to think about a spouse dying. But a fact of serving in the military is the danger and the risk of being injured or killed, even in peacetime training. I always think that if I have our life insurance and will in order and have talked about the consequences with my spouse, then nothing will happen. In my mind, the day he goes off without preparing is the day something will happen. It isn't easy, but you must be ready for the one thing you hope never occurs.

Discuss communication expectations.

Letter writing

❑ Decide how often to write. Be realistic. "I'll write every day" may or may not work.

❑ Agree on the extent of bad news to write about and how to handle potentially negative or stressful information.

❑ Set up a system to number letters.

❑ Discuss use of postcards (quick and easy, saves on postage, but lacks privacy).

❑ Service members: Make a list of your family's special days (birthday, anniversary, holiday). Buy a stack of cards and address and stamp the envelopes. Paper clip each card/envelope to the page in your planner two weeks (depending on mail delivery) before the special day to remind yourself to mail it. Or, if your family has access to the Internet/e-mail, preorder e-cards to be delivered on the dates you choose.

❑ If you move during your spouse's deployment, such as accepting on-base housing, make up labels with the new address and send them to your deployed spouse.

Audio/video tapes

❑ Acquire two identical-sized tape players, plenty of blank cassettes, and mailers for the cassettes.

❑ Find out if a video camera and VCR will be available.

❑ Ask if a computer will be available for viewing digital home movies on CD-ROMs or DVD.

Phone calls

Determine if a phone will be available and how often.

❑ Set up a basic time of day or night most convenient for each of you. Discuss time zone differences.

❑ Discuss frequency and length of calls, keeping in mind budget restrictions.

❑ Agree not to discuss unresolvable issues over the phone or to bring up a subject you aren't prepared to explain clearly in a short amount of time.

E-mail

There are many advantages to using e-mail, primarily its relative immediacy. If the service member will have e-mail available, get an e-mail account at least for the deployment. There are many free e-mail services, including Yahoo! (http://mail.yahoo.com/) and Hotmail (http://www.hotmail.com/), that are great for temporary accounts and are accessible from any Internet connection.

Even with reliable and easy e-mail, keep in mind there is nothing quite as special, reassuring, and personal as a written letter. Don't let the ease of e-mail preempt the intimacy of letters.

MARS radio

Determine the availability and discuss procedures ("I love you!...Over!") and the lack of privacy.

Care packages

❑ Agree on a budget for care packages.

❑ Discuss what types of items to include.

❑ Consider the amount of time for delivery and circumstances. Certain foods may not make it due to extended delivery time (e.g., homemade cookies after three weeks), or due to weather conditions at the destination (e.g., chocolate in the desert heat).

Photos

❏ Acquire a camera for each of you. It doesn't need to be expensive.

❏ Agree that both of you will take photos at regular intervals throughout the deployment and mail them or e-mail (digital photos) to each other. It might be easier for the deployed spouse to send back undeveloped film.

See Chapter 6 for more communication ideas.

Parenting/Children

Discuss discipline and other parenting issues with each other and with children. If a single parent or both parents are leaving, clearly communicate your expectations and give guidelines to caregivers. Explain to the children that the new caregiver is now the mom or dad, or both, for the time you are gone.

Encourage children to be a part of the preparation process and to give their opinion of how things should be handled while a parent is away. Talk through ground rules and any new chore schedules that account for one family member being absent. Keep as close to the normal routine and rules as possible.

In addition to group and family portraits before the deployment, take a picture of each child with the deploying parent. Have each child give a copy to the parent who is leaving and keep the other copy. When the child looks at the picture, not only will he think of the parent, but he'll also imagine the parent thinking of him.

Have the deploying parent make an audio or video tape before he or she leaves. The child can listen to the parent's voice over and over. A favorite for many children is to fall asleep listening to a parent "read" bedtime stories. And all young children love to see themselves on video, especially playing with a parent.

See Chapters 6 and 7 for more ideas.

Emotional Preparation

Adjusting to change and developing positive coping strategies are the two most important aspects of emotional preparation.

Have you noticed that your niece, nephew, cousin, brother, or sister changes his or her hair, height, and personality every time you go home for the holidays? Everyone changes over time and throughout life's experiences. Those changes are more noticeable when they occur in the absence of another. During a deployment, expect and prepare for change. Talk about how family roles and responsibilities will change. Recognize the separation period as an opportunity for everyone involved to grow personally.

The emotional cycle of a deployment is very similar to the grief cycle experienced with all significant losses. A part of you is leaving. It's normal to feel guilty about leaving or angry with someone for leaving you. Even when the reason for a deployment seems justified or is accepted by both partners, sometimes the spouse left at home will still feel guilty for being angry. Although everyone has these feelings, they are not conducive to positive communication or the basic enjoyment of life during extended separations. Overcoming guilt, anger, self-pity, and denial is the first step in positive coping. It's difficult to think of being separated from your best friend and your family as a positive experience. But it can be if you let it.

Guilt

When Ginger Taylor's husband told her he was going to Okinawa for a year, "he seemed guilty, really sad." He told her the good news and bad news all at once. "He tried to smooth it over," she said. "He just started rambling about how it was a great career move, and about all the things he'd do for me before he left. I think he just felt a tremendous amount of guilt."

There are at least three kinds of guilt:

❑ The deploying spouse feels guilty for leaving.

❑ The remaining spouse feels guilty for wanting to get the goodbye over with and for feeling relieved that the deploying spouse is gone.

❏ And, though hardly anyone admits to it, some spouses feel guilty because they *look forward* to the separation.

Consider each of these:

Feeling guilty for leaving?

❏ Accept orders to deploy as ORDERS. ("Roger...Out!")

❏ Acknowledge that no one in the family wants to be *separated from each other*. It's the *opportunity* the deployment or separation will bring that we sometimes look forward to.

❏ You won't be home to do your share of the work. Take time to help your spouse prepare for the added responsibilities that will now be placed on her shoulders.

❏ Help and encourage your spouse to develop a support network. You won't be there to provide the hugs and daily support.

Feeling guilty for wanting the goodbye to be over, or for feeling relieved when the deployment is actually underway?

❏ Reassure each other that the reason you want to get on with the separation is because you love each other and it hurts to say goodbye. It's human nature to want to run away from pain.

❏ Express your thankfulness for the extra time you do spend together before saying goodbye.

❏ Acknowledge that you're relieved to be past the goodbye stage because you are one step closer to the end of this painful (yet rewarding) experience. Explain that you want to get on with it because the sooner your spouse leaves, the sooner he'll be back.

❏ Accept the departure as tangible evidence the deployment has actually started and your great adventure has begun. Now you can get on with the task of making the best of your time apart.

Feeling guilty for looking forward to the separation?

❑ Understand that in some way, you *do* want to go on this adventure together, even though you are in separate places. There are opportunities for everyone to discover something new about themselves. It's healthy to be selfish once in a while.

❑ Encourage each other to admit that some good will come of this separation. It's OK to want to leave or to want your spouse to leave for this relatively short period of time. Not everyone becomes depressed at the prospect. Many couples see deployment as a forced but needed vacation, a time to refresh themselves individually so they have more to offer their relationship and family.

❑ Reaffirm your love. Talk.

Anger

Anger often stems from *jealousy*. Katelin Hodge went through periods of "really being angry" when her husband got orders to a Middle East training facility. "I was angry that he was provided with a housekeeper and a cook. She did his laundry...I got stuck at home with four kids and a big house to take care of."

Agree not to play "who has it worse" games. Each of you will have both good and bad aspects of your separation. On one deployment, the service member may have the opportunity to visit foreign ports and exotic beaches. On another, that same service member could go for weeks in the hot desert without a real shower, home cooked food, or even mail delivery! The spouse at home may suffer through sick children and car problems. Or that same spouse may enjoy taking a new class, working a new job, and meeting new friends. If the grass looks greener, be happy for your spouse. Life is too short. You should want and encourage each other to enjoy it.

Other times, anger surfaces from a sense of *lack of control*. Jim Partridge felt this anger when his wife was sent to Operation

Iraqi Freedom. He explained, "I have always been supportive of my wife's career, but this forced me to reevaluate our priorities. We have two little girls [ages 4 and 2]. I'm doing my best, but I'm not a mom. I just keep thinking that is no place for [my wife] and that we need her at home. I understand her duty in light of war, but was still pissed off at the Army for giving her those orders."

If you must be angry, be angry at the intangible, ever-present military. Blame someone you don't know in the vast darkness of "orders land." But don't blame or be angry with your spouse.

Positive Coping

Accept the responsibility for developing positive ways of coping with the stresses of separation. Tell yourself you *will make* this deployment a positive experience. (See Chapters 4 and 5.)

Address the issue of loss. Most couples find if they discuss and prepare for this possibility, they don't worry about it as much.

Involve children in "helping" the parent prepare to leave. This can be as simple as putting stamps on the envelopes that the parent will mail home. When the child receives the card or letter, he'll remember that he put the stamp on.

Work together to make the transition easier on your children. Talk with them. Encourage them to express their feelings. They are probably feeling the same hurt, loneliness, anger, or sadness that you are. Deploying parent: Explain why you must leave. Children sometimes misunderstand the situation and blame themselves for a parent leaving. Tell each child that you love them but you have to leave to do your job. Reassure children that you'll return. Be aware that children at different ages will understand and respond differently.

Make routine changes in family life something positive. Involve children in these decisions. Invite their ideas and comments. Make them feel a part of the solution.

* * *

Life is a wonderful adventure. If you look, you'll find at least one good thing happens each day.

Chapter 3
What a Bargain

Most of us are uncomfortable discussing finances. It seems the less money we have to play with, the more we consider it a private matter and a stressful topic. If we really want an entertainment center or need a new mattress, we, of course, deserve it and should have it! The difficulty comes when we're having trouble paying the bills (we can't afford either new purchase) or we disagree about priorities (we can afford *one*; will it be the entertainment center *or* the mattress?). Credit cards, which encourage us to buy both now and pay later, compound the problem.

Now add to the everyday, sometimes uncomfortable money decisions the fact that during a deployment you may have to take on new money management roles, live by a completely different budget, and decipher confusing changes in military pay allowances and deductions. Creating a deployment financial plan together is a necessity.

Define Financial Roles

The first step in your financial preparation is to define financial roles and responsibilities. Logistically, it is easier for the person who is not deploying to pay the bills. Utility bills, for example, are usually mailed to the home where the utilities are used. It doesn't make sense to have that mail forwarded to the deployed spouse for payment. Mail can be very slow, and it can be lost or misdirected. The payment will take longer getting back to the utility company. And if there is a late or lost payment, the last thing you need is for a warning from the utility company to be sent to the deployed spouse.

However, defining financial roles is not as simple as just saying you (the non-deploying spouse) will pay the bills. Perhaps you already pay the bills, but aren't aware of the many income and expense changes during a deployment. Or, if you have not had the bill-paying responsibility recently or ever before, it may not be clear what time of the month the bills are generally due, what the procedures are to avoid late charges, or how to budget your money so that all bills can be paid. Adjustments also need to be made for couples with separate bank accounts and investments. Couples solve these problems in different ways.

Sergeant Kate Jennings and husband Bill Harte exchange financial responsibilities frequently. When Kate deploys, Bill takes control of the finances, then hands the task back when she returns. Before a deployment, they create a list of items that need to be paid, along with a time schedule. "The hardest financial decisions to make usually have to do with unexpected house or car repairs or an unusual expense with one of the kids," Kate said. "We set up basic rules we both agree to and I trust Bill will make the best decision at the time."

Tammy and Colonel John Stellor each have their own checking and savings accounts. "We pay some bills out of his account and others out of mine," Tammy explained. "Since we keep our checkbook records differently, I had twice the paperwork the first time John deployed. Now I transfer all the money into my account and pay the bills that way when John's gone."

Gunnery Sergeant Red Petrie took over the finances completely when he married Ginger five years ago. "She was reluctant to give it all to me," Red said, "but after all this time she has confidence in what I do." When Red got orders to go overseas unaccompanied for one year, all that confidence was dumped into Ginger's lap. "He does things with the stock market and I have no idea where all our money is," she confided. How did they sort it out? She paid the bills and took care of regular finance issues for a full month before he left in case she had questions and to "get back in the swing of things." While Red was overseas, he kept track of the stocks himself, through U.S. newspapers and an online brokerage account, and called Ginger if any changes needed to be made that he couldn't make online.

Captain Aaron Robinson and his wife, Emily, set up online bill pay. Most recurring bills were taken directly out of their checking account each month, and the few bills whose amounts due changed slightly were set up as regular accounts and Emily simply typed in the amounts when those bills came in. That left a set amount each month for Emily to manage for expenses such as groceries, gas, and miscellaneous.

Regardless of your individual financial situation and current roles, one thing is certain: the bills will still have to be paid. In addition, you want to be prepared for any unforeseen money-related problems that arise during the deployment. Two things most couples who successfully manage deployment finances have in common are:

❑ They do a "trial run" before the deployment.
❑ They create, discuss, and *live by* a deployment budget.

Create a Basic Budget and a Deployment Budget

A *basic budget* should be a part of everyone's financial planning, regardless of deployment status. Budgets often are uncomfortable to create; after all, you are balancing what you *want* against what you *can afford*. But a good budget is the blueprint for building your financial future. A carefully planned budget ensures you won't run out of money now, and that you'll have enough money later to pay for lifelong goals.

Start with your basic budget first. Once you have the basics set, it's much easier to factor in all the changes to create a separate *deployment budget*. Look at the budget worksheets for each on the following pages. Then read the section on *"What's in a Budget?"* and fill in your own budget amounts. Pay special attention to those things that *change* in the deployment budget.

Basic Budget

INCOME
_____ Military base pay
_____ BAS*
_____ BAH*

_____ Other*

_____ Civilian pay (service mem.)*
_____ Civilian pay (spouse)*

_____ Dividends, interest
_____ Rental income
_____ Child support/Alimony to you
_____ Other

_____ Total Income

DEDUCTIONS
_____ Federal tax (FITW)
_____ Social Security tax (FICA)
_____ State tax
_____ Service Group Life Insur. (SGLI)
_____ Dependent dental
_____ Allotments*
_____ Child support/Alimony you pay
_____ Advance pay reimbursement
_____ Other

_____ Total Deductions
_____ Income minus deductions
        (Net Income)

EXPENSES
_____ Savings*
_____ Housing (rent/mortgage)*
_____ Utilities*
_____ Food & household needs*
_____ Transportation*
_____ Medical/Dental*
_____ Insurance*
_____ Clothing*
_____ Work-related expenses*
_____ Debt payments
_____ Education expense*
_____ Memberships/Subscriptions*
_____ Entertainment*
_____ Charitable contributions
_____ Cushion
_____ Other

_____ Total Expenses
_____ Net Income minus Expenses
Positive (surplus) or negative (deficit)?

*may change during deployment

Deployment Budget

INCOME

_____ Military base pay

_____ BAS*

_____ BAH*

_____ Career Sea Pay*

_____ Imminent Danger/ Hostile Fire Pay*

_____ Family Separation Allowance*

_____ Other*

_____ Civilian pay (spouse)*

_____ Dividends, interest

_____ Rental income

_____ Child support/Alimony to you

_____ Other

_____ **Total Income**

DEDUCTIONS

_____ Federal tax (FITW)

_____ Social Security tax (FICA)

_____ State tax

_____ Service Group Life Insur. (SGLI)

_____ Dependent dental

_____ Allotments*

_____ Field Rations*

_____ Child support/Alimony you pay

_____ Advance pay reimbursement

_____ Other

_____ **Total Deductions**

_____ Income minus deductions

(Net Income)

EXPENSES

_____ Savings*

_____ Housing (rent/mortgage)*

_____ Storage/ Relocation*

_____ Utilities*

_____ Food & household needs*

_____ Transportation*

_____ Medical/Dental*

_____ Insurance*

_____ Clothing*

_____ Work-related expenses*

_____ Debt payments

_____ Education expense*

_____ "Spouse missing" expenses*

_____ lawn maintenance

_____ maid or laundry service

_____ babysitter

_____ care packages

_____ Memberships/Subscriptions*

_____ Entertainment*

_____ Charitable contributions

_____ Cushion

_____ Other

_____ **Total Expenses**

_____ Net Income minus Expenses

Positive (surplus) or negative (deficit)?

*may change during deployment.

What's in a Budget?

To create a budget you need to know three things: your sources of income, how much you spend, and how to make the difference between the two a positive number.

There are some basics of military pay and allowances that everyone should be familiar with. This chapter will help you understand enough to plan and implement a basic budget. Keep in mind that new proposals to change military pay allowances are introduced each year. The *Uniformed Services Almanac,* published annually, has more detailed information. You can get the *Almanac* at most base exchanges for under $10, or by ordering direct from the publisher at http://www.militaryalmanac.com/, P.O. Box 4144, Falls Church, VA 22044, or 703-532-1631.

You can also learn more about military pay at various official military Web sites: start at the Secretary of Defense's Military Compensation site at http://www.dod.mil/militarypay/. This site has all the current charts for military pay and allowances. The central military pay office, the Defense Finance and Accounting Service (DFAS) can also help, at http://www.dod.mil/dfas/. Each of the services also has useful links to pay information; start at http://www.defenselink.mil/, then follow your service's link.

One essential monthly information source for your budget is the Leave and Earnings Statement (LES). This statement outlines Entitlements (basic pay and allowances), Deductions (what you don't get out of the paycheck, such as taxes, SGLI payments, and monthly TRICARE premiums), and Allotments (money you are getting, but which you are having deposited somewhere else). The Summary section tells you what the actual "take home" pay should be. You'll find exactly what taxes are being withheld, along with other important entitlement information. Become familiar with the LES; arrange to see a copy of it each month. It may be sent to your spouse at his or her deployed address. Check with the unit to get a copy for yourself.

Direct deposit is the electronic transfer of pay directly into a bank or financial organization account. Since it is required for almost all active duty military members, you should already have it. Direct deposit is extremely reliable and you *know* your military pay is in the bank on each payday. It makes financial management easier. Direct deposit is also available for many civilian jobs. If you don't have it, get it.

Income

Military Basic Pay

Basic pay is a military member's basic salary and is determined by time in service and pay grade. Publications such as the *Air Force Times*, *Army Times* or *Navy Times* print a copy of the pay scale each year, as this is public information. It is also available on military Web sites, as discussed earlier.

In addition to basic pay, there are two other types of income from the military. Allowances are provided for specific needs, including housing, food, and clothing; most are not taxable. Special/incentive pays recognize critical skills and increased danger. Not everyone gets all types of income, and changes occur depending on duty status, location, type of assignment, and so on.

Another important part of military pay are Combat Zone Exclusions: any military pay earned while in a combat zone is non-taxable. You won't see these exclusions specified on the LES, so they won't be directly factored into your budget worksheet, but they will have an impact on take home pay. The exclusions are unlimited for enlisted service members, and for officers is limited to the maximum enlisted pay amount. Combat zones and dates are set by Presidential Order.

Basic Allowance for Subsistence (BAS)

This is a non-taxable food allowance intended for the service member, not family members, so BAS is paid regardless of family status. There are three standard amounts: one rate for officers, regardless of pay grade, and two rates for enlisted members, depending on whether circumstances prevent or require eating at a government facility. Since all service members get paid BAS, all service members have to pay for any meals eaten in government facilities, such as the "chow hall," or provided by the military, such as "hot chow in the field," or world famous Meals-Ready-to-Eat.

Basic Allowance for Housing (BAH)

This is a non-taxable housing allowance intended to partially pay for housing expenses in civilian communities. It is generally not paid if you live in government quarters. The amount of BAH is determined by location, pay grade, and whether you have dependents. The location that determines BAH is your duty station, not where you actually live. The exact BAH rates are determined by surveys of rental rates in each area, and are set so that everyone in the same pay grade pays about the same out-of-pocket expenses, regardless of location. Rates in high-cost areas will be quite a bit more than in low-cost areas, but the average out-of-pocket expenses should be about the same. In 2002, for example, a married E-5 anywhere in the U.S., had, on average, $106 in out-of-pocket expenses. The Defense Department adjusts BAH over time, anticipating that eventually there will be, on average, no out-of-pocket expenses for civilian housing.

Regarding dependents and BAH, there are only two categories: with or without. The *number* of family members—one or seven—is irrelevant. For example, in 2002, a married service member in pay grade E-4 stationed in San Diego with no children received $1,132 per month BAH; a single parent in pay grade E-4 with two children also received $1,132 per month; a single service member in pay grade E-4 with no qualifying family members received $766 per month.

When both spouses serve on active duty and have a child, the senior ranked spouse draws BAH at the "with dependents" rate and the other spouse receives the "without dependents" rate. In a dual-service marriage with no children, both draw the BAH at the "without dependents" rate.

Service members stationed overseas who are not living in government quarters are eligible for an Overseas Housing Allowance. If the tour is unaccompanied, then BAH is paid at the "with dependents" rate based on where the dependents live in the U.S.

There are also some additional twists on BAH that depend on special circumstances. Partial BAH is paid to members without dependents living in government quarters. BAH-II is paid to members in particular circumstances, such as returning from overseas tours, or to reservists on active duty less than 20 weeks. BAH-Diff is paid to those assigned to single-type quarters, but who pay child support.

Family Separation Allowance

FSA is a tax-free allowance paid monthly to service members who are involuntarily separated from their families, such as when on deployment or on temporary additional duty for over 30 days. The payment is intended to defer some of the additional housing expenses resulting from these separations. There are several types and subcategories of FSA, and various conditions that must be met to qualify. Dual-service couples are also eligible for FSA.

Clothing Allowance

When they join the military, enlisted personnel are issued basic uniforms and are paid an allowance to buy required personal items that aren't issued. Officers get a one-time allowance to purchase a small portion of their military clothing. Enlisted personnel (but not officers) also receive an annual clothing replacement and maintenance allowance. Clothing allowances are not taxable.

A one-time special clothing allowance, determined by location and duration of assignment, is paid to service members in jobs requiring civilian clothing. There are also special clothing allowances for duty assignments such as recruiting and drill instructor billets.

Special and Incentive Pay

There are more than 50 kinds of extra pay for service members who take on special duty or who serve in critical fields. Here are a few common pays:

Enlistment or Reenlistment Bonus

May be offered to enlisted service members serving in certain critical positions or skill fields.

Flight Pay

Paid to qualified aviation personnel in a flight status. The amount is based on years served in flying assignments, pay grade, and time in service. Several types of flight pay, including Aviation Career Incentive, are paid to pilots, navigators, and flight surgeons.

Hazardous Duty Incentive Pay

Paid for certain assignments considered to be hazardous, such as parachuting, diving, explosive ordinance disposal, assignments on an aircraft carrier's flight deck, air weapons controllers, and demolitions work. Some of these pays are flat rates, while others depend on pay grade and time in service.

Career Sea Pay

Paid to qualified personnel assigned to a ship, ship-based staff or ship-based aviation unit while the ship is away from homeport. Pay is based on cumulative years of sea duty. All officers and enlisted members in pay grades E-4 and above are eligible.

Separate from career sea pay, submarine duty pay is based on grade and years in service and is paid to all members on submarine duty even if the sub is in port awaiting its sea assignment.

Imminent Danger / Hostile Fire Pay

This is a flat rate paid while the service member is serving within an officially declared imminent danger/hostile fire zone. Also known as combat pay.

Special Pays/Bonuses (Medical)

Many officers in the medical field (doctors, dentists, nurses, optometrists, pharmacy, veterinary) receive various special pays under various categories (accession, incentive, board certification, retention, etc.).

Per diem

This is a tax-free, daily allowance for the added expense of meals and lodging while traveling on government business or serving a temporary duty assignment at another base.

Other Sources of Income

In many cases you have additional income that isn't paid by

the military. These may apply to you or your spouse.

Civilian Pay

This includes income from all civilian jobs held by both spouses. This is a very important part of your budgeting because for many families take home pay is *lowered* during a deployment. For example, the deployed service member will have to quit any part-time civilian job. Faced with child care costs and increased responsibilities during the deployment, some non-deploying spouses reevaluate their current job and either quit, reduce their hours, or work the same but incur higher child care costs. Pregnancy complications or sudden illness can also force you to quit a job. When a spouse is deployed, be prepared for the possibility that this second income could be reduced or taken away completely due to unforeseen and often uncontrollable circumstances. As you can see, if this happens, your *deployment budget* will be quite different from your normal *basic budget*.

Dividends, Interest

Count on this only if it is regular and substantial. An example would be interest from a Certificate of Deposit or payments from stocks and bonds. Don't count this money in your budget if you reinvest it.

Rental Income

If you own a house/apartment/condo and rent it out, count the rental income here and include the mortgage payment under "Expenses: Housing."

Child Support/Alimony Paid to You

Include any such payments to either spouse. Any child support/alimony either of you pay to someone else is included under "Deduction: Child Support/Alimony you pay" or "Expenses: Other."

Other

Include any other source of income not listed here.

Total all income.

This is your **Gross Monthly Income**.

Deductions

Deductions are not really expenses or spending, but rather downward adjustments to your income. These are the most common deductions:

Federal Tax (FITW), Social Security Tax (FICA), Medicare Tax

Make sure the amount taken out of your paycheck(s) for these taxes is correct. Generally, your goal is to neither owe money at tax time, nor get a refund. While some people get excited about a big refund, remember that it is your money that you didn't have access to or earn interest on all year! To get to this balanced goal, complete a tax return early in the year based on your expected income and deductions and see if the amount of tax you will have paid out of your paycheck is approximately the same as the amount of total tax owed on the return. If it's not, you can adjust the number of exceptions you claim or adjust by a lump sum how much tax is withheld from your pay. Talk with a tax advisor to determine if you are claiming an appropriate number of exemptions on your W-4 form. Since the purpose of these tax *exemptions* is to make sure you are withholding the right amount of money, it may not be related to the number of *dependents* you have.

State Tax

Service members pay state income tax to the state of their legal residence. If your spouse does not live in that state during the tax year, ask your attorney or a tax advisor whether the service member is exempt from paying state tax. Non-military income, which includes wages earned by non-military spouses and wages earned by military personnel at a civilian job, is taxable in the state in which it is earned. The *Uniformed Services Almanac* mentioned on page 60 has useful examples that address this, as do many state tax instruction booklets. A few states do not have state income taxes, but do tax property.

Allotments

Allotments involve automatic transfer of money to an account, person, or organization for a specific purpose. Allotments are set up with the military pay office, which sends the money, and a bank, credit union, insurance firm, mortgage company, etc., which receives the money. Do not confuse allotments, which are deducted directly from military pay before depositing the remaining paycheck, with automatic bill payments, which your bank can make to an account, person, or organization, using money from your bank account just as you would write a check.

There are several types of military allotments, for various purposes, for example:

❑ To provide income to a family member. Highly recommended during a deployment. If the service member is declared missing-in-action, injured, or killed, there may be a disruption to pay but this allotment does not stop. This allotment can be made to the family member's account at a financial institution.

❑ To pay loans, such as for a car.

❑ To purchase savings bonds.

❑ To purchase commercial life insurance on the life of the service member or family members.

❑ Mortgage or rent payments.

❑ Payment of pledges for Combined Federal Campaign or a service Relief Society.

❑ Deposits to the Post-Vietnam Veterans Educational Assistance Program.

❑ Repayment of loans to a service Relief Society or Red Cross.

❑ Payment of delinquent taxes.

Check with your unit administrative office for a complete list of allotments available to you and how to set them up.

Field Rations

Deducted from pay when a service member is deployed, this is a charge for the meals your spouse is provided while in the field, on a ship, or otherwise deployed.

Child Support/Alimony You Pay

If these payments are deducted directly from your paycheck, write in the amount here. If you pay them with your monthly bills, write the payments under "Expenses, Other" to remind yourself that the payment needs to be made each month.

Advance Pay Reimbursement

If your spouse elected to take advance pay when joining the service or when moving to a new duty station, the repayment of that advance will automatically be taken out of your spouse's pay in monthly increments. Use this benefit with caution; many budget problems are caused by taking advance pay and then having a lower paycheck while paying it back.

SGLI

All active duty personnel are insured for $250,000 under the Servicemen's Group Life Insurance. The monthly premium is deducted automatically. If you do *not* want the coverage, you must submit a written request.

TRICARE Plan

While the active duty service member gets free medical and dental care, family members wanting to take advantage of this program must be enrolled in the TRICARE health plan, which requires monthly premiums.

Other

List here any other automatic deductions taken out of gross income. Don't forget to include deductions from non-military sources of income.

Total all deductions.

Gross monthly income - deductions = net income.

Your net income is the amount available for savings and expenses.

Savings

Savings is an essential part of every budget. It's an *expense* item, but it's better to think of it as an investment for *income* in future budgets! Pay yourself first by saving at least 10% of your family net income. You need savings for emergencies and for short- and long-term goals. Many people set up an automatic payment to savings by allotment, so they aren't tempted to spend it. Savings allotments are especially valuable during a deployment, when the temptation arises to spend money allocated for savings.

The amount of savings is not as important as getting in the habit of saving. If you don't already have a savings plan, set aside at least $25 a month as a start. Get in the habit of increasing this amount periodically. There are many online tools to help you figure out the projected return and yield on your savings.

The Basic Savings Plan

Your basic savings should go into four separate funds: emergency, reserve, goals, and retirement.

Emergency Fund

Always a part of your regular savings plan, an emergency fund is especially important during a deployment. Separation can make difficult decisions seem overwhelming. Financial hardship coupled with an emergency can make matters even worse. An emergency fund is an easily accessible cash reserve. A death in the family, sudden illness, accident, prolonged unemployment, major car repair, or major home repair are a few examples of emergencies that can arise. At least one month's net pay is recommended for an emergency fund, although three to six months' pay is ideal. It can be set up in a separate checking or savings account or as part of your regular account (subtract it from the total available balance so you aren't tempted to spend it).

Realize that it will not be possible or practical for most people to establish such a fund in a matter of weeks before a deployment. That's why it's important to start planning early and include an emergency fund in your regular savings plan. However, if you find yourself facing a deployment with little or no savings, contact a financial advisor or your base family center for help. An advisor can consider your individual circumstances and recommend the best plan of action.

Reserve Fund

A reserve fund keeps cash available for routine expenses you know you'll have but are infrequent enough that they are easy to forget. Insurance premiums and taxes are two of the most common types of payments made from a reserve fund. If you find it difficult to maintain a reserve fund, arrange to pay a portion of the expenses monthly. There is usually a charge for the privilege of paying monthly instead of quarterly or semi-annually. On the other hand, don't use your reserve fund for monthly payments for furniture, appliances, and similar purchases; you'll pay a lot of money in interest charges. Instead, save the money first in your goal fund and then pay cash. Not only will you not pay someone else interest, you'll earn interest for yourself.

Goal Fund

When you develop a savings plan, you should set short- and long-term goals that encourage you to look to the future and save for that future. Goals can include vacations, buying a car, buying a home, financing a college education, or paying for a wedding. There are many ways to save and invest money for these more expensive short- and long-term goals, since this money does not have to be easily accessible like the other funds. Examples are mutual funds, money market accounts, bonds, Certificates of Deposit, and low-risk stocks. Also look into special savings accounts, such as 529 education savings plans or custodial accounts.

Be sure to share some of your goals with parents and other family members. Next time they're looking for great gift ideas, they can consider contributing toward one of your goals.

Retirement Fund

Even though the military has a pension plan, everyone should have a separate retirement account. The military only pays its pension under specific conditions, the first being 20 years of service. It's wise to plan on other income. An Individual Retirement Account (IRA) is a good place to start. There are basically two types of IRAs: regular (contributions are not taxed, withdrawals

Financial Goals Worksheet

Short term goals

Goal	A: Target date (# of months from now)	Cost*	B: Balance (Amount you still need)	B÷A= Monthly savings required to reach goal
for example: Pay off credit card	5 months		$1,000	$200 + finance charge
New couch	6 months		$600	$100

Long term goals

Goal	Target date	Cost*	Current amount saved	Balance left to save**	Amount to save this year	Amount to save each month
for example: Trip to Europe	3 years	$5,000	$2,300	$2,700	$900	$75
John's college	10 years	$60,000	$7,000	$53,000	$1200	$100

Note: These figures do not account for *inflation or **interest on your savings. Refigure your cost and amount saved at least annually.

How to figure yearly & monthly savings plans

<u>IDEAL</u> amounts for **each** goal:

1. Decide when you want to reach the goal   ____years
and how much money it will take to reach it. $____

2. Divide the total amount of money needed by the number of years.

$_____/ _____years = $_____ **per year ideal**
savings to reach goal. Enter this amount on Yearly Savings Plan Worksheet.

3. Divide the yearly savings needed by 12 months.

$_____/12 = $_____ **per month ideal** savings
needed to reach goal.

Since all figures are in today's dollars, you need to adjust the figures each year. You should reevaluate your savings goals and savings plan a few times a year.

<u>MINIMUM</u> amounts for **each** goal:

1. Prioritize your goals within each fund.

2. Separate immediate needs from future wants.

3. Under the Reserve Fund, list the minimum yearly payments for non-negotiable items, such as insurance and taxes.

4. In your Emergency Fund, list one month's pay as the minimum for the entire fund (all goals).

5. Add your Reserve Fund and Emergency Fund minimum totals. Divide by 12. This is your **<u>minimum</u> monthly** savings to enter in your **basic budget**.

6. After you finish creating your basic budget, determine whether you have a positive or a negative balance. If it's positive, allocate the surplus to your other savings funds (on your savings worksheet) in the order you prioritized.

7. Periodically evaluate your spending and distribute extra money to your savings plan. The closer your minimum savings payments are to your ideal payments, the sooner you will reach your savings goals.

Yearly Savings Plan Worksheet

Type of Savings	Annual Amount Needed		Monthly Contribution
	Minimum	Ideal	(Annual/12)
	1 mon. pay	3-6 mon. pay	
EMERGENCY FUND (death, illness, accident, unemployment, repairs)	_____	_____	_____
RESERVE FUND (insurance, taxes)			
_____	_____	_____	_____
_____	_____	_____	_____
Subtotal	_____	_____	_____
GOAL FUND			
Short-term Goals (vacation, furniture)			
_____	_____	_____	_____
_____	_____	_____	_____
Long-term Goals (New car, home, education)			
_____	_____	_____	_____
_____	_____	_____	_____
RETIREMENT FUND (IRA, 401K)			
_____	_____	_____	_____
_____	_____	_____	_____
_____	_____	_____	_____
TOTAL	_____	_____	_____

are) and Roth (contributions are taxed, withdrawals are not). Your
financial counselor or a bank representative can give you information on IRAs and help you to set up an account. Certain companies also offer retirement plans such as a 401K. If you are self-
employed, look into a SEP-IRA.

Remember, it is not necessarily the *amount* of money you save,
it's the fact that you do save *regularly* that matters. Work with
what you have. But don't cheat yourself; pay yourself first.

Expenses

Housing

Include here the total cost of all housing payments, such as
current rent or mortgage payment, mortgage payment on a rental
property, and homeowner's fees.

This expense may change during a deployment depending
on where you decide to live for that time. For example, some
spouses choose to live with parents or to share housing with a
friend.

Storage of Personal Possessions in Commercial Facilities

This is a common addition to a single service member's deployment budget. If possible, save money by storing belongings
in a friend's garage or spare room. Consider sharing storage expenses with another single deploying member. (Make sure it's
someone trustworthy, in case your return dates differ.) Keep your
renter's insurance current; let your insurance company know the
location of your belongings.

Relocation Expense

This is most common for those families who move without
authorized orders. For example, some spouses choose to move
overseas (e.g., to Okinawa, Japan) to be with service members
during an unaccompanied tour. Some spouses choose to move
away from a duty station during a deployment to live with their
parents. If you choose to move on your own, you'll need to plan
for this expense as the military will not pay for these moves.

Utilities

Include all utility expenses. Practice energy-wise techniques, especially when your budget is tight. Tips to lower utility bills:

Gas/Oil/Electric:

- ❏ Check furnace, air conditioner, and water heater before every season for cleanliness and proper functioning.
- ❏ Wear sweaters instead of turning up the heat. Most energy companies recommend setting the thermostat at 65°F to 68°F when you're home and 58°F when you're sleeping or away.
- ❏ Turn off lights in unused rooms. Use energy-efficient light bulbs whenever possible. Cook in a toaster oven if you're cooking for one or two instead of heating up the oven. Hang clothes instead of using the dryer. Do not run the TV or radio unless there is a specific show you want to watch or listen to.

Water/Sewer:

- ❏ Use the water level settings on your washing machine.
- ❏ Turn off the shower water when soaping yourself. (My husband thinks all spouses of shipboard sailors and Marines should have this eye-opening experience!) Most hardware stores have inexpensive shut-off valves for shower heads. Consider water-conserving shower heads that regulate the flow of water.
- ❏ Do not run dishwater continuously. Don't run the water when brushing your teeth or washing your face.
- ❏ Operate outside sprinklers manually to avoid over-watering.

Cable:

- ❏ Write down the programs your family watches to see if they are network or cable shows. If they are mostly network, consider using a good antenna for reception rather than paying for cable. If they are cable shows, check with your local company to see if it offers program packages. Some companies let you customize your programming and pay for fewer channels. Do you really need those premium packages?

Telephone:

❏ During a deployment, be prepared for higher telephone bills. Budget *at least* double your normal expense. Calls from overseas are expensive. Use letters, tapes, or government-sponsored services. See Chapter 6 for other communication ideas.

❏ Many times during a deployment you'll feel down and want to talk with an old friend or Mom or Dad. Let others know you would like to hear from them more often and take turns calling.

❏ Compare long-distance plans and cellular options.

Food and Household

Include all trips to the commissary, exchange, supermarket, convenience store, and drug store. In addition to food, count money spent on:

❏ toiletries and personal care products (e.g., hair and skin care products, deodorant, toothpaste/brushes, contact lens or eye glass supplies, make-up, razors, feminine hygiene)

❏ cleaning supplies (e.g., detergents, sponges, vacuum cleaner bags)

❏ household supplies (e.g., light bulbs, sheets, shower curtain, desk supplies)

❏ pet supplies and food

During a deployment, it's especially important to keep food and household expenses under control, since routines and habits change after your spouse leaves. A few tips:

❏ Make a menu. Base it on sale or coupon items.

❏ Use coupons. Write your grocery list, based on your

menu, on the front of an envelope. Then keep the
coupons for that list in the envelope.

❏ Try generic or store-brand items. They often taste just as
good and are significantly cheaper. Use off-brands for
combined dishes (e.g., generic tomato sauce for lasagna
or store-brand tuna in a casserole).

❏ Buy bulk sale items when possible (e.g., a 12-pack of
light bulbs instead of one bulb; a big box of paper towels
when on sale).

❏ Consider using a membership store (e.g., Costco, Sam's).
The disadvantages are the membership fee,
unpredictability of stock, and sometimes they are
crowded. The smallest size they have may be too much
for your needs. On the other hand, they have many great
buys. Shop prudently.

❏ Organize and consolidate shopping trips. Avoid making
several small trips; they don't always save you money. It
just seems less expensive because you aren't spending it
all at once.

❏ Use a calculator while you shop. When you've reached
your budget, stop shopping. If you still have essential
items to buy, put back items that you need less.

Transportation

Include public transportation as well as personal vehicle use.
Include licenses, gas, bus/train passes, tolls, and maintenance costs.

If you plan to travel while your spouse is deployed, budget for
the additional expense.

Medical/Dental

Know your benefits and use them. Use military hospital or
clinic facilities whenever possible. Consider all options available
to you, such as on-base family clinics. When using outside providers, be aware of TRICARE coverage limitations. Set aside a
minimum of $10 per month per person for insurance co-pays,

fillings, medications, or unexpected illnesses not covered by insurance or military facilities. Remember, sickness can be more frequent during a deployment due to stress, poor eating and sleeping habits, and emotional roller coaster rides.

Does your civilian employer offer a health care reimbursement account? An HCRA lets you set aside pretax dollars out of your salary to pay for health care costs that aren't covered by your insurance. To determine the amount you should set aside, carefully estimate the cost of services you know you will use, such as eye exams. Look at what you've spent each year for the past two years as a guide. Also consider large expenses you know you'll incur this year, such as orthodontics work or having a baby. Include only your out-of-pocket expenses. It provides a nice tax break, but remember that if you don't spend the money, you don't get it back.

Insurance

Include here any insurance payments not already accounted for under Deductions. This includes:

Auto: In high cost areas, it may be financially beneficial to take the insurance (except theft) and plates off a vehicle you won't be using. Check your state Department/Bureau of Motor Vehicle's insurance and liability policies.

Life: Do you have life insurance for the non-deployed spouse? Many couples are so concerned about the risks of military life (and take SGLI for granted) that they overlook financial hardships that could result from the death of the non-military spouse.

Personal: Include renter's/homeowner's insurance if not already included in your monthly rent/mortgage payment, as well as personal rider policies (e.g., jewelry, computer equipment, personal business equipment).

Medical/Dental: Include regular or supplemental insurance payments not already deducted from pay.

Clothing

Take into consideration any special uniform or clothing needs for the service member deploying to a new area (e.g., desert battle dress utilities—BDUs/"cammies"). Also count in clothes for school if you have children, and for yourself for work and pleasure. Even necessities such as underwear and socks can be a surprisingly large expense. Clothing savings tips:

- ❏ Many consignment and thrift shops have reasonably-priced second-hand clothes in very good condition. This is an especially good option for inexpensive children's play clothes.
- ❏ Learn to sew. It's fun and easy to make your own clothes. You can find beginner patterns and inexpensive material at any general fabric store.

Work-related Expenses

Total the costs of child care, business attire not accounted for under clothing, dry cleaning, commuting costs not included earlier under transportation, and meals related to work. Compare it to your individual take home pay: how much are you really making? Many spouses look at this figure critically to see if there is a real gain in income, especially during a deployment. Child care savings tips:

- ❏ Does your civilian employer offer a child care tax credit or reimbursement account?
- ❏ Check with your family center for on-base child care options.
- ❏ Trade child care services with a trusted friend or neighbor so you can both save money.

Debt

Include all monthly payments to all creditors. Examples of common debt: credit cards, bank loans (personal or business), vehicle loans, education/student loans, and furniture/electronic/appliance payments (try to avoid these). Debt management tips:

- ❏ Reserve credit cards for emergencies.
- ❏ Suppress the urge to overspend your means, thereby

acquiring more debt. (See the debt-to-income ratio chart on next page.)

❑ Keep your total bill to an amount you can afford to payoff in full each month. If you already have a balance on your credit cards, plan to pay more than your minimum monthly payment required by the credit card company or bank. The minimum payment often barely covers the finance charge assessed on your previous month's balance. Even if you can only pay $10 more, it will pay the bill off sooner.

❑ Consider a consolidation loan (if the rate is lower) to pay off credit cards. If you do this, don't use the credit cards again to build up more debt!

❑ For other purchases, such as furniture, plan ahead rather than impulse buy. Save the money first by putting the monthly payment into a savings account. Then when you have enough saved, pay cash for the item. This will save you large amounts of money in interest charges. It also gives you time to make sure you really need an item and to shop around for better prices.

"Spouse Missing" Expenses

You won't find this expense in most budget counseling literature. But there are times when having only one adult in the house is more expensive than two. For example, during a deployment, one spouse cannot always assume both spouses' responsibilities. Write down all of your spouse's responsibilities, such as lawn maintenance, house cleaning, laundry, or baby-sitting. Then consider which ones you will not have the time or energy to do (be realistic) during a deployment. Add up the cost of hiring someone else to take on those tasks that were not accounted for in your regular budget. You should also include the cost of postage, stationery, and care package items.

Education

Include committed education expenses such as tuition toward

Debt-to-Income Ratio

Knowing your debt-to-income ratio helps you make decisions regarding future debt, such as a new car payment.

$$\text{Debt-to-income ratio} \quad = \quad \frac{\text{installment credit*}}{\text{net income}}$$

*Add up all monthly charge card payments, car payments, and other loan payments; do not include rent/mortgage, utilities, or insurance.

When you have figured your ratio, multiply it by 100 to get a percent, then use these guidelines:

less than 15%: You can afford to incur additional debt if it doesn't put you over 20%

15%-20%: Fully extended. Don't take on additional debt.

21%-30%: Overextended. Stick closely to a budget and take steps to reduce debt.

greater than 30%: Seriously overextended. Make changes or see a financial counselor.

Example:
    Monthly payments:
    Credit card A $ 50
    Credit card B $100
    Car payment $320
    Loan payment $150
    Total $620
    divided by net monthly income of $2000 = .31
    .31 x 100 = 31%, overextended

a certificate or degree and special training or professional development expenses.

Memberships/Subscriptions

Add up dues for social clubs, athletic clubs, or professional associations. Also include newspaper, magazine, and newsletter subscriptions.

Entertainment

Include money you spend on having fun, treating yourself, or doing something extra, such as:

- ❏ eating out or ordering pizza
- ❏ going out to or renting movies
- ❏ sight-seeing or traveling
- ❏ taking a ceramics or photography class
- ❏ golfing or bowling
- ❏ any other hobbies or special events

Contributions

Include charitable donations, such as church offerings, you give regularly.

Cushion

Allow a cushion for some flexibility. A realistic amount is $25-$50 per month plus $10-25 for each additional family member. Give yourself room to cover unexpected items, such as replacing a child's lost gym bag, paying a parking ticket, or accepting an invitation to lunch with a friend.

Other Expenses

Keep a log of what you spend. Keep all of your receipts to help complete your log. Write down even a $2 trip to the drug store. You'll be surprised how quickly $1 vending machine trips add up, not to mention those $3 lattes! Include what you spend on haircuts, outside laundry or dry cleaning, cigarettes, and impulsive and compulsive spending. You may have budgeted for some of these; does your budget match the true expense? Using this log, you can more accurately create and stick to a budget for miscellaneous items. Cut excess or unnecessary expenses as much as possible without cutting out the fun.

Total all savings and expenses.

Subtract your savings and expenses from your net income. The result is either a balanced budget, budget surplus, or deficit.

Balance Your Budget

If the result of your budgeting is a positive number (surplus), stick to your budget, review it each month to make adjustments as needed, and stay on track. Use the extra money for additional savings (put it into one of your four savings funds), to pay off debt, or for travel, household items, or extra care packages to your loved one. Reevaluate your savings plan if this extra is more than $100 per month. Remember to pay yourself first. You can reach those future educational, home, or new vehicle goals sooner.

If your balance is negative (deficit), you need to adjust right away. Don't get depressed about trying to give up something or needing to get a new job. Here are a few ideas to look at:

Check your income.

- ❑ Are you receiving all your military pay and allowances?
- ❑ Are you claiming the right number of exemptions on your W-4s for withholding?
- ❑ Are any allotments about to expire?
- ❑ Consider part-time employment or turn a hobby into income.

Decrease your expenses.

In addition to the savings tips given earlier:

- ❑ Use your military benefits, facilities, and services.
- ❑ Separate *needs* from *wants*. Make spending changes if one spending category is excessive, an activity becomes habit instead of fun, or achieving a goal can be done at a slower pace. Swap talents or skills with friends, neighbors, and co-workers so you can all save money.

Pay Adjustments During Deployment

Factor into your deployment budget the probability that military pay will most likely NOT match the monthly budget you created. Plan for known pay, allowance, or deduction changes during the deployment *regardless* of what the LES reads.

There is a "period of adjustment to pay" during which relevant administrative facts may not have reached the finance system in time to actually adjust current pay. This period of adjustment may take several pay periods. Many spouses are surprised that a paycheck is short when they have figured out an increase in pay during the deployment. There can be several reasons for this. Let's look at an example:

Carol's husband, Jack, a Marine Sergeant, will deploy for six months. During this deployment Jack will not get his Basic Allowance for Subsistence (BAS). Let's say Jack's BAS is $241 per month. Carol is planning on $241 less in Jack's next paycheck. But the finance system doesn't know Jack is deployed yet, so Carol receives the $241 that Jack does not rate. Jack's following paycheck is $482 less than Carol expects; it is reduced by the $241 he didn't rate the first pay period plus the $241 he doesn't rate for the following pay period. If Carol has not planned accordingly and already spent that $241 of "extra" pay that came in the first paycheck, she'll have trouble meeting her budget.

If we add to Carol's trouble the fact that Jack is now entitled to Family Separation Allowance (which finally showed up on his following paycheck), but his Basic Allowance for Housing (BAH) is reduced on his next paycheck (because his room on ship is considered government housing), Carol has a potential budgeting nightmare.

Plan according to the changes that are *supposed to be there.* Don't hesitate to ask for help or reassurance that the pay *will* get straightened out. Bring pay problems to your family center during a deployment or to the unit family readiness officer.

❏ Experts say you can increase your spending power by 10-15% if you follow a spending plan. Once you create a realistic budget, follow your own spending advice.

Reduce debt.

❏ Make managing debt your first priority. Don't take on new debt until old debt is paid. Compare interest rates.

❏ Refinance a debt, if applicable. First, call your creditors and discuss your situation. Many creditors are more willing to work with you if you take the initiative to contact them before your payment is overdue. Some will even revise the amount and due date of your monthly payment.

❏ Learn to control your finances. This is the best defense, and reading through this section may be enough to get you started. But don't hesitate to take advantage of free services available to you. The Consumer Credit Counseling Service (CCCS), at 800-338-CCCS (2227), or http://www.debtadvice.org/, provides money management information and can work with you and your creditors to get your debts under control.

Become a Wise Consumer

My friend Jodi can spot a bargain a mile away. But she also knows that being a wise consumer is more than knowing that a product has a reasonable price tag on it. Researching the product or company, being aware of potential scams, and using common sense over emotion when making important purchase decisions are skills wise consumers master.

Do your homework.

Before you make a big purchase:

❏ Talk to your friends and neighbors about it. Ask if they have bought a particular brand or used a particular merchant you are considering.

- ❑ Read *Consumer Reports* magazine and annual buying guide for product ratings and safety evaluations.
- ❑ Call the Better Business Bureau or go to http://www.bbb.com/ and look up the company you plan to purchase from. The BBB can tell you how long the company has been in business, if the company has had any complaints registered against it, and if those complaints were resolved.
- ❑ Comparison shop for price and quality. Look at competitors' products and services. What's different from the one you are considering?

Recognize potential scams.

Beware of stores that make incredible claims that sound too good to be true. Just because it's in print, does not mean it's true. Although there are certainly many reputable companies offering such deals, look for common scams in these areas: photo clubs, telemarketing sales, mail order fraud, used car sales, some health spa memberships, prizes offered through the mail or e-mail, credit card frauds, multi-level marketing offers, and door-to-door sales.

Use common sense and trust your instincts.

- ❑ Protect your credit card. Never give your credit card number over the phone unless you initiated the call and know exactly to whom you are speaking.
- ❑ Think it over. Take at least 24 hours or more to think about a major purchase before making a final decision. This will give you time to think more clearly and evaluate if you can afford it, if you need it, and if there is a better alternative. Don't fall for the line, "This offer won't be good tomorrow." Any offer you get today is good tomorrow from a reputable company.
- ❑ Get all promises in writing. Never sign an incomplete contract, and always read the fine print. Don't sign what you don't understand. If you feel uncomfortable with a

contract, have a legal officer or trusted friend review it. Get a copy of any contract you do sign as well as any guarantees or warranties offered.

Protect Your Credit

When creditors want to know what kind of credit risk you are, they ask you to fill out an application that allows them to do a credit check or *inquiry* at a credit bureau. The bureau generates a report that tells creditors how well you've paid current and past bills, including payments for credit cards, department store cards, student loans, bank loans and accounts, medical accounts, and much more. Information is kept for seven years or since the date of your most recent bad credit incident (if any). If you've been denied credit within the past 60 days based on information in a report, you're entitled to a free copy of your report. If you want a creditor to remove an incident such as a late payment from your record, contact the creditor directly to discuss the possibility. If you find an incorrect item on the report, contact the bureau. The bureau will contact the creditor and if the creditor agrees there's an error, the bureau will remove the item from your report.

Common reasons you could be denied credit include:

❑ missing or late payments, especially if this is a pattern

❑ too many credit inquiries within the last 12 months (some creditors view excessive inquiries as negative, even if your record is immaculate)

❑ too high an amount of unsecured debt (e.g., outstanding credit card balances, personal bank loans, and other money lent to you without collateral. Secured debt means the lender can take the attached "security" or physical property if you fail to make payments; common examples are vehicle loans and home mortgages.)

❑ a credit card or unsecured credit line where the balance is too close to the credit limit.

Get a copy of your and your spouse's credit report, even if

you've never had trouble obtaining credit. It's a good education to see how you are listed by your creditors, what type of accounts generally show up on a report, and how joint accounts affect your individual record. It also helps you to understand why paying bills on time is important. If you discover you need to establish a credit history, you don't have to have your own credit cards to get one. You can be an authorized user of a credit card (make sure the bill's paid each month) and you can put some monthly bills such as utility bills in your name.

There are three primary credit bureaus, each specializing in different regions of the country. If you've moved around a lot, it would be interesting to compare records from all three bureaus. The cost of a report varies by bureau, state, and how many copies you request in one year; usually, reports cost about $10.

The three major credit bureaus are Experian, Equifax, and TransUnion. Depending on the bureau, you can request a copy of your credit report online, by phone, by fax, or by mail. You'll usually need your full name (and any aliases or former names), current address, previous two addresses, social security number, date of birth, current employer, and contact phone numbers.

Experian
P.O. Box 2002
Allen, TX 75013
888-397-3742 (888-Experian)
http://www.experian.com/

Equifax
P.O. Box 740241
Atlanta, GA 30374-0241
800-685-1111
http://www.equifax.com/

TransUnion
P.O. Box 390
Springfield, PA 19064
800-916-8800
http://www.tuc.com/

Don't Underestimate the Value of Good Financial Management

Having reviewed budgeting and financial planning in some detail, you may be wondering if it is worth the time. Consider below the military family financial experiences during Gulf War deployments. While each deployment situation is different, about a third of these families, regardless of pay grade or service, *did* experience more financial burdens. For the majority of those families, the burden was more than $500 and for a third, it was more than $1,000.

Were there any additional financial burdens on the family resulting from Operation Desert Shield/Storm?

Percentage* reporting additional financial burden due to Operation Desert Shield/Storm

	E1-E4	E5-E6	E7-E9	O1-O3	O4+
All services	35%	41%	38%	31%	31%
Army	31%	42%	46%	35%	36%
Navy	30%	31%	27%	24%	27%
Air Force	42%	48%	42%	35%	28%
Marine Corps	37%	43%	38%	31%	33%

	Female	Male
Spouses with children	41%	34%
Spouses without children	26%	26%

Of those who reported an additional financial burden:

8% reported the burden was	Less than $250
22% reported the burden was	$251-$500
11% reported the burden was	$501-$750
6% reported the burden was	$751-$999
35 % reported the burden was	More than $1000

Source: 1992 DoD Surveys of Officers and Enlisted Personnel and Their Spouses

*percentages are rounded

While we can't generalize too much from the Gulf War experience, you can see that financial burdens resulting from deployment are normal, widely experienced, and sometimes expensive.

In a survey of active duty military members a decade later:

- ❑ 55% were married; 5.9% were married to someone else in the military (joint-service)
- ❑ 46% had children; 6.1% were single parents

The top two member/family concerns for base commanders were:

- ❑ Young enlisted money management (62%) and
- ❑ Financial indebtedness (58%)

In addition,

- ❑ 20% of Navy and Marine families found a "great" financial hardship of deployment
- ❑ 57% of military families said managing bills was the highest money concern of deployment

To ease the burden on your family's pocketbook, which will in turn help emotional and relational burdens as well: plan, budget, and manage your finances.

Financial Planning Checklist

❑ Define financial roles and responsibilities: who does what, when, and how.

❑ Discuss financial concerns.

❑ Become familiar with Leave and Earnings Statements.

❑ Create or review an existing basic budget.

❑ Set up or continue an existing savings plan.

❑ Discuss which pay allowances or expenses you expect to change during a deployment; create a deployment budget by making these adjustments to your basic budget.

❑ Do a "trial run" of paying the bills.

❑ Practice energy-saving, money-saving habits.

❑ Learn to be a wise consumer (e.g., use coupons, consult *Consumer Reports*).

❑ Know where to go for help if pay is incorrect or if you need budgeting or financial assistance.

Separation

Who wanted to creep along in comfort when there was one chance in a thousand of flying?

—*Gail Godwin*

Chapter 4
The Super Spouse

Ask any veteran deployment survivor what happens the first day your spouse leaves, and the answer might go something like this: The garbage disposal breaks (after you've filled it), you catch the flu, the toilet plugs up, the dog breaks through the fence, the car dies, the basement floods, and your youngest child loses his favorite toy. You set one less place at the table, crawl into an empty bed, and realize that was just the first day!

Dorothy Windsor is married to a Marine with broad shoulders, a square jaw, and the ability to grunt "Ooh rah." In their 12 years of marriage, she estimates he's been deployed at least half of the time. Dorothy herself is a cross between a superhero and Marilyn Monroe. She's too busy treading water to notice, but her friends who have watched this suddenly single spouse work full-time, mow the lawn, raise three kids, patch the fence, change the oil, program the VCR, and file the taxes while remaining a happy and fulfilled person have stopped to admire.

Deployments present many challenges, including learning how to fix things you didn't realize could break, balancing work and play, finding time for yourself, and keeping the right perspective on your life events. There are also many opportunities: you might develop new skills, discover hidden talents, find new interests, and gain a better understanding of yourself and your loved ones.

So how do you meet these challenges and take advantage of the opportunities? What does it mean to be suddenly single yet happy and fulfilled? What does it take to become a Super Spouse?

You don't have to leap tall buildings in a single bound. But you do have to choose the buildings you want to leap and then leap with confidence.

Handiwork

The most common complaint among Super Spouses: "everything breaks" when their spouse deploys. What are your options?

1. Fix it.

2. Live with it broken.

3. Pretend this isn't happening to you.

Choice number three, pretending this isn't happening to you, is usually the preferred choice on day one. It's simply a way to allow yourself to get some much needed sleep. Click your heels three times and say, "This isn't happening to me." You might convince yourself it's all a bad dream and everything will be better in the morning. (Living in Kansas with a dog named Toto is also helpful.)

On the second day, you realize it's not a dream. Yet with your new found rest and creativity, you decide choice number two, living with it broken, might actually work for some things. For example, if the garbage disposal *wasn't* full when it broke, you could start a compost pile in the garden instead of fixing the disposal. So what if the television picture went black, you've been meaning to catch up on your reading anyway.

Sooner or later, you will come to choice number one. It is, after all, one of the great hallmarks of a Super Spouse. Of course "fix it" is open to interpretation. There's fixing it for now and fixing it right. More importantly, there's fixing it yourself or finding someone else to fix it for you.

One year we invested in a Time-Life book series on do-it-yourself home repair. As luck would have it, my husband was on a six-month deployment when our toilet decided to run water continuously. So I read the plumbing book. The picture in the book didn't look anything like our toilet, but the problem matched the description of needing a new *ballcock*. I had no idea what that meant, so I called a plumber. Just for kicks, when the plumber arrived, I said, "I think we need a new ballcock." He looked it over and said, "You sure know your plumbing" and replaced the ballcock (whatever that is).

This event gave me confidence when our kitchen faucet started leaking. I went shopping at Home Depot, picked out a Delta faucet, and embarked on a new career. What I discovered is that putting in a new faucet isn't as easy as it should be. First, you have to find the right tools. Second, there isn't any room to maneuver around under the sink (a person can get a serious headache banging her head under there). Third, there are so many hoses and pipes *all in the same location*, it's nearly impossible to fit the tools, once you find the right ones, in between the hoses and pipes... But after two or three or who's counting hours, I had a new kitchen faucet, no leaks, and a new respect for plumbers.

No matter what the repair, whether you are a do-it-yourselfer or not, it's important to have a "fix-it" plan. Begin with regular maintenance (go back to your pre-deployment checklists). Expect things to break. Determine what maintenance items and repairs you want to do and are expected to do yourself.

If you live in military housing or rent an apartment or home, the maintenance department or property manager will take care of most maintenance and repairs for you. Keep their numbers handy, especially the after-hours number.

If you own a home, consider a home warranty, or home protection plan. This is especially helpful if you recently purchased your home. When we bought our first home, we didn't want the possible expense of repairing or replacing a water heater or other major appliance. So we paid approximately $300 per year for a home protection plan. Anytime a major appliance needed a repair, we called the insurance company. We paid $25 for the repair visit and the insurance company paid to fix or replace the appliance. The policy paid for itself when the microwave control panel needed to be replaced and the toilet needed that new ballcock.

Mostly, it paid for deployment peace of mind.

Make a helper list of friends and neighbors who are willing to be called for certain tasks—just remember this approach may cross the "fix it now" or "fix it right" line. Keep a list of handymen—look in the yellow pages or call a local real estate agent. Call your local utility companies. Some are willing to clean or replace filters and give free yearly checkups on a furnace at the beginning of winter or an air conditioner at the beginning of summer. Others will at least send you information about the maintenance that you should do yourself.

Learn to watch for signs of possible breakdown. Most spouses complain about auto maintenance and repair. Here are a few rules of the road to keep in mind. Make yourself similar lists for other areas of maintenance.

Car maintenance tips:

- Check tire pressure at least once a month. Watch for signs of uneven wear. Have tires rotated about every 5,000 miles (many places will do the rotation for free if you bought the tires there). Keep your spare tire in good condition, with proper air pressure, and keep it in the vehicle! Learn how to change a tire.

- Watch for electrical problems. If lights dim when you start the car, for example, you might have a weak battery. Trouble starting the car could indicate worn out spark plugs or a clogged fuel pump.

- Make sure all lights and turn signals work.

- Change oil or take it in to be changed regularly; every 3 months or 3,000 miles is generally recommended. If you take your car to a quick-change station, ask to see the old filter and the dipstick when they're done to make sure they've actually changed both the filter and the oil. The dipstick should show clear-light brown oil to the full line.

- Keep your windshield washer reservoir filled.

- ❑ Check fluids twice a month; recognize fluids by color. Motor oil is brown, black if you've put off changing it for a while. Coolant is green, pink, or yellow. Transmission fluids are red. Brake fluid is clear brown. Oil, coolant, and power steering leaks usually occur at the front of the car. Shiny streaks inside tires may indicate your brake or wheel cylinders are leaking or that a CV boot is torn.
- ❑ Inspect hoses and connections for signs of wear and leaks.
- ❑ Replace air filter at least every 25,000 miles.
- ❑ Maintain regular checkups, usually every 30,000 miles.
- ❑ Know how to handle common auto problems on the road, including:
  - — car won't start (common cause: dead battery, clogged fuel pump, worn out spark plugs, or electrical problem): keep a set of jumper cables in the trunk and know how to use them
  - — radiator boiled over (possible causes: low fluid level, a leak, broken thermostat, not enough antifreeze in the fluid): keep a gallon of antifreeze in your trunk if your car does this. Check the level in the overflow tank; that's where you add new fluid. Be careful checking the radiator—it's hot!
  - — door lock frozen (don't wash the car if the air temperature is 40°F or below): keep a can of de-icer in your home and office
  - — locked keys in car: give an extra set to a trusted friend; call a service station, auto club, or locksmith
  - — flat tire: practice changing a tire; join an auto club that will come to you and change it for you
  - — ran out of gas (this usually only happens once!)
- ❑ If your car is prone to problems, or you are worried

about its reliability, consider joining an auto club. They dispatch tow trucks, bring a gallon of gas, sometimes fix problems on the spot, open a locked door, or tow you to a repair shop. AAA is the most widely known, and costs $40-60 per year, which can pay for itself in one tow or lockout.

Car Emergency Kit:

- ❏ cellular phone
- ❏ tire puncture sealant (noncombustible)
- ❏ full-size lug wrench
- ❏ jumper cables (know how to use them)
- ❏ flashlight (check monthly; batteries can lose life quickly)
- ❏ first-aid kit (with snake bite kit)
- ❏ work gloves
- ❏ screwdriver, pliers
- ❏ electrical and duct tape
- ❏ flares
- ❏ survival gear in case you are stranded. You can keep this in a box or backpack to reduce trunk clutter

Always include:
   —water (a box of bottled water is fine)
   —food (a good use for your spouse's leftover MREs!)
   —extra clothes (old jeans or sweats)
   —shoes (an old pair of running shoes)
   —sweater/jacket
   —tarp and some string or twine (in home supply stores; many uses, such as for shade, shelter, blocking a broken window, or visibility if you are off the road)

in hot climates, add:
—hat
—sunscreen

in cold climates, add:
—fire starting kit
—shovel
—warm clothes, hat, gloves
—blankets/sleeping bags

The Balancing Act

Maintenance and repairs, unfortunately, will not be your only time-consumers during a deployment. Suddenly, just you will have all the responsibilities of two people. Whether that means taking on chores you once shared with your spouse, or becoming a single parent, it requires a delicate balance between work and play and a conscientious effort to learn your limitations and make time to stay healthy and happy.

Signs you may be doing too much:

- ❏ It's 10 o'clock at night, you're exhausted, and insist on getting just two more things done.
- ❏ You've stopped seeing any of your friends because you don't have time.
- ❏ You forgot your child's name.
- ❏ You eat smart and get plenty of sleep, but you're still tired most of the time.

Signs you need more to do:

- ❏ You dust your house with a Q-tip twice a day.
- ❏ You're making your 11th phone call this morning, and that's below average.
- ❏ Your list of favorite television shows grows longer by the day.

So, are you still waiting for those extra five hours a day to finally complete your to-do list? Or are you bored?

Either too much or too little to do is not healthy nor is it any fun. Super Spouses find a balance between work and play, between time for others and for themselves, and they find out and respond to their own limits.

Where Does the Time Go?

Whether you are trying to delegate a few extra responsibilities, looking for valuable experiences to fill your time, or attempting to juggle the new with the old, the first step is to honestly assess your situation.

Keep a log of how you spend your time. The easiest way is to buy an inexpensive notebook that you can carry with you. Write down in small blocks of time the type of activity you did and how you felt doing it. Try to write while you are doing an activity or soon after completing it. Consider this scenario:

From 7:00 a.m. to 7:30 a.m. you made breakfast for the kids and sent them off to school. You normally do that every day and it makes you feel like a great parent. Except this morning, the kids asked some hard questions about your spouse being gone and how life will change. They were moody and sluggish. Half way through breakfast, you realized you forgot to turn on the lawn sprinklers at 6:30 (a task your spouse usually takes care of). The kids almost missed the bus and because they were late, you also left for work late. You arrived just in time for your 8:15 meeting, but you felt rushed and unprepared; you missed your first cup of coffee.

Isn't it amazing how one half hour in the morning affected the rest of your day? During your lunch break, you made the time to write down and think about what happened that morning. Your family's daily routine during this deployment has the potential to be a negative experience. But instead of letting it get you down, you think of things you can do to make it better. For example, you can get an automatic timer for the sprinklers or tape a reminder to the bathroom mirror. You can have a nice long, open discussion with your kids tonight and really talk out their fears and confusion about your spouse being gone. And you can change breakfast time to 6:45 instead of 7:00 to give everyone a little more time to get dressed and feel good about getting out the door on time.

Obviously, everyone's daily routine is different and this example may seem simplistic. But this technique will work for almost any situation. Keep in mind it might take some time for a pattern of feelings or occurrences to develop before you realize what the source of the problem is. By writing down (and later thinking about) what happened, what you did, and how it made you and others in your family feel, you can begin to find solutions to make your life easier. Write down the solutions, too, so you can refer back to them. They might give you ideas when you think you've run out of good ones.

Once you have a better overview of what you really do with your time and what kind of new activities and responsibilities fill your time, you may find you need to make adjustments. Your goal is to mix necessary responsibilities with personal choices in a way that gets the needed jobs done, while leaving you enough time for things you want to do for yourself.

Too Much Time in the Wrong Places

Is your day filled with so many activities that you don't have time left for yourself or your loved ones? Whether you've decided to take on additional tasks or been given new responsibilities as a result of the deployment, having too much to do can increase stress and eventually cause burn-out.

Crystal and Larry Martin shared the responsibilities of their house and children—until Larry deployed on a ship for six months. They put their house up for sale in anticipation of orders upon Larry's return. Crystal had to keep the house ready to show to buyers and meet with real estate agents on call. She had to keep the lawn clean cut. And when the school year ended, she had to taxi their three children back and forth from day care to sporting activities. The problem? Crystal also had a full-time job. When the day was complete, she found herself frustrated, exhausted, and with no energy or good feelings left for herself or her children. She was even too tired to write letters to Larry. It was a difficult, agonizing decision to make on her own. But after looking over their finances and writing a letter to Larry explaining the situation, she decided to quit her job. She worried that Larry would think she couldn't handle things back home. He surprised her one Saturday with a phone call, saying he understood and was behind her all the way. He had confidence she knew the situation better than anyone and had made the right decision. Crystal spent the summer in the gym and at poolside with her children and found the relaxation she needed to counter the stress.

Quitting your job is not the answer for everyone. Crystal would have quit her job in a matter of months anyway when they moved. In the meantime, little was left from her paycheck after paying child care costs. The family's monetary loss was minimal. Her gain—time for herself, her children, and the real estate agents—was worth millions.

For Deanna Shoemaker the issue was finding a good day care facility near her office or a reliable nanny. "I'm not good at staying home," she explained, "I don't have the discipline." She says that

> As of March 1995, according to the U.S. Department of Labor, 422,000 military wives, 54.5 percent of all military wives, were employed. The study did not include male spouses.
>
> According to a 1992 survey by the Defense Manpower Data Center, 61 percent of all military spouses who worked were employed full time, 30 percent part time, and 9 percent self-employed.

especially during her husband Tom's deployments, she would "go crazy" without the structure and distraction of work. She finds she has a lot more love to give their 5-year-old son when she has meaningful time away from him. "He can tell I'm a happier person," Deanna says.

While Kathy Wane says her family sure could use the second income, she can't make enough at a job to pay child-care costs for their four children. And her husband's schedule, even when he's not deployed, is very unpredictable so she never knows if he can be home to care for them.

Ginny Clark found out that extensive training schedules have many of the separation emotions of a longer deployment. Her husband, John, was transferred to a unit that specialized in running field training exercises for new recruits. To help her family adjust, Ginny accepted a half-time computer training position at the company where she used to have a full-time director position. "The pay is still good and I'm keeping my skills up-to-date," she explained. "But I'm home when my kids (ages 7, 12, 15) get home from school. They're all in different schools (elementary, middle, high), each going through different growing pains right now. I felt they really needed some continuity and a strong parental presence, especially with John's new training schedule."

The decision of whether or not to work is made by dads, too. James Ludson quit his job when his wife, Kim, deployed to the Persian Gulf. Their two children were barely toddlers. When Kim returned to the states, her hectic schedule made for some long work days. James continued caring for the children during the day, cleaning the house, and making dinner. "Some of our friends, even our parents, kept asking when I was going to stop living off my wife and get a job. They thought something was wrong," James said. "They didn't get that we were doing this for the kids. The kids needed some consistency. They were at such a critical age. I'm really glad we could afford for me to stay home. More fathers should try it; it's very rewarding." The couple decided to keep the arrangement regardless of deployment status until both children were in school.

The key to the decision of whether or not and how much to work, according to these military spouses, is to know and respond to your limits. By delegating some of the necessary responsibilities (e.g., hiring a babysitter once a week to give yourself a break; contracting with a gardener/lawn maintenance service during the deployment; giving some household chores to older children; paying an accountant to do your taxes; or exchanging cooking nights with another "single" spouse), you can open up time for yourself, regardless of your employment status.

Time for Yourself

Some Super Spouses use the time they create for themselves to try something new or to tackle that project that's been hiding

Tips for Busy Professionals

Some spouses have demanding professional careers that don't offer flex time or the option of taking a year off. If you're on the fast track to CEO, you still need to find balance in your life in order to succeed at work. Since you're married to a service member, you already deal with the challenge of maintaining your professional status as you follow your spouse around the world's duty stations. With the added stress of a deployment, you may begin to feel like Sisyphus, the mythological king doomed forever to roll a large boulder up a hill, just to have it roll back down again. Here are a few things to try:

❑ Make appointments with yourself. Treat the time as seriously and delicately as you would a meeting with your most important client, your supervisor, or your staff. Turn off the phone, accept no interruptions.

❑ Take regular breaks and go for a walk, outdoors if possible. This is especially important when you have a busy schedule. You're much more productive when you're fresh and in a good frame of mind.

❑ Remove minor irritations from your work environment. Eliminating a flickering fluorescent light, a loud computer fan, a pile of clutter, or a shortage of office supplies will help you focus on your work.

❑ Communicate with peers within and outside your office. By participating in professional associations, you gain new ideas and a chance to share your own expertise with colleagues in your field.

❑ To remind you of your success and to encourage you to continue achieving, keep signs of achievement, such as awards, letters from appreciative clients, professional certificates, diplomas, etc. within sight of your work area.

in the closet for months. Remember, this is time for *you* and what you do should be something you really enjoy.

Staying in balance allows you to try new activities or to engage in projects you've wanted to do for a while but couldn't. It makes your months alone seem more complete. You feel better about yourself and your accomplishments.

For example, during deployments, Nancy McKenzie uses "organizing" as both a coping technique—she has less idle time to think about missing her husband—and as a way to clear her mind (and house!). "Everything in my house has to be reorganized," she says. "Closets, cabinets... My husband is almost afraid to go. He'll say, 'now don't touch anything in this closet while I'm gone.'"

Jill Kepling signs up for community classes whenever her spouse deploys. Ceramics, pottery, and photography are her favorites. She says, "They encourage me to be creative and to meet new people."

Richard Trent has his own consulting business. He tends to take on several more clients when his wife is deployed. "I like to fill my schedule to the max," he explains. "I don't have to worry about coming home late because we don't have kids. It gives me the opportunity to learn more about my business and to make some extra money."

Take out a calendar and block off milestones for the deployment. For each block, write a goal for accomplishing a certain project, spending time on a hobby, or learning something new. As you finish each block, you'll be one step closer to reunion. Here are just a few ideas:

- ❑ Go to the library and catch up on your reading (magazines, mysteries, short stories, poems, classics...).
- ❑ Walk in the mountains, on the beach, in the park, around the neighborhood.
- ❑ Bird watch.
- ❑ Write in a journal.
- ❑ Write a children's story.

- ❏ Go fishing.
- ❏ Get together with friends and catch up on things that have happened in your lives since you last spoke. Write letters or send e-mail to old friends.
- ❏ Join a church group.
- ❏ Get involved with your local family support network.
- ❏ Volunteer your time and talents. Be a pool assistant or teach water skills at the YMCA. Work at the thrift shop or in a relief center. If you know how to sew, knit, or crochet, relief organizations always need items for their emergency kits or programs like "Baby's First Sea-bag." Check local schools, youth camps, and volunteer centers for opportunities. Some companies organize volunteer activities for their employees to participate in, such as Meals on Wheels, tutoring, Big Brothers/Sisters, and Habitat for Humanity.
- ❏ Learn woodworking. Build something simple, even if it's a workbench for future projects.
- ❏ Visit your base auto hobby shop. You can use the tools and equipment to repair your car. Some shops sell supplies such as oil filters. And there's usually someone around to give you a few tips.
- ❏ Plant a vegetable garden or flowers.
- ❏ Learn how to cook something new.
- ❏ Take a class. Work on a degree or take enjoyable community classes, such as scrapbooking, photography, painting, ceramics, or creating Web sites.
- ❏ Learn to play an instrument.
- ❏ Go to plays, movies, or museums. Find discount nights or matinees.
- ❏ Join a ball team, bowling league, or golf club.
- ❏ Visit the base recreation areas for archery, horseback riding, swimming, nature activities, or boating.

Staying Healthy

When an airplane taxies to the runway, flight attendants brief passengers about the safety features of the aircraft, including oxygen masks. Passengers are told that in the event oxygen is needed "and you are traveling with a small child, please assist yourself first, then assist the child." Well, it works the same on the ground; when you are breathing, you are better able to assist yourself and others. Grabbing the oxygen mask translates into many things, but the bottom line is to take care of yourself first. This isn't just a matter of selfishness: if you are not healthy, you can't take care of your kids, your job, your home, or your deployed spouse.

A Healthy Body
Nutrition

Eating right takes discipline, especially during a deployment. One bad habit many spouses fall into is eating out or ordering out for fast food. Aside from the fact that it's expensive and can destroy your budget, fast food can drain your energy and quickly add unwanted pounds. The problem is, it's hard for many spouses to get up the energy to cook a full dinner just for themselves or for their children (who also love "greasy spoon" menus!). Here are a few healthy ideas:

- Take a multivitamin every day.
  Your doctor or pharmacist can recommend the best brand or combination vitamin for your body's needs. The vitamin is to *supplement* your well-balanced eating habits and give you extra insurance during this stressful time. Do not substitute vitamins in a pill for vitamins in food!
- Always have healthy snacks available.
  Fruits and non-starchy vegetables are no-fat, no-cholesterol sources of fiber and fluid and 100 percent pure energy. Clean and cut fresh fruits such as cherries, grapes, watermelon, cantaloupe, strawberries, raspberries, blueberries, and kiwi; throw them all in a big bowl,

cover with clear wrap and refrigerate. Clean and cut
fresh vegetables such as celery, carrots, cauliflower,
broccoli, peppers, and radishes; place in water in a
sealed plastic container and refrigerate. Have apples,
oranges, grapefruits, and bananas on hand. Make salads
ahead of time. Prepare all this on a lazy Sunday afternoon. If your budget allows, buy ready-to-eat snacks,
such as low-fat nutrition bars and low-sugar instant
drinks. When you or the kids are hungry for a snack, a
healthy, delicious one is already prepared!

❏   Eat low-fat foods, even if you're not dieting.
    We need fat in very small quantities for lubrication and
    for transporting fat-soluble vitamins (A, D, E, K). In
    excess, fat increases your risk of certain diseases,
    elevates your blood pressure, makes you feel sluggish,
    and makes it more difficult to stay thin.

❏   Drink 8 to 10 eight-ounce glasses of water each day
    (more if you're an active athlete or live in a warm
    climate). Drink fruit juice instead of colas.
    Water cleanses and hydrates your body, helping it to
    function more efficiently. If you really crave colas, drink
    caffeine-free. Caffeine can keep you awake at night and
    make you tired in mid-day. Some other snack foods and
    candies have the same sluggish effect. If it's the fizz
    you're after, mix 100 percent fruit juice with sparkling
    water; it resembles soda but is far more nutritious.

❏   Eat breakfast.
    Think of your body as a campfire. It barely burns at
    night while you sleep. When you wake up, you need to
    stoke the fire with good wood or the fire will go out. If
    you skip breakfast, the body turns to muscle mass, not
    fat, for energy. When you eat later, the food is stored
    mostly as fat because your body isn't burning at a fast
    enough rate. In effect, you're dumping wood on a dead
    fire.

❏ Eat every three to four hours.

I eat every two hours when possible. I eat a meal, then a snack, then a meal, then a snack, and so on. Distributing food evenly throughout the day prevents your blood-sugar level from dropping and keeps your metabolism rate high. Your blood sugar normally crests and falls every 3-4 hours. As it falls, so does your energy, your mood, your concentration, and your ability to handle stress. Also, several small, healthy meals a day deposit less fat than one or two large meals.

❏ Eat balanced meals.

Learn the food groups and how many servings a day you should eat. Determine serving sizes and calories according to your weight and lifestyle. Eat in modera-tion—not too much or too little. For example, if you cut out red meat completely because you want a low-fat diet, you may be cutting needed iron sources.

Always have a carbohydrate with a protein, such as rice with beans, otherwise your body will burn the protein for energy. You need that protein for building muscles, fighting infection, and growing healthy skin, hair, and nails.

❏ Plan simple meals that don't take a lot of preparation but go a long way. For example, pasta dishes usually involve little more than boiling water and are inexpen-sive and filling.

❏ If eating alone is your culprit, work out a schedule with a friend or neighbor. Plan to eat together at least once a week. Take turns cooking for two.

If a whole unit is deployed, get together with other spouses from the unit and plan a common meal once a week. The host can choose a theme for the dinner and prepare the main entree. Other spouses simply R.S.V.P. with what they'll bring to ensure a balanced meal. This is also a great way to get to know other spouses. You can

The Foods You Eat

The U.S. Department of Agriculture and U.S. Department of
Health and Human Services have designed a food guide
pyramid with recommended daily servings. The pyramid
shows how to build a healthful diet by eating a variety of
foods each day.

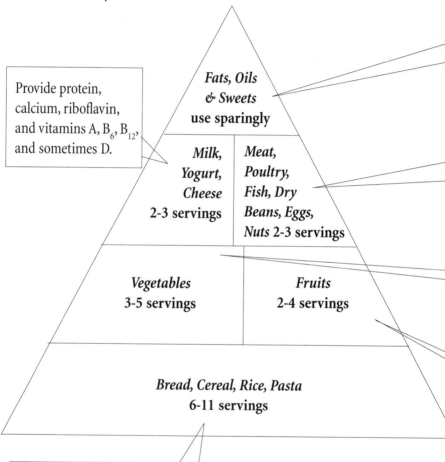

Provide protein,
calcium, riboflavin,
and vitamins A, B_6, B_{12},
and sometimes D.

Fats, Oils
& Sweets
use sparingly

Milk,
Yogurt,
Cheese
2-3 servings

Meat,
Poultry,
Fish, Dry
Beans, Eggs,
Nuts **2-3 servings**

Vegetables
3-5 servings

Fruits
2-4 servings

Bread, Cereal, Rice, Pasta
6-11 servings

Grain foods, such as brown rice, oatmeal, whole wheat bread,
tortillas, and pita bread, supply carbohydrates, a good source of
energy. Nutrition experts recommend eating the most from this
group. These foods also provide protein, B vitamins, iron; whole
grains supply magnesium, folate, and fiber.

Fats have very few nutrients in proportion to calories; vegetable oils supply vitamin E and essential fatty acids. Eat fruit to satisfy your natural craving for sweets; save chocolate for a special treat.

Provide protein, phosphorus, vitamin B_6; meat of animal origin provides B_{12}; meat, dry beans, and peas provide iron; liver and egg yolk provide vitamin A; dry beans, peas, and nuts supply magnesium.

Vegetables provide carbohydrates, fiber, vitamins A and C; certain dark green vegetables such as spinach, romaine, broccoli, and kale provide riboflavin, folate, iron, magnesium, and calcium; deep yellow vegetables such as carrots, sweet potatoes, and pumpkin are good sources of vitamin A.

Fruits provide carbohydrates, fiber, vitamins A and C, and essential minerals. Orange fruits (apricots, cantaloupe) have lots of vitamin A; citrus fruits and strawberries vitamin C. Oranges have folate. Bananas, dried apricots and prunes are great for potassium.

Pregnant Women Eat For Two

If you are pregnant or nursing, you need extra nutrition. In addition to regular, well-balanced meals, be sure to get enough:

- ❑ Extra calories (300-500 more per day) to provide energy for your growing baby. Get this by eating more of good foods, not candy bars and other sweets.
- ❑ Protein to help the baby's tissue growth, increase the blood supply for both of you, help the placenta grow, and maximize your baby's brain development. Eat milk, cheese, eggs, meat, fish, poultry, beans, nuts.
- ❑ Calcium to help the baby's skeleton and teeth develop. Eat milk, yogurt, cheese, whole grains, leafy vegetables.
- ❑ Vitamin C to help heal wounds, repair tissue, develop teeth and bones, and aid both mom's and baby's metabolism. Eat citrus fruits and juices, tomatoes, strawberries, melons, peppers, potatoes.
- ❑ Folic acid to decrease the risk your baby will be born with certain defects. Eat dark leafy vegetables, citrus, fortified breads and cereals, whole grains, liver, dried beans, and peas.
- ❑ Iron to prevent anemia and increase mom's blood volume. Eat green leafy vegetables, fortified bread and cereals, meat, fish, poultry, beans, nuts, eggs.
- ❑ Fluids! Drink at least 8 glasses a day to help build the baby's cells and develop the circulatory system, deliver nutrients to the baby, and help excrete waste. Lots of fluids will also help mom avoid urinary tract infections. Drink water, fruit juice, and vegetable juices.

Also:

- ❑ Avoid alcohol and drugs, which can seriously hurt your baby.
- ❑ Check with your doctor about *any* medications.
- ❑ Don't use or at least cut way back on caffeine.
- ❑ Don't smoke, since it has been linked to low birth weight and premature delivery.

Kids Need to Eat Right Too

Help young children develop healthy eating habits that will last them a lifetime.

❑ Even though young children's appetites and tastes may change daily, offer a variety of foods, including new foods.

❑ Use the basic Food Guide Pyramid, but adjust the number of daily servings for very young children:

—Two servings from the Milk, Yogurt, Cheese group

—Two servings from the Meat, Eggs, Beans Group

—Three servings from the Veggie Group

—Two servings from the Fruit Group

—Six servings from the Grains Group

Each young person's serving should be about 2/3 of a regular serving. A good rule of thumb is to serve a variety of foods from the five major groups and let your kids decide how much to eat.

❑ Serve enough calcium, which younger children need for growing bones. In addition to the obvious sources (milk, yogurt, cheese), serve breakfast cereals and fruit juice with added calcium, pudding and soups made with milk, and dark leafy veggies.

❑ Young people also need iron, so try serving lean meats (especially beef), cereals with added iron, turkey dark meat, enriched whole wheat bread, cooked dry beans (especially kidney and pinto), and that perennial favorite, spinach.

❑ Remember that 2- to 3-year-olds are at risk of choking until they learn to chew and swallow better. Use smaller amounts, prepared to make it easier for them: cut hot dogs into thin strips, slice meat into small bits, cut carrots into sticks, cut grapes or cherries (no pits!) into pieces, spread peanut butter thin (no spoonfuls). Be careful with chips, raw celery, nuts, seeds, raisins, popcorn, marshmallows, pretzels, large pieces of fruit, round or hard candy.

plan different events (teach a crafts project, invite a
speaker, play board games) for after dinner as well.

❑   Prepare a large portion for several meals.
    Make a big pan of lasagna, a roast, or a big pot of soup.
    Keep enough for one or two meals that week and freeze
    the rest in individual-sized portions. The easier you make
    it to pull out a ready-made meal that's healthy and inex-
    pensive, the less tempted you'll be to go out or to skip
    dinner altogether. Remember, it's cheaper to cook for two
    or more and eat one portion at a time, than it is to cook
    for one each night.

Physical fitness

The second factor of having a healthy body is to stay fit (you
thought "P.T." was just for service members?). Physical training
can be as simple as taking a walk in the morning or evening, or as
elaborate as spending three hours a day in a weight room, gym,
and pool. You decide how much time you can spend each day and
what resources are available to you. Many base gyms hold aerobics classes and have weight-lifting equipment as well as individual fitness programs, including specialized classes for pregnant women. Many are offered at no cost or for nominal fees. A
low-cost program in the community is an alternative. Beware of
contractual programs at larger spas. It may cost more than you
really need to spend. Check out your local YMCA; many have
special programs for children and families. Or share a video with
a friend and work out together at home. A few exercises or a walk
or bike ride a few times a week is enough to get started.

Create a schedule with goals for your workout (a 1-mile walk,
20-minute jog, 40-minute aerobic tape, or 20 laps in the pool).
You'll stick to it better and won't be as likely to give up early if you
have it written down. Actually write the workout on your calendar just as you would a doctor's appointment.

Vary your workout so you don't get bored. You want it to be
fun and something you look forward to. Keep track of your

progress. Workout ideas:

- ❑ walk/run/hike
- ❑ bike (stationary, road, mountain)
- ❑ skate (ice, roller)
- ❑ aerobics (gym/classes, video tape)
- ❑ aerobic machines (stepper, cross trainers, rowing, tread mill)
- ❑ muscle exercises—make sure you learn the proper techniques. Bad form not only doesn't help you get in shape, it can cause injury. Learn some exercise secrets. For example, if you tighten your muscles as you work, you work them twice as hard. If you tighten your abdominal muscles while you exercise or lift weights you won't need to do so many situps.
- ❑ weight training (Nautilus, Cybex, free weights)
- ❑ join a team (basketball, tennis, volleyball, softball/ baseball, soccer, swimming, golf—no carts; also a great way to meet people)
- ❑ mow the lawn with a hand mower
- ❑ canoe, kayak
- ❑ swim/surf/bogey-board

If you let your body become undernourished or out of shape, you open yourself up to feeling run down or depressed more easily. Working out and eating right not only helps you to look and feel better, it aids in building your immune system which combats illness. It gives you extra energy and clears your mind for more positive thinking.

A Healthy Mind

Five minutes is about the time it takes for the sports segment on the evening news, for a bag of microwave popcorn to pop, or for a song to play on a compact disc. Relatively, a short amount of your day. Yet most people don't give themselves just five minutes a day to relax. In fact, parents often spend the time they do get to themselves "getting things done" that they can't accomplish with children around.

Your mind needs time to relax and recuperate from all the good and bad stress of the day. Keeping your mind relaxed will help your body stay healthy and will help you face each day with more energy.

What do you do with these five minutes? Go to a quiet place. If you have children, try to do this early in the morning, at night, or when they take a nap. If they are old enough to understand, let them know you need a little time to yourself and ask them not to disturb you. Close the door to distractions. Simply relax. Five minutes alone with yourself can seem like an eternity. The first time you try it, you may want to set a timer for five minutes to help you concentrate on yourself instead of the clock.

Sit in a comfortable chair or lie on your back with your legs bent. Close your eyes. Tune out all other noises. Concentrate on your breathing. Try to feel your heart beat. Breathe slowly and be conscious of only one thing at a time. Focus on your breathing, your heart beat, how relaxed your body feels. Some people focus on a calming word or an inspirational and relaxing phrase or verse ("Be still and know that I am God"—Psalm 46:10).

This is not a waste of time. Remember, it is only five minutes! You'll be surprised how much doing this each day will help you to relax and think more clearly. It simply gives your mind and body a chance to consciously relax. If you fall asleep, you probably needed the nap!

Some people follow this five minutes with a "think nap." My brother takes one each day. He lies in a comfortable position and sometimes dozes off but concentrates on one problem or situation. He thinks about the different options. It helps him to make clearer decisions or to feel better about the decisions he's made.

Other people use the time after their five minutes to write in a journal. No one has to know what you are thinking or writing. It is for you. Some of my journal entries I've never read through again. But they helped me to sort out my thoughts and to get things off my mind at the time. Some I have read again and I'm amazed at what I've learned or how engrossed I was in some particular problem that has since become less important.

Some people also encourage their children to have quiet time during this five minutes. Then they get together and talk about their day, what they learned that day or an observation they made. And then they write to the deployed loved one together or separately. (It's important to be as peaceful, calm, and clearheaded as possible when writing. Anger, resentment, and guilt can all come through in a letter and be very confusing to the reader who receives it weeks later.)

Other ways to keep your mind healthy:

❑ Maintain an active brain: read, write, and engage in meaningful conversations.

❑ Get involved. Don't sit alone and feel left out. Volunteer. Do something for others.

❑ Prioritize what's critical and then pace yourself to accomplish only those things. Be realistic when making your "to do" list. Break up long-term goals into shorter ones so they seem more attainable and you can see your progress.

❑ Take quiet lunch breaks; don't eat quickly or talk about work.

❑ When something starts to get to you, set it aside and come back to it later.

❑ Stay around happy people. Have as little contact as possible with negative people.

❑ Accept compliments.

❑ Explore ways to relax: take a hot bath, listen to music, or meditate.

❑ Avoid self-medication. Chemicals such as alcohol can temporarily mask stress symptoms, but they do not help to solve the source of your stress. Many are habit-forming and can cause more damage than stress itself.

Be Creative!

Want a new outfit but it's not in your budget? Sew what!

Fabric: Try old curtains, remnant pieces, or off-season sale fabric.

Pattern: Have an outfit that's getting worn out but you love the way it fits? Carefully cut the threads in all seams and make a note about the order in which pieces were sewn together. Use the old pieces as your pattern.

Can't find a pattern you like? Hold an old sheet up to you and draw the basic shape you're looking for on the sheet with a pencil. Cut out the shape, leaving extra room for seams and reshaping. Sew the sheet pieces, try it on, and adjust the seams until it fits the way you want it to. When it fits, trim the seams to 5/8" all around. Then take apart the seams and use the pieces as your pattern. It really works; I made my wedding dress pattern this way!

❑ Get enough sleep. Lack of sleep makes you irritable and less able to deal with stressful situations. Most people need at least seven to eight hours of sleep in any 24-hour period.

❑ Get up earlier. Go to bed earlier.

❑ Talk out troubling matters with a trusted friend, a chaplain, priest/pastor/rabbi where you worship, or a counselor.

❑ Accept what you can't change. The hard part is knowing whether or not you can change it.

❑ Make friends with yourself the same way you make friends with anyone. Find something good about yourself to admire, and be kind and patient as you deal with your lesser qualities. Think of things you'd like to do and places you'd like to go.

❑ Find something positive about each day (even if it's just that the day is over.)

❑ Eagerly accept an invitation from a friend, even if it's climbing a mountain this weekend. You never know what you'll love doing until you try.

❑ Remember that progress is not always steady nor always forward.

❑ Make the best with what you have. Instead of wishing you had more, take pride in being creative with meals and decor. For example, with all those military moves, surely you've figured out something to do with boxes. Early American cardboard decor can be quite handsome with fabric remnants. Plank boards and crates or cement blocks are hard to break in a move and make great shelves. Remember, you aren't the "Jones"—and who would want to be anyway?

❑ Laugh. Humor takes the tension out of any situation.

❑ Be yourself. Accept your limits. Even Superman was vulnerable to kryptonite.

What Happened During the Deployment: Events/Problems Most Frequently Mentioned by Spouses

Event/ Problem	Percent Experiencing	Of those who experienced, percent who found it extremely stressful
Fears about spouse's safety	93%	42%
Not knowing what was going to happen	90%	45%
Fears about spouse's physical health	83%	34%
Rumors about return date	82%	38%
Problems communicating with spouse	70%	40%
Snow removal at home	57%	33%
Pregnancy while spouse was away	12%	56%
Death of close friend/family member	11%	47%
Giving birth while spouse was away	3%	58%
Violence in the family	2%	45%

Source: A 1993 field study of spouses whose Army soldiers stationed with the 10th Mountain Division at Fort Drum, NY deployed to Operation Restore Hope in Somalia.

How Spouses Coped with Life Demands: Health and Safety

Percent Coping Well or Very Well

Life Demand	Operation Desert Shield/Storm - CONUS deployed	Operation Restore Hope - Deployed	Operation Restore Hope - Not deployed
Maintaining safety of home	70%	74%	65%
Taking care of their own health	52%	65%	65%
Handling their own emotions	—	44%	48%
Handling fears about their soldier	—	40%	41%
Handling their loneliness	30%	40%	45%

Source: Same as p. 122, plus 1991 Survey of Army Families II, which included spouses of soldiers deployed to Persian Gulf.

Of Those Spouses Who Were Employed, What Effect Did Operation Desert Shield/Storm Have on Spouses' Employment?

Percentage Reporting Effect of Operation Desert Shield/Storm on Paid Work

Effect	Spouses Without Children		Spouses With Children	
	Female	Male	Female	Male
No effect	74%	71%	61%	69%
Lost/quit job	6%	5%	6%	6%
Worked less	5%	1%	10%	7%
Worked more	10%	18%	6%	10%
Took a job	6%	3%	6%	1%

Source: 1992 DOD Surveys of Officers and Enlisted Personnel and Their Spouses

What Specific Problems Did Spouses Have During Operation Desert Shield/Storm?

Percentage Reporting Very Great or Great Problems with….

Communicating with spouse	35%
Sending packages to spouse	25%
Emotional well-being	21%
Having money to pay bills	16%
Getting car or household repairs done	13%
Children's emotional well-being	13%
Taking care of emergencies	10%
Time with family	9%
Physical health	9%

Source: 1992 DOD Surveys of Officers and Enlisted Personnel and Their Spouses

Chapter 5
Plungers & Other Survival Gear

Super Spouses wouldn't think of going on this adventure without a fully stocked tool box. A few things you'll need:

Plunger

Get the industrial plunger. It costs about $10, versus $2 for the wood-stick rubber-end kind, and is well worth the extra bucks. Leave it by the toilet and you're sure to get laughs from guests. This accordion-style, cone-shaped (usually blue) plastic tube is not just for toilets (although it'll fix *any* toilet clog). It clears clogs in sinks, garbage disposals, and tubs. Warning: it's powerful; be ready to smell the depths of the drain! Find in home supply stores.

Rubber "Gripper"

An essential if you have weak hands and normally rely on your spouse to open jars. This flat, flimsy piece of rubber has ribs on one side and grips the jar top to help you hold while you turn. Available in most discount or kitchen supply stores.

Cordless Screw Driver

It makes holes, screws and unscrews screws, and does much more as you'll quickly find out. It even untwists paper for crafts.

One of Your Spouse's Shirts

To maintain your spouse's presence and a sense of intimacy, cuddle up to familiar items personally associated with your spouse.

Wear your spouse's T-shirt, move to his side of the bed, spray his cologne on a towel.

When my husband deployed, I didn't wash the sheets for a couple weeks; I liked having the smell of him there. I sent one of my sweatshirts with him, sprayed with my perfume. He used it as a pillow.

Journals

Journal entries, like letters, can be very personal, silly and short, or creative and philosophical. Most importantly, they should be honest. Recognizing the truth and being honest with yourself about your feelings is often the hardest part.

Write when you go to bed, when you first get up in the morning, when your young child is taking a nap, or during a break at work. Your writing can be elaborate or simple.

During Bob's six-month shipboard deployments, the midway point (Marines and sailors call it "hump day," as in over the hump) was always the hardest for me. At that point, I usually concluded, "Okay, I've learned all the lessons I'm going to learn, you can come home now." My journal entries often got shorter during that time and reflected something new I learned, a silly dream, a philosophical thought, an observation of a person, or just a series of little doodles that represented my utter confusion or tiredness over the separation. This is an example of an entry I wrote midway through Bob's first six-month deployment:

frustration
ugliness
loneliness   *dum de dum*   *ho hum*
woe is me
struggling   *what to do   hmm anxiety*
confusion   *in love*

Solutions: workout, eat good meals
hair cut...shorter...healthier...change
forge on one day at a time - 79 more days!
save $, don't spend
get more sleep zzzz
write, paint, read, smile   talk about it.

even my plants are droopy.

The trick to keeping a journal is to make it an enjoyable habit every day. Whatever time of day when you have 10 free minutes, reflect on everything that's happened in the past 24 hours. Explore your feelings. Sometimes we have no idea why we feel the way we do. There have been nights I've dropped into bed exhausted after doing nothing, and was ready to cry at nothing.

Treat each page as a person who will really listen to you, without judgment. Don't worry about correct grammar, handwriting, or the possibility of someone else reading it. This is for *you*, to help *you* sort out your true feelings and to reflect and grow. If it makes you feel better, write on the first page: DO NOT READ THIS. That's usually a good sign that if someone picked it up by mistake, they would surely get the message that it's personal. Are you intimidated by the journal's blank pages? Write anything to get some ink on the page and get the pen rolling. Some people start with quotes or Bible verses. Others just write anything that comes to mind, including countries they'd like to visit or good names for dogs.

The journal itself can be anything that works for *you*: loose leaf paper that you put in a binder as you write, a spiral notebook, a small notepad, a diary or blank journal from a stationery store, or I've even used old paper bags and wrapping paper! A computer works well if you like to type as you think and you can use a password to keep the file private. A friend of mine types her journal at an old typewriter. If writing in general intimidates you, try talking into a tape recorder. Do whatever makes you comfortable and allows you the most freedom to express those pent up thoughts. Get to know yourself. You may decide to stay in touch when the deployment is over.

A Domestically Challenged Attitude

One of the most humorous housecleaning articles I've read was written by Ginny Hanson, a freelance writer married to a retired Air Force Office of Special Investigations agent. In the May 20, 1996 edition of *Married to the Military*, she writes about being "domestically challenged." If she can still see the carpet, the room doesn't need tidying; if there are clean dishes in the cabinet, she doesn't have to do the ones in the sink yet. A few of her tips will work wonders for your sanity on those days when you simply don't have the time or energy or don't want to notice.

- ❑ If a room is messy, shut the door; it makes a home look cleaner in seconds.
  "If a visitor wants to open one of the doors, explain that you haven't found the pet tarantula that escaped that morning. But tell them to go right in if they feel the need to. Trust me. They won't."

- ❑ Throw everything—newspapers, socks, toys—into the bathtub and close the shower curtain.
  "Anyone nosy enough to look behind a drawn shower curtain deserves the shock they surely will get."

- ❑ Make use of the dust on the furniture.
  Can't find a pen and paper? Use your finger. "Gone to the store" or "Don't forget to buy milk" fits easily on a typical dusty coffee table.

Nonmilitary Involvement

Many spouses join groups outside the military community. Civilian groups offer a different kind of support, a different perspective, and the opportunity for friendships and projects that help you have a life outside your deployment situation. The most popular include religious groups (such as home fellowships and specific-purpose ministries), and special interest groups such as book reading clubs, investment clubs, professional networks, sports associations, political campaigns, recreation centers, community theater, and school groups.

Encourage your deployed spouse to stay busy with valuable non-military activities as well. Especially for those deployed on a ship, there are often hours of inactivity and boredom to go along with the long hours of duty. Your spouse can take a correspondence course, work on a hobby, catch up on reading, or take advantage of port visits and sign up for tours.

Pets

The character of a police officer played by Bruce Willis in the movie *The Last Boy Scout* told his unfaithful wife, "If you're lonely, get a dog."

One of the toughest aspects of separation is loneliness. You can be in a crowded room of people and still feel alone if you don't know any of them well. You can be surrounded by caring friends, family, and support groups but still feel lonely because your best friend is a world away.

"You'll always be a little lonely, because you miss your husband or wife so much," says Patricia Gains, an Army wife for 18 years. "But if you can limit those lonely times as much as possible, the time flies by a lot quicker."

Pets offer companionship, the responsibility and joy of caring for another living being, and a good dose of compassion.

Staff Sergeant John Keener gave his 7-year-old son, Greg, a puppy before he left for a six-month tour. He asked Greg to try to teach the pup some tricks before he got home. A walk or romp in the yard each day with the puppy helped Greg to take his mind off missing his dad. He filled his leisure time with caring for the dog rather than sulking or being bored. Often, a child doesn't realize or won't admit to the fact he's depressed or not doing well in school because of a parent being gone. He may say it's because of a friend, a certain test, and so on. A distraction and responsibility such as this helps.

If your lease agreement, living space, or budget restricts you from having a larger pet such as a cat or a dog, consider getting a parakeet, turtle, or gold fish. They aren't quite as cuddly, but they're still great listeners.

One of the best companions I had while my husband was deployed was a parakeet. Bob brought it home one day as a surprise. He thought it would make a great companion for me while he headed off to war in Iraq. It may sound corny, but that little blue parakeet, Jake, became one of my best friends. I was alone in a town where I didn't know any one person well enough yet to cry in front of, yell at, or read letters to.... Jake was it for me. That bird heard so much about my fears, frustrations, and joys. He moved to California with us and was my friend in our new home when Bob spent many weeks at a time in field exercises.

Same-Gender Friends

Some spouses say that being around same-gender friends allows them to talk more freely without adding to their spouse's anxieties. They walk around the block each evening with a neighbor or join an all-male or all-female ball team or fitness club.

Why same gender? One wife explained, "If I spend too much time with any other male, my husband worries that the man is taking his place." Sometimes, this "substitute" does eventually take the real spouse's place. A subject that is so often hushed but well-known in gossip circles is the statement that "So & So" had a guy over not even a week after her husband left and she'll kick him out a week before the homecoming. The big question in that circle then becomes which guy she'll keep in the long run.

Remember that when you marry, it is for better or worse. In the military, you will run into the "worse" part more often than you care to think. It is not an easy way of life. And separation (which means no sex) is part of the deal. Trust, faithfulness, love, and discipline should all overcome physical urges. Spouses who've confided in being unfaithful say it was due to loneliness and having someone convenient to talk to and eventually become intimate with. Because their spouses weren't there, it was easy to justify why the new relationship was so much better. Their advice now: Make your marriage number one priority, even though sex and companionship with your spouse must sit on the back burner until homecoming. Substitute intimate letters to your spouse. Keep your love alive in other ways. And use "safe" people, such as same-gender friends, to help you combat loneliness.

Family Members, Friends, Neighbors

Let's face it: They care. They want to help. They have no idea what to do.

As a bystander to spouses left behind during deployments, I've fallen into this dumbfounded state myself. And I *know* what it's like to go through it! My neighbors Ed and Julie prepared for a month for Ed's year-long unaccompanied assignment. I saw them once or twice in that month. Not because they were gone on vacation or hibernating somewhere, but because I struggled with whether or not they *wanted* to see me. I kept thinking they wanted to spend time together alone, not with pesky neighbors who don't know what else to say except, "So, how are you handling things? Are you getting ready? When do you leave? Is there anything I can do?" The day Ed left I practically avoided Julie because I thought she wanted to be alone. I didn't want to upset her, but I didn't know whether or not she wanted company.

If you don't want your family, friends, or neighbors to visit, let them know. Otherwise call them. Help *them* to know what to do to make it easier for *you*. Get together to eat pizza, play board games, or watch a video. Invite a good friend who lives far away to take her vacation to your house this year. Each pitch in for it.

Include family, friends, and neighbors in your support of your spouse. Kevin Rea was my husband's best friend in high school. The two lost contact for several years. When Kevin heard that

Bob was in Iraq, he sent him a big package. One item was a Bart Simpson figurine that had traveled to several other countries with Kevin as his good-luck talisman. He asked Bob to bring Bart home safely. The package was a wonderful surprise for Bob and the restart of a great friendship.

Holiday Spirit

Holidays are a hard time to be apart. Changing *how* you celebrate might make it easier. For example, simply change the way you decorate: substitute decorations hung from the fireplace

---

Holiday Alternatives

Janice Baker, in a November 1990 *Military Lifestyle* article, offered these suggestions for coping during the holidays:

Holidays: they're supposed to be family time, right? So what's that empty chair doing at the head of the table? Don't let the holiday blues get the best of you. Though the military has put a crimp in your usual holiday plans, make some *un*usual ones:

If your spouse is ready to leave now or has just returned, have an early or late holiday celebration and then a mini-festivity on the actual holiday.

If your spouse misses a holiday altogether, set up your own rituals or do something completely different. One Marine Corps wife had a slumber party on Easter Sunday.

Surround yourself with people. Remember all those other families in the same boat as you, and get together.

Whatever you do, videotape it, photograph it, record it, or write about it so your spouse can experience your holiday, too.

Challenge your thinking about holidays. If you are convinced that they will be a total loss without your spouse, then that may happen. Instead, be upbeat, decide you can enjoy the day, and have your spouse there as much as possible by telling him about your celebration.

mantle or put up a smaller Christmas tree. Send small decorations to your spouse. Ryan McKenzie sent an igloo ornament to his dad in Somalia.

Friends and neighbors may invite you over and if you're like me you'll be tempted to decline. I didn't want to impose on their family time just because my family wasn't together. But after spending too many lonely and depressing holidays at home as a "deployment widow" I finally gave in to an invitation to go to our next door neighbors' for Christmas morning festivities. Once I got over the guilt of having fun while my husband ate MREs and went day number 14 without a shower, I was able to see that it was in fact a better alternative to sitting at home by the phone (I was just next door, so I brought the cordless phone with me!).

As for birthdays and anniversaries, you'll learn that it's not the date that really matters. Nancy McKenzie and her husband spent two wedding anniversaries together out of 13. Nancy said they've learned to accept that birthdays and anniversaries happen whenever they can closest to when Mac's home. "That's the way our life has been," she said. "One year Mac was home for our anniversary, and we didn't know what to do. We sat there looking at each other and asking are we going to go out or what are we going to do?"

Calendars

A good way to mark the days on a scheduled deployment is to keep some kind of calendar. During Bob's first deployment, I made a backwards calendar. Each day I ripped off a square until the last day on the calendar was homecoming. In situations where there's a good likelihood of delay, this kind of calendar could be a bummer. But in general, it helps to build milestones.

Jeremy Hopper marked time by adding a paper link to a chain that hung from one corner of his room. He had measured the distance across his ceiling and knew that as the chain got closer to the door, his dad would be coming home. He hung a few letters and pictures from his dad on the chain loops and wrote the date on each link as he added it.

Use your imagination to create your own calendar milestones. One wife told me she counted how many menstrual cycles her husband would be gone. She bought enough tampons to last one month more than that. When she was down to the last box, he was on his way home across the ocean.

The possibilities are endless. The trick is to pick something easy and meaningful that helps you count the days in a positive way. Many spouses do not begin the calendar countdown until they hear the official return date is less than a month away. This is a good idea if you have young children who don't really understand the concept of time. Otherwise they might get tired of waiting and decide the homecoming really isn't going to happen.

Time will pass on its own; don't urge it to go faster. I remember in January saying to my dad, "I wish it were April; then Bob would be home." He said, "Hey, I don't have as many years left as you do. Don't be wishing my life away by asking time to fly." When you look back at this deployment, you'll want to remember more than simply all the energy you spent wishing for it to be over.

Security

Many strong spouses, even those who say *they* (not their military spouse) would be the one to save the house and family from disaster, feel less secure when their military spouse is gone. Part of this insecurity comes from potential deployment scams. For example, during Desert Storm, in Jacksonville, North Carolina, thieves called military families and told them their loved one was coming home that day. When the families left to pick up their service member, the thieves burglarized their homes. Other thieves used "winning a family portrait" to lure families out of their homes. Feeling less secure can also stem from the heightened awareness that *you* have to defend yourself and your children without your spouse's daily support.

The key to feeling secure is to have a plan. What would you do if someone broke into your home at night? during the day?

Have you practiced a fire escape plan? What would you do if someone grabbed you or your child on the street?

If you can answer questions like these, you're off to a good start. Think through each step of each plan, including little things like turning on the lights to big things like calling 911 or shooting a gun. Safety tips other spouses follow:

- ❑ I've got my own system worked out with the kids. There's a telephone in my daughter's room and if she hears me having a problem she can sit up and call 911.
- ❑ I sleep with a baseball bat and a cell phone next to the bed.
- ❑ I keep the house well lit outside and plenty of night-lights inside. I leave the dog out as long as I can and then keep her in the garage so I can hear her.
- ❑ I check every window and door lock before I go to bed.
- ❑ I try to make sure there's no pattern when we do things. That way no one really knows what we're up to all the time.
- ❑ I carry a little flashlight and a squeezable horn on my key ring. I can get into my car quicker at night and I'd be able to make a sound if my arms were being held.
- ❑ I always park and walk in well-lit areas. Whenever possible, I have an escort.

Contact your local police department or on-base Military Police. They may have home/personal security pamphlets or courses. Some departments will provide an assessment of your home's physical security and give you recommendations.

Sheep to Count

Insomnia is a common deployment problem for spouses, even during short field exercises. Try these ideas:

- ❑ Take a hot, relaxing bath.
- ❑ Drink hot, caffeine-free herbal tea.
- ❑ Don't eat late at night.

❑ Keep a pen and paper by your bed. Write down what's on your mind: things to do or remember the next day or something that's worrying you. Then forget about it. You can pick up your list of worries in the morning, after a good night's sleep.

❑ Read. Stay away from horror or anything too stimulating or upsetting. Boring text books should put you to sleep.

❑ Feel safe. Get a watch dog. Double check all locks and lights throughout the house. Sleep with a phone and baseball bat next to the bed (make sure you tell your spouse not to make any surprise homecomings during the night!). Go ahead and check the closet and under the bed to make sure the boogie man isn't waiting.

❑ Listen to soft, mellow, familiar music.

❑ Sleep on your spouse's side. Add extra pillows and blankets for that bulk and warmth that's missing. Sleep with your arm around a stuffed animal or the extra pillows.

❑ Put a photo of your spouse on your nightstand. It takes away the anxiety some spouses feel during a long separation when they can't quite remember what that dimple looks like.

❑ Spray your spouse's cologne or deodorant on a comfortable shirt and sleep with it.

❑ Clean the house or do a workout tape until you're tired.

❑ Get up at the same time every day to establish a sleep routine. Go to bed when you're tired, even if it's 8 p.m. If you're well rested, it will take you a few minutes to fall asleep at night and you'll wake up no later than one hour past your normal wake-up, even on the weekends.

❑ If all else fails and you still can't get good sleep, see your doctor. There are safe, short-term sleep-aid medications that may help.

News

I've always been one of those people who has to know everything. That includes what my husband is doing while he's deployed. During military conflict especially, we all want to know what's going on. Where to get the information is the question. It's a matter of opinion whether or not to watch the news all the time. Bob usually preferred that I waited to read the news in his letters. He claimed to be a more accurate reporter than most journalists and he figured by the time the letter got to me, the danger had probably passed.

Sometimes your local media will do a good job covering deployments, such as Navy ship movements. For example, the San Diego *Union-Tribune* published a map of the Pacific and Indian Oceans, with grid coordinates, at the beginning of the deployment of two ship task forces, a carrier group and amphibious group. Throughout the deployment, the paper provided updated grid coordinates. Spouses used this information with their children to find out where the ships were and lessen the uncertainty. Suggest this to your local paper if they don't do it. Or this could be a rewarding project for you to do in conjunction with your local military public affairs office.

Most spouses do prefer to rely on e-mail, letters, and occasional phone calls for information. They don't want any reason to worry more than they already do. If their spouses don't tell them everything that's going on, they assume they aren't supposed to know. One night I got a "hook flash" (phone call through an operator) from Bob in Mogadishu. I heard a lot of noise in the background and asked if everything was OK there. He said, "Yeah, it's just the generators making a lot of noise." The noise was actually gunfire just outside the U.S. compound. But I didn't need to know that. He assured me he was safe; that's what I needed to know. Six weeks after Bob's return, we found ourselves glued to CNN as the violence in Mogadishu rose up again. I quietly thanked God Bob was safe in our living room, watching the fighting with me.

When e-mail is restricted, mail is slow, or when events are likely to change daily, it's hard to fight the "CNN syndrome." Spouses admit to listening to and reading every piece of news they can get hold of, even though they know it's better to get it from the unit or their spouse. Gwen Gerdes, whose husband, Tim, deployed to Somalia, agrees: "The news drove me nuts. Every hour I watched CNN and you just can't do that. But when it takes 2-3 weeks for a letter, your imagination gets going." In their letters, Gwen and Tim compared the news she saw on television with his experiences.

If you have questions about the validity of news items, call your key volunteer, ombudsman or unit rear contact person. Sometimes a news item may be correct for some military members but doesn't affect your spouse. Other times, news reports are simply wrong or overdramatized.

A Different News Focus

Your spouse wants to know all the news from home, too. As you peruse the newspapers, look for interesting items that have nothing to do with the deployment.

While Bob was away, I cut out articles on major world events or local interests. For example, during a 1989-90 deployment, we had the big San Francisco earthquake, the Berlin Wall came down, a McDonald's went up in Moscow, San Francisco won over Denver in the Super Bowl, Nelson Mandela was freed, there was no opening day of baseball, my sister Tammy made the high school volleyball team, and my parents bought a new truck. Collecting such clips and family news showed us "how much time" had passed in six months and gave us a different perspective when looking back at our own changes during that time.

An Ounce of Faith

We all worry at some point about the health and safety of our service member. Whether it's armed conflict, a routine deployment, or a training exercise, the military is a dangerous job.

Media Relations

If something good or bad happens to your spouse's unit, you could be contacted by the media. Family members who reside off base are very accessible and, especially during highly visible missions, are likely to get unwanted media attention.

The public has no absolute right to information about service members or their families simply because they are topics of current events. Any media person who says the public has such a right is mistaken.

The Joint Public Affairs Office at Camp Pendleton, California, offered this advice for those who choose to speak with the media:

- ❑ Don't speak for everyone in the group.
- ❑ Don't speculate on ongoing or upcoming operations.
- ❑ Keep letters from your loved one to yourself.
- ❑ Support what your service member is doing.
- ❑ Speak only from personal experience.
- ❑ Before granting an interview, contact a Pubic Affairs Officer to receive advice about whether or not to do the interview, for help getting rid of unwanted media, or for assistance conducting the interview.

Fear of loss is a very real emotion spouses wrestle with. During Bob's high-conflict deployments, I would cry myself to sleep some nights, telling myself I should just accept the fact he wasn't coming home. Every time he was delayed, I thought it was a sign something awful was going to happen to him.

Dealing with this fear is an individual task, but there is a lot you can do together to prepare. Being legally prepared often relieves some of the anxiety. Discuss wills. Talk about where you and your spouse want to be buried, where to go for help in managing the funeral, how to collect death benefits, and so on. It's not a fun topic, and it's best if you can discuss it first outside of a deployment or other high risk situation.

Also discuss the possibility of loss with children who are old enough to understand and who bring up the fears themselves. Beth Weiss explained that when her son Abe watched the news while his dad was in Afghanistan, "he would ask questions like, 'Dad could get killed, couldn't he?' and I'd say 'yeah.' He'd say 'I hope Dad has that gun loaded the right way and knows what he's doing before he does anything.' I would explain that his dad thinks before he does anything but sometimes there are accidents. And you can't control that. More people have been killed doing something like riding a bike. He realizes that."

Loss is difficult for your spouse, too. The danger and reality of their jobs surround them daily. In a letter from Iraq in May 1991, Bob wrote: "Looks like it'll be a few more days before we move south. Had a depressing end to yesterday; a Marine died from an accidental discharge and another got wounded from the same bullet. What a waste. The Marine that died found out two days ago he's a new daddy! What an absolute shit sandwich!... I'm OK, I'm not taking any crazy chances."

Your spouse has had specialized training and uses plenty of safety equipment. Ask your unit for a demonstration of some of the equipment or for a copy of some of the safety precautions for your spouse's job. It may help you and your family feel better about his safety. In any case, an ounce of faith will take you far. Believe and think positive.

Casualty Reporting and Notification

When a service member is killed, injured, gets sick, or is hospitalized, he or she becomes a "casualty." It is important to know that being a casualty can mean anything from having been killed in combat to having an attack of appendicitis.

Once a casualty occurs, this starts a systematic series of reports, which serve many purposes, including notifying the service member's family or next of kin.

Who reports the casualty?

❑   The service unit closest to the location of the incident reports the casualty to the parent unit, which then prepares and releases a Personnel Casualty Report (PCR).

❑   PCRs are sent immediately to the service headquarters in Washington, DC, and other commands.

❑   PCRs provide the information used to inform the next of kin that a casualty has occurred.

❑   Information on the PCR comes from the member's service record, especially the Record of Emergency Data (that's why it's *critical* for service members to update the RED before deployment), hospital reports, and accounts of the incident.

Who is the next of kin?

The person most closely related to the casualty is considered the primary next of kin; this is usually the "unremarried surviving spouse." Other next of kin are recognized in the following order:

❑   Children (natural and adopted) in order of seniority

❑   Parents in order of seniority

❑   Remarried surviving spouse

❑   Blood or adoptive relative granted legal custody of the person

❑   Brothers or sisters of legal age in order of seniority

❑   Grandparents in order of seniority

❑   Other relatives of legal age in order of relationship, then by seniority

❑   Persons standing *in loco parentis*

How is the next of kin informed?

A local military unit near the next of kin's residence appoints a casualty assistance officer. In the Navy, Marines, and Coast Guard, this is a Casualty Assistance Calls Officer (CACO); in the Army, a Casualty Assistance Officer (CAO), and in the Air Force, a Casualty Assistance Representative (CAR). In addition to serving as messenger, the casualty assistance officer is also a resource coordinator and administrator. The officer:

❑   *personally* contacts the primary and secondary next of kin (primary next of kin is usually a spouse or child; secondary next of kin are parents; see above)

❑   will *not* contact the next of kin by telephone

❑   will usually be accompanied by a Chaplain, fellow service member or assistant, will wear the service "A" uniform, and in most cases be an officer

❑   is sent as soon as possible, but unless the situation is extremely urgent, will not call on the next of kin between midnight and 6 am

❑   is the representative to the next of kin and keeps the family informed of everything concerning the casualty. Casualty assistance officers keep liaison with hospitals and parent commands, and will be available to the next of kin to answer questions or provide support.

What happens after notification?

❑   In injury or illness cases, the casualty assistance officer will continue to monitor the situation and keep the next of kin updated. If the unit commander and the attending physician believe that the next of kin's presence is necessary for the health and welfare of the service member, they both must request in writing that the command approve funding for transportation for the next of kin.

❑   In death cases, the casualty assistance officer will coordinate all the necessary or family-desired arrangements, including funeral support; travel and transportation; monetary benefits such as arrears of pay, death gratuity, and Servicemen's Group Life Insurance; and all household goods shipments and personal effects collection. In all death cases, a formal investigation will also be completed by the command and copies of the completed investigation, with certain restrictions, will be made available to the family.

Empathy

Camaraderie is unsurpassed in the military community. A special bond, first developed among its service members, soon reaches beyond to the families included in its holds. When we find someone in our situation, empathy comes fairly naturally.

At the same time, military members and their families are proud. And human. Blame, resentment, and feeling like a martyr are easy emotions to develop during a deployment, especially when other service members and families have the greener side of the fence.

> *We both were uniformed servicemen of roughly the same age, yet one of us would shortly be looking into the jaws of death on an almost daily basis, while the other would be polishing his surfboard in air-conditioned comfort. I thought wryly of the differing degrees of sacrifices demanded of a pig and a chicken when forced to contribute to a breakfast of ham and eggs.*
>
> — Lewis B. Puller, Jr., *Fortunate Son*, p.66

Lewis Puller's description of his feelings prior to his Vietnam deployment mirrors what many spouses feel when their service member is asked to contribute to the ham side of the breakfast. Sometimes it's the sacrifice of deploying versus serving at a home base or the sacrifice of staying on active duty longer. I know I had mixed feelings about the homecoming parades at the "end" of the Gulf War. While I was happy for the support given to those troops, my Marine wasn't due home for at least four more months. I resented those who thought everyone was home and who stopped watching the news, saying their prayers, and hanging their yellow ribbons.

On the other side, I know people who don't want to just supply the eggs. The supporting role, though very important to the mission, certainly isn't as glamorous or fulfilling as front line duty. Elaine Wilner said she can't stand to live with her husband when he doesn't get assigned to a conflict, "He's unbearable to be around." Linda Johnson, however, will take her husband anytime. "He's deployed often enough. I just remind him it's someone else's turn this time. His chance will come soon enough. He's needed at home, too."

Whatever situation you find yourself and your spouse in, realize that the surface is not always the depth. Like a basketball team that needs its coach as much as its point guard and center, each one of us plays an important role in protecting our great country. As a spouse, your role is to support and encourage your service member and show empathy for other members and their families, no matter what role they're playing or what they're bringing to breakfast.

Chapter 6
Communication

"She'll wish there was more, and that's the great art o' letter writin'."
—Charles Dickens, *Pickwick Papers*

Although there are many aspects to a positive deployment experience, the level of happiness you, your spouse, your marriage, and your family enjoys is intimately connected to how effectively you communicate.

There are many ways to communicate during a deployment. In your preparation, you discussed your communication expectations and agreed on guidelines, such as how often to write or call, what to write about or discuss over the phone, how to handle e-mail, and how to resolve and communicate important issues while apart.

Letters

Letter writing is the age-old favorite and often most reliable form of communication in any deployment situation.

Write often. Write as soon as you can.

Days can seem like months when you're counting the amount of time since you last received a letter. It's especially hard to be patient at the beginning of the deployment when communication channels are slow or nonexistent. Lots of short letters, with an occasional long thoughtful one, are usually better than infrequent longer letters. When Pete's wife Allison was deployed with the Navy to Antarctica for five months, one of the things that made the long separation bearable was that she got something from him *every* mail call.

Date your letters. Let your spouse know how long it took for a letter to arrive.

Besides giving you something to complain about, knowing how long it takes to get mail to one another can help you make communication decisions. For example, if you really need to get information to or from your spouse within the week, the unit may have a better way of achieving that than mailing a letter.

Number your letters (and cards, tapes, packages, etc.) to avoid confusion about the timing of events.

Mail will not always arrive in the order it was mailed! Getting a letter about Sue's cast coming off can be startling to a parent who hasn't received the letter explaining she broke her wrist. If you number your letters (on the outside of the envelope and on the letter itself), your spouse will know if a letter is missing. My husband, Bob, has often received letters #1 and #2 three weeks or more after receiving letter #20. No one can explain the mail system during deployments. Just understand that your letters won't get there when you expect them to and it will take longer than you hope to receive a response.

Honor a letter writing agreement. Share your expectations.

What kind of letters did you say you wanted? How often is often? If you made a letter writing agreement, it was probably made idealistically during a stressful and hurried preparation, and many things will change for both of you during a deployment. Do your best to honor the agreement. If you can't, explain why (e.g., "I know I said I'd try to write every day but I was just assigned additional duty and I'm beat at the end of the day. I'll write as often as I can. I think of you several times a day."). If your spouse digresses from your agreement in a way that bothers you, tactfully express your feelings. If you need to make major changes, re-negotiate the agreement, don't just let it collapse.

If you don't have an agreement, it's important to let your spouse know if you're hoping for something other than what you're getting. For example, Kelly wanted Joe to be romantic in his letters. Gerard expected more letters from Darnice. Each got what they wanted because they let their spouse know. Do you want bare facts, details, emotions, hopes? Remember that some people have a hard time expressing themselves, especially in writing. Also, it's hard to be intimate in a letter; it takes practice. Effective communication is two-way. Help each other.

Answer all questions.

Reread letters and make sure you addressed everything. An issue or question may seem insignificant or incidental to you, but if you don't answer, it's frustrating to the person waiting for the answer or input.

Share what life is like. Exchange questions and information about routine and daily activities.

Chances are, during a deployment, you and your spouse will live in very different worlds. I always wanted to get a sense of what life was like where Bob was deployed and what role he played there. His letters often had both mundane details and philosophical perspectives. It helped me to better understand the demands, stress, and learning opportunities in his work. His descriptions ranged from comments like "I could really go for a cheeseburger," and "I miss taking a nice hot, relaxing, private shower" to more elaborate insights into the reason he's there:

> *28 April 1991, Kurdish refugee camp, Northern Iraq*
>
> *"Had another scare; Iraqi (Kurdish) kid came up and showed us a grenade. Tried to get it from him; no go. Had to get an adult who spoke English. Found out this kid knows where there's <u>lots</u> more; told him we'd trade MREs for grenades. He showed up with 30 or so in a few minutes! Gave him a case of MREs and told him to shove off. All these grenades have been rigged by the Iraqis with 0-second delay; pull the pin, let spoon fly and <u>BOOM</u>!*

> *...The kids are <u>everywhere</u>, yelling 'Meestah, Meestah,*
> *wan, wan, Meestah' meaning one MRE. It's pitiful! But*
> *give a kid an MRE and 10 kids jump on him and kick the*
> *shit out of him! We've got our ROWPU [Reverse Osmosis*
> *Water Purification Unit] set up by the river in town*
> *making fresh water and passing it out in 5 gallon jugs.*
> *Also have medical set up doing a type of 'sick call' there;*
> *saw over 500 people (mostly kids) in two days. Quite a*
> *few have chronic illnesses that can't be treated by our*
> *corpsmen, require hospitalization! What a vicious circle!*
>
> *Will mail you pictures of a mural of Saddam we found.*
> *Those are bullet impacts on it! The gesture I'm making is*
> *the most appropriate I could think of at the time!"*

For Carol Statesman, the most difficult aspect of her husband's Somalia deployment was the lack of communication in the beginning "because you had no idea what they were going through," she said. "You'd see it on CNN but you didn't know what was directly happening to them, what city they were in, in the embassy or going out on patrols." Once she found out more about where her husband was and what it was like for him, she felt much better. "I could write about specific things. Before, I wanted to send him something but I felt helpless. Once we had communication, I knew that even if it took three weeks to get there, I could 'take action.'"

Similarly, Bob wanted to read about both familiar and new events at home. He asked about what treats our pet bird was eating and whether the kitchen faucet still dripped. Although those things seemed dull to me compared to his adventures, I knew it was important for him to read about "normal" life. Think about what you would share at the dinner table or as you retire for the evening if your spouse were at home. Jot down those thoughts and send them off frequently.

Don't forget the "little things."

"I missed you at the grocery store. I didn't buy any Oreos

because you weren't there to ask with those puppy dog eyes."

When you write, don't leave out something because you think it's too silly. Telling your spouse about the little things that make up your day keeps you connected.

Give news about friends, relatives, and neighbors.

Even though you've given your spouse's address to these folks, they'll probably only send a letter or two during the entire deployment. Those few letters are certainly cherished ("someone other than my spouse misses and thinks about me!"), and you should encourage them to write ("Bob would love to hear from you about your new car!"). But rarely do they provide all the news your spouse would like to hear. So whenever you learn of someone's new job, baby, engagement, or outrageous hair cut, pass it along.

Supplement longer letters with postcards, greeting cards, and short notes.

It's tough to write long letters, especially if you're trying to write every day or several times a week. Keep a few stamped and addressed postcards ready for quick notes like "The peach tree blossomed this week. The peaches should be nice and juicy when you get home," or "Steven scored a goal today!"

If you're tired of writing the same old stuff, make a greeting card. It can be serious or silly. One time when Bob was at a four-month training school, I drew stick figures on a paper bag and wrote:

> *Jane goes to work. Jane comes home from work. Jane thinks about her plump, cool, feather pillow and soft, warm, cuddly quilt.*
>
> *Then Jane remembers he's in Virginia. See Jane cry. See Spot lick her tears. See Dick soon I hope.*

Commercially made greeting cards express "I love you and miss you" messages in romantic or humorous ways that give our own creative juices a break. Stock up for those times you need a writing break but don't want to break the writing habit.

Write quick notes on Post-its as you think of something during the day. Stick the notes together and throw them in an envelope. Not only is this a fun "letter" to receive, your spouse can take out favorite messages and post them by a desk or bunk.

Send photos.

Send people photos or everyday life photos. For example, I laminated a fun photo of me and Bob and sent it to him to hang by his cot. I also sent before and after pictures of the garden, a room I rearranged, and other projects.

Order double prints when you develop film and send one set to your spouse. Or tack two or three photos to a sheet of paper, make a color copy, and use the white space on the copy to write a letter. If you have a digital camera or scanner, print out black & white or color prints with fun sayings or captions. Or upload the digital photos to an online service and have prints mailed directly to your spouse.

Sometimes it's easier for the deployed person to send home film to be developed or to send the film directly to a mail order film developer and have the pictures mailed to your home address. For Bob's six-month ship deployments, he mailed his film to the developer and ordered double prints to be sent to me. He put a date on the address label with the order. Then in a separate letter, he told me where the pictures were taken and the date he mailed the film, so I could match the pictures with the location. When I received the pictures, I reread his letters and relived his adventures. I put one set of pictures in an album and split the doubles between letters to Bob and family and friends.

Use unique stationery to send messages.

Why limit yourself to stationery or legal pads when there are paper bags, leaves, rocks, art projects, sides of a tissue or cereal box, and much more. Bob once sent a postcard made from the side of an MRE box. He was in Iraq, had no paper and envelopes, so he improvised. Make letter writing interesting and fun!

Don't write when you're depressed, frustrated, or angry.

Try to write when you feel good. Emotions come through in letters and you don't want to cause worry if there's no need. If you aren't doing well, then of course it's important to tell your spouse. But most of the time, whatever has upset you or put you in a bad mood will go away long before the letter reaches its destination. Think about what you want to hear in a letter: probably that your spouse is doing great and is being well cared for, even though he misses you. Chances are your spouse wants to hear the same from you. It's okay to write about the situation that upset you; it puts your spouse at ease to know that it's past tense and you're doing fine now.

Carefully choose which unresolved problems to write about.

Many day-to-day problems work themselves out in a short period of time. Ask for advice only when you need it and make sure there's enough time for return correspondence before you need to implement the advice. For example, if it takes two weeks for your spouse to receive your letter and two more weeks to get back a reply, it will only frustrate both of you if you ask for your spouse's input on a decision you need to make next week. Use your best judgment considering what you think your spouse would say, then communicate your decision, your wish that your spouse could have been involved, and the outcome. (In an emergency, know your other communications options.) When there is time to solicit your spouse's advice, explain the situation and options clearly to avoid misinterpretation.

Recognize the difficulty of using letters to express some experiences or to resolve relational issues.

Don't make major decisions or argue through the mail. Some serious discussions need to wait until you can talk face-to-face.

Keep a sense of humor.

Humor is important in any relationship or situation in life, but especially during deployments. Everyday activities can be amusing and interesting if you use your imagination. I vividly remember Bob's response to my inquiry about daily life in the Northern Iraqi desert. He drew a humorous, detailed picture of the "oil barrel shit can" where many of them pilgrimaged several times a day seeking relief from "Saddam's revenge." It was a little more information than I needed, but gave us both a good laugh. Laughter is such a wonderful gift and healer. It's great medicine for otherwise dull, uneventful, or far-too-serious letters about life.

Audio and Video Tapes

Tapes are good supplements to letters. The receiving spouse, parent, or child can listen to the cassette or watch the video over and over. Plan for this type of communication before departure by acquiring two same-size-tape players and blank cassettes (if you forgot, send a player and blank cassette along with your first personalized tape). If you plan to send videos, make sure the recipient has a VCR available.

Use short tapes.

Short tapes are easier to fill and the recipient can usually listen to or watch it in one sitting. When the tapes are longer, especially videos, it can be more difficult to find enough time to watch the entire tape or to get the equipment more than once within a short time period.

Write notes before you record.

Some people feel silly talking into a recorder or being filmed. If this is you, ease some of the discomfort by preparing yourself. A few notes can help you remember key points you want to say on the cassette or events you want to record on a video.

Record special and routine events.

The sights and sounds of home can be as elaborate as video

clips from a school play or as simple as a hidden cassette under the dinner table that captures what your spouse would hear that night if at home. Be creative. Keep it simple.

One of my fondest memories was getting together with four friends, three of whom had boyfriends or husbands deployed with Bob. We videotaped our pets, teased the men about our delicious taco salad (we filmed parts of the meal preparation, but mostly had closeups of the Mmmmms), and used the delay feature on the camera to tape a "We love you" message from three different positions on the couch. We laughed and had a great time making the tape. On the other end, the four men sat glued to the VCR with big eyes and silly grins listening intently for their girl to say something, anything, in the boring dinner conversation or to laugh or to look into the camera right into their eyes half way across the world. Interestingly, through this spontaneous, fairly uneventful video, came an important yet unintentional message. I didn't realize it until I received a letter from Chris' husband John. They had been married only a few months before he deployed. He wrote to thank me for being her friend. The video had made the men feel better knowing that we girls had each other to lean on and were helping each other to laugh.

When Jolene Franklin's husband received orders to deploy, her parents gave her a camcorder. She planned to make a tape of Gerald's friends all saying hello. Before he left, Gerald asked her not to send any tapes because it would make him too homesick. "So at the end of the tape," Jolene said, "I went around the house and filmed all the things that needed repairs so he wouldn't miss home too much."

Cassette tapes work best for the Klotz family. "I turn them on even while I'm washing the dishes," Mary said. "[My husband] Peter hears the water and the bird in the background while I'm talking. Suddenly [my son] Alan comes into the house and I'm yelling at him. That's really what our life is like and I want Peter to feel comfortable. Even the things he probably misses the most are things he hates the most. When I do a cassette tape I feel I get a truer picture of what's happening. He can actually hear the voices and can tell what kind of emotion it is and what's going on. That's much more realistic for us. Peter likes to send the tapes to us, too. When we get lonely, we have them to listen to."

Send home a video from the unit.

Service members: grab a video camera and record everyone in the unit or section saying a few words to loved ones at home. Send the tape to the rear contact person, your spouse, or someone who can invite all the families together to watch the video. Just make sure *everyone* in the unit is on the video or someone in the audience will be heartbroken. Also, the contact person can make a copy of the video for families not living at the duty station during the deployment.

Send favorite shows.

If your spouse has a VCR available regularly but can't get U.S. programming on the TV, send videos of favorite shows. Don't edit out the commercials; sometimes they're as interesting as the show to someone who hasn't been in the U.S. for a while.

Phone Calls

Phone calls may not be feasible for those aboard smaller ships (except when in port) and those in remote areas or war zones. Prepare for the possibility that phone calls may only be allowed in emergencies or as morale boosters. If a telephone is available, remind yourselves of the frequency, length of call, and subject restrictions you set up when preparing for the deployment.

Pick a time.

Set up a basic time of day or night most convenient for each of you. If possible, the deployed person should try to call only at the designated time; the spouse at home should try to be available then, within reason. If your spouse is deployed outside the U.S., late at night or early morning U.S. time usually works, if you can wake yourself up enough. To see what time it is somewhere else in the world, visit http://www.time.gov/ and look at the world map that shows time of day.

Surprise calls are always welcome and exciting, but the anticipation can be frustrating. It's hard to suppress the urge to sit by the phone day and night, just in case your spouse calls. It gets harder if you miss an unexpected call. Bob deployed one December and was unable to send out mail or phone home right away. At home, three weeks passed, including Christmas day, with no letters or phone calls. Finally, the first week in January, Bob had an opportunity to call using a satellite phone. Unfortunately, he called Saturday morning during the half hour that I was out running errands. He received his own voice on the answering machine. In this case, he couldn't have gotten word to me about the call; he just hoped I would be home for the one chance he happened to get that month. It was wonderful for me to hear his voice and to know he was okay, but I felt terrible that he didn't get the same opportunity. I had to fight that urge to sit by the phone day and night, just in case he could call back.

Keep notes beside the phone.

Whether the call is short because of your agreed upon time/budget restrictions, the instability of the line (such as MARS calls or phone patches), or many other deployment factors, you usually don't have time to "think" on the line. As you think of things you want to discuss on the next call (whether or not you know when that will be), write down a few notes and keep them by the phone. When your spouse does call, the notes will remind you of what you want to ask or say, and will also help keep the conversation brief.

Keep a pen and blank paper by the phone, too. You'll want to keep notes of important things your spouse may tell you or ask you to do, or little things he says to you, to make it easier to remember later.

Keep it simple and focused

Do not discuss unresolvable issues over the phone or bring

up a subject you aren't prepared to explain clearly in a short amount of time.

Keep in mind budget restrictions.

When preparing for the deployment, you discussed frequency and length of calls. For some, you won't have a choice. It will be "maybe I can call once or twice." For those in situations where frequent or lengthy calls are an option, such as unaccompanied tours to Japan, it's extremely important to stick to the phone budget you've determined for the deployment. Stories of couples with $2,000 phone bills are not just sea-stories. Find out the rates before you call. If you need a reminder, set a kitchen timer to tell you both when time is up.

Learn how to say goodbye.

It's so great to hear each other's voices. It's so hard to say goodbye. The first thing Bob and I said after the jump-up-and-down "Hi!!" was usually "I love you and miss you" just in case the call was cut short. Then we talked quickly about all those "list" things. Then... silence. Who wants to say goodbye? It's the hardest part. Find out when the next phone call opportunity might be. Say you look forward to it. Express love, hugs, and so on, and agree to both hang up. Don't listen to the dial tone. Don't pick up the phone to see if someone is still on the line. Just enjoy that strange feel-good, feel-let-down feeling behind your silly grin and glossy eyes.

E-mail

Many units offer individual electronic mail addresses. Others have a unit address and can print out messages for individuals whose name appears in the subject line. If your spouse has this opportunity, and you don't already have one, it may be worth getting an e-mail account at home for correspondence during the deployment. In the end, e-mail provides a quick response like phone calls, offers the time to think and compose like letters, and is less expensive than either!

Find out your spouse's e-mail environment.

Will your spouse access e-mail via a private or shared computer? Is the e-mail account an individual or shared inbox? Is it a military e-mail address? Can messages be stored on a computer or diskette; if so, for how long? Is it an option to view messages on an Internet server without downloading them (e.g., a Yahoo or Hotmail account)? Does your spouse have access to a printer to print messages? Are incoming or outgoing messages monitored or screened for content? How often can your spouse check and respond to e-mail? Answering these types of questions helps you decide what information is appropriate to send via e-mail.

Send to the right address.

Keep your spouse's e-mail address in a nickname folder or electronic address book so you don't have to retype it each time. This helps prevent misaddressed/ undeliverable messages.

Type your spouse's name in the subject line
("For Sgt Bill Smith").

For private or password-protected individual accounts, this isn't necessary. But if your spouse shares an account, receives mail through a unit account, or has an account that's easily accessed by someone else, this subject line alerts the person pulling up the message that the content is for your spouse only.

Be aware of privacy issues on shared accounts.

Like postcards, e-mail on a unit or shared account can be read by someone else. Most likely, the message will be printed out for your spouse rather than left on the machine for your spouse to check later. This is especially true in remote areas where there may be a large number of troops but only a few computers.

Keep it brief.

Think of an e-mail message as a postcard or phone call, even though you technically can write as much as you want without increasing the cost. Your spouse may have limited time to read the message on screen and may not have the opportunity to print your message to read later. If you keep the message short and to the point, chances are your spouse can read it and respond in the same session.

Make it readable.

Write short sentences and paragraphs, with line spaces between paragraphs or major ideas.

Messages sent over the Internet through secure firewalls usually lose formatting (no bold, italic, or tabs), so you have to emphasize words and make the piece readable in other ways. The easiest way to keep it readable is to hit the return key twice (add a line space) to separate ideas, questions, or information. Use quotes " " or asterisks * * around words you would normally boldface or italicize. Use all CAPS only when you want to SHOUT.

Proof for clarity.

Reread your messages before sending them. Since e-mail is so quick, it's easy to be thoughtless. Proofread what you write for grammar and punctuation, but most importantly for clarity and content.

Don't send attachments unless you're sure they can be received.

Some systems, especially those with a firewall for security reasons, will not accept attachments from the external Internet, even if it accepts attachments from an internal intranet.

The most common attachment people want to send is photos. Even if attachments are allowed, you have to be aware of file size limitations. Unless your spouse's unit has shared specific guidelines for attachments, it's best to either mail the photos or include a link to a family Web site.

Web Sites

A really fun way to keep your spouse up to date, if he has Internet access, is a family Web site. There are several easy-to-use software tools that help you create and manage Web site pages. Most Internet service providers give subscribers free or low-cost space on a server. There are also many inexpensive hosting services that offer enough server space for an average photo-filled site for a low monthly fee.

Learn about Internet safety: do not include personal correspondence or personal contact information; do not reference your spouse's deployment in connection with your family. Remember that anyone in the world can access your Web site, so take reasonable steps to protect your privacy. That said, it's a great way to post scanned or digital photos of your daughter's soccer game, your new living room curtains, or the tree damage from the storm. Include a link to new photos or pages in your next e-mail.

If your spouse's whole unit is deployed, suggest they put up photos on a Web site, too. Often, the rear unit team or spouse support network can maintain the unit or deployment site.

Care Packages

Everyone loves to receive a package. There's always something that would make your spouse's deployment more comfortable or more like home.

Find out what your spouse really wants or needs, then send a little extra.

When Bob was in Somalia, certain items became more difficult to obtain, especially as units' return departures were delayed. He asked for things like deodorant, Wet Ones, and *The Wall Street Journal*. After reading what his daily life was like (e.g., handwashed cammies that hung dry in blowing sand), I also threw in new underwear, socks, a towel, and wash cloth, all freshly washed, rinsed with fabric softener, and fluffed dry.

Expect your package to be shared.

Sending homemade chocolate chip cookies to the ship? No matter where your spouse opens the package, someone will be there to share. This isn't all bad; in fact, I often felt good about Bob sharing goodies with some of the single members who didn't receive packages from home. I've received some nice thank you letters from Marines I'd never met who loved my cookies!

For holidays, it can be fun to join forces with other spouses and create packages for the whole unit. Small items that go over in a big way include M&Ms and lollipops for Valentines Day and a little desk tree or other decorations for Christmas.

If sharing becomes a problem (e.g., your spouse is one of the few getting packages and you're tired of supplying the unit's goodies), send "bait." Throw in a bag of candy for your spouse to share while hiding the gourmet coffee. Or send one package that's labeled "to share" and label all the others "private."

Stick to a budget.

Like other forms of communication, packages can get expensive. Keep in mind that normally the military provides the basics such as drinking water, basic meals, and some personal care items available through a supply tent. Limit care package items to those you know your spouse needs, can't get there, or would really enjoy. Choose the lightest version possible (e.g., powder sports drink instead of liquid).

Consider delivery time and local climate.

Certain foods may not make it due to extended delivery time (e.g., homemade cookies after three weeks), or due to weather conditions at the destination (e.g., chocolate in the desert heat).

Send convenient, individual packages.

Most field and ship living spaces are cramped, troops often have gear limits, and there's not always a clean utensil handy. Popular care package items that come in individual packets include:

- ❑ powdered sport drink, health drink, or fruit juice drink mixes
- ❑ dried fruits
- ❑ hot sauce, garlic powder, cooking spices (especially good for field exercises or when MREs are the main meals)
- ❑ favorite snack foods (check first what's already available: candy, chips, peanut butter, etc., are often available on

ships)

❑ "field comforts" such as skin lotion, powder (foot, jock itch, baby), wet wipes, laundry soap, clothes pins, and clean underwear

If your spouse is deployed where the not-so-primitive facilities include an exchange and most of the above is available for purchase, send more personal items such as the local newspaper, a new novel from a favorite author, or customized video tapes. Disposable items are still preferred.

General Communication

Communicate often.

No matter what communication vehicle you choose, you can't express love too often. Send hugs, draw hearts, or say "I love you." Whatever your style, do it every time you think of your spouse, and more often than you think is necessary.

Write clearly. Say what you mean.

If you're both always straightforward, you won't have to read between the lines or try to interpret what hidden meaning might be there. Take the guess work out of communication.

Express your appreciation for letters, tapes, and so on.

Say thanks and mention one or two things specifically. For example, "Thanks for your April 15 letter from the Kurdish refugee camp. It helps me to know what your daily life is like and it's good to know you still have a sense of humor. I especially appreciate your description of the 'toilets.' Your drawing was very helpful; the neighbors agreed to a similar setup in the back yard when you return, to help with your transition."

Participate in changes.

Think about the excitement of watching an 11-month-old toddler trying to take his first steps. Now imagine that the last time you saw this child, he was a 5-month-old infant who could barely sit up on his own. The change is dramatic.

If your communication with your spouse throughout the deployment is reserved, the changes you, your spouse, and your family experience will appear as stark as the difference between the 11-month-old and 5-month-old. If you communicate openly and frequently, many of the changes will be expressed naturally.

I remember being excited about Bob's first six-month deployment. I thought it would be a good time for me to concentrate on my graduate studies. And, it would be a great opportunity for Bob to see the Mediterranean. A good friend, Gene Peters, was on a separate deployment. He wrote to me from the USS Nassau with this advice:

> *"As for you and Bob, well, separations can be beneficial. But remember to communicate. Six months is a long time. You'll both change a lot in that time. Be sure the other is a participant in those changes, no matter how small a role. Of course, a lot of the changes in Bob will be superficial, the result of living with a thousand other dirty, smelly, crass jarheads! Mail will be slow. For a while my letters were taking over a month to get back to the U.S."*

More isn't always better.

Everyone communicates differently. Don't compare with other spouses the number of letters or phone calls you receive. Focus on what you need from each other, not on how often another couple communicates.

Involve each family member.

Encourage communication between your deployed spouse and each family member. It's important for each child to hear from the deployed parent and to have an opportunity to write their own messages back to the parent. Tapes are a good way to communicate. A favorite for many younger children is to fall asleep listening to a tape of the parent "reading" bedtime stories.

Encourage children to send unique letters and include pieces of their lives such as drawings or school papers. Teens can include a magazine article about a common interest with the parent, photos from a camping trip or sports event, or a tape from a recital. It's important for the deployed parent to acknowledge *everything* a child or teen sends. Young people put more thought into the correspondence than you might realize and need to hear that their thoughts were appreciated.

If you have an opportunity for planned phone calls, try to arrange a call when everyone can at least say hello and hear your spouse's voice. Explain the reason it has to be brief. Usually, one or two sentences means the world to them.

Respect privacy.

It's important that parents let children and especially teens have "secrets" with the other parent. If a 15-year-old son is used to talking to dad about girls it might not be so easy to suddenly talk to mom about it. Mom shouldn't ask to read letters from the son to the dad or vice versa; it's private. In the same way, your children shouldn't read your personal, romantic letters.

Stay connected with the unit.

Know your rear contact person and key volunteers. Use the unit hotline, telephone tree, newsletter, and other communications to stay informed, especially during mail delays or hostile circumstances. The media may have incorrect or incomplete information.

Stay in touch with friends.

I wouldn't have survived all of our deployment experiences without Bob's great communication efforts. But some of the greatest sources of support for me during deployments were notes from people Bob worked with or had been stationed with in the past. Just a line or two saying "hang in there, he'll be home soon. I know this last part is tough" meant a lot coming from someone who had deployed before. Bob's deployment to Somalia was the most difficult separation for me. About a week before his homecoming, I received a letter from Kevin, a Marine who had worked with Bob in a unit that deployed to Iraq. We had not seen Kevin

and his wife, Deb, for about a year and a half as they were assigned to Seoul, Korea. He wrote:

> *"I shot Bob a letter about a week ago but, as*
> *Mogadishu mail goes, who knows if he'll ever receive it.*
> *Anyway, I hope this finds you well and in good spirits,*
> *despite the absence of Bob. I know it's probably of little*
> *consolation to you but I feel much better knowing Bob is*
> *on the job in Somalia. He was absolutely instrumental in*
> *my efforts to keep my sanity for a long time, and I'm sure*
> *he's keeping others sane and, more importantly, out of*
> *harm's way while he's there. ...*
>
> *I hope that by the time you get this you're way too*
> *busy with homecoming celebrations to read it. Hang in*
> *there and keep the faith. ..."*

It also helped me to stay in touch with other spouses. In March
of 1991, many troops came home from Desert Shield/Storm to
parades and television cameras. Chris Taraschke, whose husband
was deployed with mine in Northern Iraq, lived away from the
base most of the deployment and corresponded with me for information and support. Through her honest, emotional letters, I
found equal support in our developing friendship. Her March 13
letter expressed my feelings exactly: "It's been hard for me watching all those teary reunions on TV. I really miss my sweetie and I
want him to come home so we can be a normal married couple."
The July homecoming seemed so far away; we spent the next four
months helping each other get to our own teary reunions.

In a similar way, friends outside the military provided balance in my life. Without trying to understand what I was feeling,
they simply called, visited, and made sure life went on. They helped
me discover that while communication is an important part of a
deployment experience, it's important not to let the deployment
be your only communication. There is more to life.

Chapter 7
Children

"Dadda, Dadda!" Katie, age 2, pointed and shouted up at the airplane. Every airplane. Every airplane she saw during the four months her daddy was deployed. She wondered when his plane would finally land so he could come home.

When 19-month-old Robert's dad came home from a 6-month deployment, his mom said, "Come give daddy a hug." Robert ran straight to his dad's photograph on the coffee table and gave the framed picture a big hug.

Jaci, 15 years old, refused to write to her mom for the first month of her deployment. "If she wants to know what's going on, she should come home and find out," she told her father. Once Jaci realized that not writing wasn't going to bring her mom home any sooner, she gradually started throwing a card in with her father's correspondence.

Baseball lover 12-year-old Gary decided he didn't want to play the season when his dad deployed. Two neighborhood dads stepped in and offered to practice with him and take turns going to his games. They took pictures and posted them to a family Web site for his dad to see.

Rachel, mom of three active boys, says, "The hardest part was keeping up my energy to be both mom and dad to our boys."

Young people, from infants to teens, add a new dimension to deployments. They add to your needs and have special needs of their own. As you prepare for and experience a deployment, it's worth thinking about it from your children's perspective.

Preparing Children for the Separation

Before your spouse departs, both of you should devote genuine attention to each child and that child's anxieties about the deployment. The announcement that a deployment will take place can be made to the family as a group but the preparation should be done individually.

Explain what's going to happen. Be honest and keep it simple. Talk about where the parent is going and why. Use a map or globe. Discuss the deployment mission in terms a child can understand (e.g., "Daddy's going to help people." "Some people did some bad things and Mommy is going to help make it better." "Daddy's ship has to be there in case people need help."). Talk about what the child will do during the deployment. Talk through common feelings and some things that might be hard to deal with. Together, think of solutions (e.g., the child can send photos, videos, or a detailed letter describing ball games or Scout events). If this is not the first deployment, remind the child of past happy reunions.

Give your children time to adjust to the announcement of the deployment. Some parents wait until the last minute to tell their children because they don't want to upset them or have to deal with the children's emotions when they're trying to prepare themselves. Your children need time to prepare and adjust, too.

Let them physically see the parent leave. According to Julia Threadgill, a reservist married to an active duty Marine, children need that definition. During six years, either Julia or her husband, Terry, was deployed every year; both were deployed during the Persian Gulf conflict. She says, "It's easier on the parents if the children aren't involved in the goodbye. But the children really need to see [the parent] go." Her family knew well in advance that Terry would deploy to Saudi Arabia during Desert Shield; however, her orders were very sudden, a 3-day notice. "We didn't realize they'd call reserves so quickly," she said. She found out the Friday after Thanksgiving and left the following Tuesday. Her young son, Karl, wouldn't talk to her on the phone because of the "way she left."

When Rebecca Clark's Navy husband left aboard ship for Desert Shield/Storm, after they said goodbye at the pier, she drove her children up to a high hill overlooking San Diego harbor. They watched the magnificent procession of ships head out into the Pacific. It was a memorable moment in modern history—the largest fleet sailing together since World War II. Her children all remember that dramatic moment with their father in the midst of it. Not only did the children realize that Dad's departure had actually happened, they took away a visual memory that stayed with them through his return.

From *A Survey of the Deployment Experiences of Marine Corps Spouses* by Marta Baker Garrett

The Hardest Thing about My Spouse's Deployment Was:

"My kids don't know their father and it was lonely for both of us."

"Turning into a single parent with my own Marine Corps requirements."

"Being both a mommy and a daddy to my two very active boys."

"The unhappiness of the children. Not enough contact."

"Problems disciplining the children."

"Dealing fairly with our children. My patience runs very thin and often I don't feel they are getting enough quality attention."

"Explaining where Daddy was."

"Helping teenage children make the right decisions."

"Being pregnant; I worried about his safety so much I almost miscarried."

"Hearing the children say and do things that reflect their disappointment in him being gone."

"Not having someone to give me a break with the children, especially when I needed to sleep in/nap; and worrying about my children and neglecting them."

"My child never adjusted, constantly wanting her daddy."

Meeting Children's Needs

Think about how much your life changes during a deployment. Now consider a young person who feels the same anger, resentment, confusion, or loneliness you do, but understands it even less. On a normal day, young people need your love, attention, support, and guidance. During a deployment, you can multiply that by about a thousand, give or take. Children need:

Time to adjust.

In addition to time to adjust to the idea of a parent going away for a while, children also need downtime after the departure. Expect them to be sad or just plain "feel weird." Give them space, but be available.

The period of adjustment and the impact of the separation on children depends in part on their relationship with both the departing and remaining parent. For example, mothers generally do most of the nurturing. When a mother deploys, children often miss that nurturing more than anything else. The extent of nurturing in the child's relationship with a non-deploying father will help determine the time needed to adjust.

Reassurance you're not leaving, too.

Explain why your spouse had to go work somewhere else for a while and reconfirm that you are staying home (however, dual-military couples, don't assume you won't both deploy during the same time period!). Make sure your children understand that your spouse's leaving is not a punishment and has nothing to do with their behavior. This is most convincing when the explanation comes directly from the deploying parent.

Be aware of situations that might cause younger children to cling to you or fear you won't return. For example, they may not react well to a babysitter at first (you're leaving the house and they think you won't come back for a long time). Trade babysitter services with a mother of one of your child's friends. In any case, state when you will return and don't be late.

Stability.

Your children need to know that someone will care for them, that the family won't fall apart because a parent is absent. On your weak days you might be tempted to give in to children more easily, relax rules, or ease up on expectations. While children might seem to enjoy and even encourage this slack, they may also think you aren't strong enough to hold together. Write notes to yourself. When do you usually say yes or no? How do your children react? What are the rules?

Children like routine. For shorter deployments it helps them to know that daily events such as meals and bedtime will be the same. During longer deployments, routines are more likely to change. At least provide predictability. Be consistent.

Keep traditions alive. Celebrate holidays, birthdays, and other special days.

Healthy habits.

Young people need even more food, more fluids, more exercise, and more rest than you do. During a deployment especially, they may not realize why they aren't hungry or why they'd rather lie down on a bed after school than go out and play with friends. It's up to you to keep a close eye on your children and make sure their physical needs are met. Model healthy habits.

Realistic, age-appropriate responsibilities.

Don't put older children in surrogate parent roles. Together set realistic expectations and support your children in their choice to meet those expectations.

To understand which roles change and which don't.

You are their disciplinarian, their comfort and support, their mother *and* father. Don't say "Wait 'til your father (mother) gets home." Not only does this say you aren't the real disciplinarian right now, your children might dread the homecoming for fear of punishment (they know you keep track of all the times you say that!).

Don't get into a habit of sleeping with your child or letting your child sleep with you. You both need the physical separation. And sleeping together during the deployment can lead to your children having negative feelings toward your spouse later, who surely won't want to share you in bed!

Limits; to be held responsible for their actions.

Children feel more secure when you expect them to honor rules and keep their lives in order (e.g., complete homework, clean bedroom, do chores). Teens, though they'll fight for the freedom to test them, want to know where the boundaries are and that you're strong enough to hold up the fence.

To understand more about the deployed parent's life.

Just as it helps you to know more about the conditions under which your spouse works, it also helps your children. Arrange a tour of a ship, tank, or other piece of equipment that would familiarize your children with your spouse's living space or work. Help them learn about the country, climate, or culture where your spouse is stationed. If the deployment is to a hostile zone, share nonpolitical information and encourage questions. Be realistic and objective; don't glamorize. Replace fear with facts such as demonstrating safety equipment (e.g., gas mask) or describing the extensive training that helps keep your spouse safe.

A strong role model to show them good coping techniques.

During a deployment, it's not necessarily a parent's absence that affects a child the most, it's how the other parent deals with it. Don't pretend you aren't affected by the deployment. It helps your children to know this is difficult for you, too. However, it helps more if your children see you looking for positive solutions. Be strong and cope positively; your children will follow your lead.

Support from other adults.

Visit your child's teacher. Don't ask for special treatment, just an extra set of understanding eyes. Talk about the deployment and what kind of changes you both might expect from your child.

Talk periodically throughout the deployment; don't wait for a problem.

Let your child develop closer relationships with trusted coaches, neighbors, or older friends. As much as you may want to be, you can't be all people to your child.

Peer support.

You have your outside support networks. Make sure your children have theirs. Arrange opportunities for your children to meet similar-aged children whose parent is or has been deployed. Like you, they might make new friends, or at least find out that their feelings are normal.

To know the truth.

They watch the news, listen to friends at school, and accumulate stress. Set a limit on how often and what kind of news reports you and your children watch. Interpret confusing information. Remember that the media often dramatizes a situation; check accuracy with your key volunteer or ombudsman. While some information may seem inappropriate for children, if a child asks, he wants to know. You won't protect him by lying. If you can't answer a child's question, that's okay. Say you'll try to find out the answer; don't make one up.

An outlet for their emotions.

You know how good it feels when you finish aerobics or weight lifting or write about your day in a journal. Your children need that same release. Keep them physically and mentally active. Encourage them to play outside with the dog, ride bikes with a friend, or join a sports team. During quieter times, show them how reading, writing, or drawing can relax them and take their mind off worries.

Teens, especially, need acceptable ways to act out feelings. They're dealing with changing bodies, sexual desires, and peer pressure at a time when image is of utmost importance. Drama, sports, and writing poetry are popular outlets.

A listener.

Often we don't need advice as much as we need to talk out what we're thinking or feeling. When your children talk to you, put down what you're doing and look into their eyes. Wait patiently for them to find the right words. Maintain an encouraging expression. Respond positively (sometimes a hug is enough said). Always be available to listen.

To feel emotionally safe.

Children don't really want to *hear*, "Don't worry about it" or "Everyone will be fine." They want to *feel* that they don't have to worry in order for everyone to be fine. They want to know that no matter what happens, even if they screw up somehow, they'll be loved and accepted. Everything in their lives—school, peer groups, new experiences, changing bodies—tests this. Love them. Accept them. They need to know they can always count on their family.

Something to believe in.

As children mature, their belief structure changes. Visions of Tinkerbells and magic card tricks give way to logic and physics. But the need to believe in something that's constant and inspiring never goes away. Share your spiritual resources, religious beliefs, life principles. Encourage your children to find their own personal sources of inner strength.

Control.

Young people, in general, don't get much say in things (think about how you feel when you don't have a say in your spouse's deployment). Having the information and tools to make decisions when they need to gives young people a sense of control. Let your children know where you are going, when you'll return, and how to reach you. Teach them safety procedures. Help them develop planning and problem-solving skills.

The benefit of the doubt; a fresh start.

Look at each new part of your day as a chance for a positive experience and teach your children to do the same. When you have a bad day at work do you have less patience with your children that evening than when you have a good day? Every time you come home, it's a new opportunity to have a good day; start with a fresh attitude. If you find yourself asking "Why do you *always* act this way?" or "Why can't you *ever* clean your room?" these are signs you're collecting frustrations rather than addressing a specific, present issue. Go out the door and come back in again. You're not being fair to your children who happened to make a mistake when you had less patience. Give your children the benefit of the doubt. It may not be them; it might be you.

Individual attention.

Each person is unique. Think about your best friends, your closest family members. You've spent one-on-one time with each of them. You can't have a really close relationship with anyone unless at some point you focus only on each other. It's the same with your children. Each child wants 100% of your love, wants to share with you things she hasn't learned about herself yet. The time together doesn't always have to be planned. Learn to recognize and take advantage of the five minutes in the car on the way to soccer practice, the five minutes folding clothes together.

Sometimes the best moments come unexpectedly. One day we had a wonderful rain. My son, Alexander, and I went out to the garage on our way to run an errand. As I opened the car door, he looked outside and asked, "Can I touch it? What does the rain feel like?" We caught the rain with our hands and face, sploshed in puddles, watched how it dripped from tree branches, and oooed at the brightest full rainbow as the sun broke brilliantly through the evening clouds and made all the soft drops in the air around us shimmer. A robin got a worm, all the neighbor birdies started to sing, and we completely forgot about that errand.

Stress-free together time.

Think about how drained you would be if every conversation centered around how you feel, what's going wrong, or when your spouse is coming home. You need balance! You need to laugh and just be happy. So does your family. Deployment isn't gloom. It's more concentrated life! Turn off the TV and talk with each other at dinner time. Exchange ideas without judgment. Tell jokes and stories.

To be kids.

Children sometimes feel like they have to be grown up. Help them to be kids. Set up support for yourself and give yourself time to replenish your energy, otherwise you'll seek comfort and support from your children. They can't handle that responsibility, especially at this stressful time. *You* be the parent.

Let your children have fun. If you focus on fun, positive activities, they'll follow your example. Let them have silly ideas. Let them guess and be wrong. Let them be innocent and goofy. Get dirty. Giggle. Run around. Make noise. Be kids.

Love.

Love means many things and has varying degrees. Some people feel comfortable hugging and saying, "I love you" to their children. Others prefer to show their love by spending time at a favorite activity with a child. *How* you demonstrate your love is a reflection of your own personality and beliefs. That you *do* demonstrate it is the important thing. A loving home for children is a fun and safe place to live, a place where they feel comfortable being themselves and know they will be accepted. Loving parents are consistent in demands and discipline and set an example by what they do, not just by what they say. A loving family provides each individual child with room to grow at his or her own pace.

Reactions

Young people, like adults, react to a deployment in different ways. A child may act out on purpose or without realizing it. Most reactions work themselves out as a child adjusts. Signs of severe or persistent reactions or symptoms that need immediate attention include:

❏ poor eating habits; continuously eating too little or too much

❏ withdrawal from people and activities

❏ sleeping problems such as insomnia or severe and frequent nightmares

❏ sickness with no apparent cause

❏ temper tantrums or crying spells over little things

❏ fear without real cause

❏ constant fighting or destructive behavior

❏ falling behind or not working at ability level in school

Sometimes children don't want to participate in an activity because it reminds them of the parent who is away. Nancy McKenzie decided to push her son to get involved in soccer, a sport he enjoyed. "He didn't want to sign up. I think a lot of it was that his father would miss most of the games. I told him, 'Ryan, what are you going to do, stay home and feel sorry for yourself and have no fun in life because you're thinking about your father being gone? He wouldn't want that. He'd love to see you playing. You need to get the exercise to make yourself feel better. You need to be with your friends.' Finally he agreed to it." It turned out to be Ryan's best soccer season ever. "Ryan had a coach who was excellent and kind of filled the void," Nancy said. "I think Ryan played his aggression out more than ever, that's probably why he played so well. That was his funnel for getting out his frustrations."

Lauren Lawson, age 3, experienced sleep disturbance during her dad's shorter deployments. "It's hard to have him come home after just two weeks or when he was TAD in El Toro and came home on the weekends," said Lauren's mom. "She'd see bugs and I'd have to carry her around for four hours at a time. She was real confused."

Nightmares are common for many young children because they don't understand that the missing parent is safe and will return. Geoffrey Smith, age 4, had nightmares when his dad deployed to Somalia. He told his mom, "Daddy fell down and hurt his knee. Now he can't come home." When his father called a few days later, it took a few minutes to explain to Geoffrey that he really didn't get hurt and that he was going to come home.

Younger children have no real concept of time. Julie's daughter thought her dad was still flying around in an airplane. "Every time an airplane flies overhead, she'll say 'Daddy, I'm down here. I'm eating a cookie.' And she'll wave the cookie at the airplane and she'll say, 'Daddy come home.' Or she'll say, 'let's go to the airport and pick up my daddy.' She thinks this plane is going to land and he can get off."

Sometimes it helps young people to have someone other than you to talk to about difficult feelings or situations. Sometimes they just need another role model of the same gender. When Jerry Sackley's wife, Linda, went to the field for three weeks, their oldest daughter, Sue, was 12. One week after her mom left, Sue started her first menstrual cycle. "She knew basically what was going on because Linda had talked with her and they gave her information at school," Jerry said, his face blushing. "Sue was embarrassed to talk to me about it. I called my neighbor who is a good friend of ours and she came over. It certainly wasn't a major family crisis, but I felt bad she didn't have her mom here." Margaret Humble's 7-year-old son started paying attention to the older boys in the neighborhood when her husband left for six months. "I certainly couldn't act like one of the guys for him," she said. "He just needed to hang around boys and see what they acted like I guess."

Communication

As you know from your efforts with your spouse, communication is difficult when you don't have frequent in-person experiences. Solid communication is critical to a healthy and growing relationship between your spouse and children and takes that same extra effort.

Communication ideas for strengthening and maintaining the deployed-parent/child relationship during a deployment:

Deployed parent:

- ❏ Make a cassette of favorite bedtime stories, nursery rhymes, or a legend about the people/country where you'll be deployed. Your child can fall asleep at night listening to the stories, and more importantly, to your voice.

- ❏ Before the deployment, ask your spouse to take a picture of you with each child individually doing everyday things together such as reading, watching TV, eating dinner, or playing ball. The pictures will remind each child of how much you enjoy spending time with them.

- ❏ Send a photo of yourself in uniform, on the ship or in the field, so your child can better understand what you do and where you are working.

- ❏ Write as often as possible to each child individually. Generally, you can write individual notes and put them all in one family envelope. If a child is expecting a private response, put the letter in its own envelope inside the larger envelope. Even better, address and mail it separately; the child will appreciate getting his or her own special letter.

- ❏ When you communicate, ask or answer questions specific to each child's level of understanding and interests. Ask about pets, hobbies, and school projects. Especially answer requests for a photo or a description of your day. When your children ask about these things, they are reaching out to you to help them better understand. Reread their letters to make sure you've answered their questions.

- ❏ Take with you or ask your spouse to send you schedules of ball games, swim meets, school plays, parades, and so on, so you can ask about them in letters or on the phone.

❑ If you'll visit several places, such as ports during a ship deployment, send each child a different postcard from each place. Ask your children to keep the postcards in a scrapbook and write about something they did that week. It will prompt you to exchange stories when you return.

For shorter deployments:

❑ Write the departure on the calendar and remind children so they aren't surprised. Leave a note for each child to open each day you'll be gone.

❑ If there isn't time for children to mail you letters, that doesn't mean they won't want to write. See if it's possible for them to fax, e-mail, or phone you messages. Encourage them to write down questions or issues in a journal, then set aside time when you return to talk about them.

Children:

❑ Put up a map and mark the places your parent will be going. Look up information about the places at your library or school. Even if your parent is at a desert exercise in the United States, if you haven't been to the desert, there's a lot to learn about it. In your letters, tell your parent what you learned and ask more questions.

❑ Write your own letters.

Ideas:

— Clip out and share local newspaper items or favorite magazine columns.

— Send sports scores from your parent's favorite teams.

— Play tic-tac-toe or checkers through the mail (draw the boards on a piece of paper and send the game back and forth after each move).

— Send crossword puzzles and cartoon strips.

— Send samples of school work.

— Draw pictures.

— Write about a great joke you heard.

— Send videos of games or special events.

— Make a card by cutting and pasting headlines from an old newspaper or magazine.

❑ Create a family newsletter. You can hand write or type it. Include pictures and stories from each family member. They can write their own stories or you can interview them. Send a copy to relatives or friends and encourage them to contribute news to the next issue. Or make an audio or video version.

❑ If your parent has Internet access, create a family Web site. Update it with photos. Be careful (have your parent check) not to include information about your family, home, or deployed parent that you wouldn't want a stranger to see.

When Children Are Home Alone

With your spouse somewhere else in the world, you have one less adult to help you care for your children, including ferrying them to and from activities, and supervising them after school. For some families, this means children staying home alone.

Before you hand over the house keys, assess the situation. Do your children need babysitters or can they care for themselves? Age is not always a good indicator. Look at their maturity and experience. Do the siblings get along? Do they respect house rules? Babysitter or not, check into flex time for yourself. Even if you can get home one hour earlier, that's one less hour your children are home without you.

Tips for those times when your children are home and you can't be:

❑ Ask or pay a friend to come to your house after school to start dinner. Since the friend is "helping you with dinner" the children are less likely to think of this person as a babysitter.

❑ Is there a neighbor you trust who is home after school?
   Introduce your children and ask if they can check in
   after school or contact the neighbor if they have any
   problems.

❑ Interest your children in volunteering at the local
   library or joining a community sports team that plays
   nearby after school.

❑ Set up house rules. A few examples to consider:

— Start homework right away; when done, a half hour of
   TV or video game is allowed

— No visitors

— No cooking

— No talking on the phone, except in an emergency

— Don't open the door

❑ Make it easy for them. Have a healthy snack already
   prepared. If it's dark when they get home, invest in a
   light timer or sensor.

❑ Prepare your children to meet the challenges they may
   encounter. Do they know and have they practiced fire
   escape routes? Natural disaster safety (tornados, earth-
   quakes, floods, etc.)? Procedures and circumstances
   under which to call 911? Basic first aid? Whom to call
   first with a problem (neighbor, you, police, etc.) and for
   what kind of questions or problems?

❑ Carry a cell phone or at least a beeper. Teach your
   children how to contact you.

❑ Adjust arrangements as your children's needs change.
   For example, older children tend to be more involved in
   extracurricular activities and may require transportation. Join car pools and trade favors with other parents.
   Arrange for a babysitter for younger children.

❑ Support after-school programs. Check with your school,
   community center, or church for possibilities.

How to Choose a Day Care Center:

Check the adult/child ratio. The lower the ratio the better. Use a benchmark of one adult to 4-12 children depending on age.

Who works there? Meet the staff. How are they trained (both pre-hiring requirements and ongoing training)? Are they paid well? What's the turnover rate? How does your child respond to the staff? Do *you* like the staff? Does the center director know the children's names?

Is the facility clean? Accredited? When was it last inspected?

What are the play time activities? Are there educational and developmental benefits?

Check references. Talk with parents of similar-aged children who share your values.

How to Choose a Babysitter:

Start with a good list. Ask for referrals from parents you trust. Some communities have babysitter groups that require all members to attend first aid and babysitting courses. Some day care center and elementary school teachers also babysit.

Check references. Know the sitter's family and background. Make sure the sitter is mature and understands how to handle an emergency.

Have new sitters spend time with your child while you're home. Choose a sitter you and your child like and respect.

Rules and Expectations

"It's hard for me to be the one who tells them 'no way' for one thing and then hugs them when they cry about something else," says Sue Fleming, mother of three. "It really confuses the kids. I'm mother and father. They're used to asking for permission from their father for certain things and when I say no, they get really upset that it's different when he's gone." As much as Sue tries to keep most discipline rules the same, the fact that there's only one

Setting Rules and Consequences

Rule	Reason (We have this rule because...)	Consequence (If you break this rule, then...)
Don't hit your siblings	We respect and love each other.	Time-out in your room to sit quietly and think about a better way to handle arguments.
Don't play in the street.	A car driver may not see you and you could get hurt.	You'll have to play inside for the day.
Don't throw things in the house.	You might break something.	For one week, you can't play with the toy you threw. If you break something, you'll have to pay to replace it.

Also try positive rules.

Rule	Reason (Do this because...)	Consequence* (When you honor this rule...)
Make your bed each morning.	It shows you are a neat and responsible person.	You'll get an allowance of $___ per week if you remember to make your bed every day before school without being told.
Wash the dishes after dinner.	We all need to pitch in; we need clean dishes to eat on.	You may have a treat between dinner and bedtime when you wash the dishes and help clean the kitchen without complaining.

*Consequences/rewards don't have to be tangible things. They can include praise, hugs, or a leadership award such as being the person who picks out the rental movie this week.

parent suddenly forces things to change. How do you make it run smoother and win the support of your children? Mary Wright, Army wife and elementary teacher, says it's not enough for parents to set up new rules and tell young people the way it's going to be. "The key," she explains, "is to make sure the kids have a say in the rules and that the kids think both the rules and consequences are fair." If they rebel about the changes before the deployment, chances are it will only get worse when one parent (often the stricter disciplinarian) leaves. If a child has a say in the decision process, he tends to take more responsibility for his actions. "My son agreed that he shouldn't be allowed to go out with his friends until his homework is done," explained Mary. "So he can't get upset with me when I remind him of the rule. He agreed it was fair." When a family works as a team to create and enforce the rules, the "bad" or "mean" parent role is eliminated.

There's more to discipline than doling out consequences for broken rules. Responsibility for simple household chores weighs heavier on everyone with a key person missing. It helps to divide up the chores as a family and to establish an attitude that everyone needs to put in a little extra effort and help out whenever needed. Many parents caution not to put too much pressure on any one child. For example, fathers should *not* say to their oldest son, "You're the man of the house now, take over while I'm gone." First of all, he is not yet a man and could not hope to fill a father's shoes. Yes, he can probably mow the lawn just as well, but a 15-year-old boy cannot make all of the adult decisions a husband and father has to make. Even though *you* may not expect him to make all of the decisions, *he* may think you expect it. Be specific and realistic in your expectations. If you mean "help your mother out when she asks you to," or "be nicer to your little sister and walk with her to school," then say so.

Sharing Chores

How can you split up the chores that have to be done? The maturity and physical strength of a child best determine the chores he or she is able to do. A few ideas:

2-year-olds	put away toys, sweep with a small broom or toy vacuum cleaner (it won't be clean, but makes the child feel good about helping), help water outdoor plants
3- to 4-year-olds	put away toys, help to make bed, straighten books on a shelf, put dirty clothes in a hamper, help water outdoor plants and other simple yard work
5- to 6-year-olds	make bed, pick up room, help set table, help make sandwiches, fold clean clothes, simple yard work
7- to 9-year-olds	clean tub and sink, dust, vacuum, feed and take pets for a walk around yard, help in the garden or yard, water plants, make school lunch
10- to 12-year-olds	wash the car, fix simple meals, clean up rooms in the house, take out the garbage, rake leaves, bathe dog
13-year-olds +	babysit, mow lawn, run errands, help cook and clean, wash clothes.

Be sure to explain each chore and make sure children understand that it's important to do the job right, not just get it done.

Dividing Up Chores

By spouses of the 2nd Battalion, 9th Marines.

Chore jar

Write down each chore for the upcoming week on a separate piece of paper. Each person draws out one chore for each day of the week and it's pot luck who has to mow the lawn, clean the bathroom, dust the living room, feed the dog, and so on. If you have some younger children who can't do most of the chores, have a separate jar for them. Include chores like folding clean towels or helping to pick up toys, or even something as simple as putting a stuffed animal on the bed or in a crib to "help mom or dad make the bed." The important idea is to make everyone feel like he or she is contributing and that no one gets stuck doing the same chore all the time (or if they do, it's pure luck of the draw!).

Refrigerator chart
Make a list of all the jobs that need to be done during the month. Create a chart for rotating some responsibilities by the week. Take turns on the least desired jobs. A weekly change usually results in fewer arguments than daily changes. For example, if you change who washes dinner dishes each day, a typical argument might be that one person always gets the easy night (cook on the grill, paper plates) while the other always gets lasagna night. When someone washes for a whole week, it tends to even out. If one child has a ball game every Tuesday, he or she can trade one night or trade a chore.

(M=Mom, S=Sara, D=David, C=Charlie)

List of chores	Week 1				Week 2				Week 3				Week 4			
	M	S	D	C	M	S	D	C	M	S	D	C	M	S	D	C
wash dishes	X					X					X					X
dust		X					X					X	X			
vacuum			X					X	X					X		
clean bathrooms				X	X						X					X
pick up bedroom	X	X	X	X	X	X	X	X	X	X	X	X	X	X	X	X
mow lawn	X					X					X		X			
feed the dog				X			X					X		X		

Charlie's too young to mow the lawn, so he gets double duty on feeding the dog. Everyone has certain jobs regularly like cleaning up their bedrooms.

Winning Cooperation

You've set up rules and consequences and divided chores. You've discussed them as a family and agree that they're fair. One parent leaves. The children *will* test the program you've all set up. And sometimes circumstances will change and you may all agree to change the original rules somewhat (make sure you change them together, not unilaterally). The key to success is to be consistent and firm. Remind children that they helped create and write down the rules. In fact, win their cooperation in enforcing rules. There are several techniques promoted by the Navy Family Service Center in Hampton Roads, based on the work of Katherine C. Kersey, Ed.D., professor of Early Childhood Education, Old Dominion University. The following list is adapted from their recommendations:

Techniques we often use with children that ***invite trouble.***
DO NOT USE.

Embarrassing.
To neighbor: "Johnny's too weak to pick up his toys today."

Taking away favored things.
"You didn't pick up your toys, no TV."

Labeling
"He's such a shy boy!"

Arguing
"Don't tell me you're not going to pick up those toys."

Repeating commands.
"Pick up your toys." Five minutes later "Pick up those toys." Later and louder, "I told you to PICK UP YOUR TOYS!"

Threatening.
"If you don't pick up your toys, I'm going to ___."

Psychological punishment.
"If you don't pick up your toys, I won't love you anymore."

Inconsistency.
"Don't worry about picking up your toys today, honey."

Saying what you don't mean.

"I'm going to throw away one of your toys if they're not picked up now."

Pleading, begging.

"Come on now, help mom, ple-e-e-ase pick up those toys."

Losing your cool.

"Damn you, kid! I always have to trip over your things."

Being vague.

"Time to clean!" or "Be a good girl or boy."

Allowing dangerous or destructive behavior to continue, such as hitting a playmate.

Rewarding misbehavior.

"Stop throwing a fit and come get this cookie."

Allowing a child to manipulate an adult.

Rewarding whining/demanding in store: "I want some candy!"

Expecting a child to read your mind.

"The room was a mess. You knew we were having company. I shouldn't have to remind you all the time."

<u>Techniques to use with children that **invite cooperation**:</u>

When/Then

"When you put away your game, then you may go outside."

Abuse it/Lose it

"You went into the street again. I'm afraid you'll get hurt. You'll have to stay inside this afternoon."

State expectations in advance.

"We will leave to go to the commissary when the next commercial comes on TV, so please have your shoes on."

Give clear directions.

Don't say: "Stay close to me." Instead, say: "Hold my hand when crossing the street."

Set limits.

Tell each child what the limits are and stick to them.

Ignore minor misbehavior.
Unless it is embarrassing, such as whining.

Stop dangerous or destructive behavior.
"I won't allow you to hit your brother."

Issue an instruction only once.
"Stay out of the street." If the child disobeys or forgets, bring him or her inside.

Follow through.
Take action. Don't talk; enforce the appropriate consequence.

Offer verbal, physical, or tangible (maybe) incentives for appropriate behavior.
"I really like the way you listened. Good listener!"
(Hug.) "Thanks for helping me."

Plan ahead.
"The next time he whines, I'm going to go into another room."

Restructure time.
"I see you're getting tired, we'll go to the store later."

Rearrange the environment.
"I won't let you hurt my favorite knick-knack so I will put it on the high shelf."

Make substitutions.
"You can throw this ball in your room, but not the soccer ball."

Use natural and logical consequences.
"Oh, oh, an accident. Here's a paper towel to wipe up with."

Parenting is tough enough in normal times. During a deployment, it can be a much bigger challenge and requires even more of your energy and focus. When your children demonstrate erratic behavior and you're sure it's associated with the deployment, don't punish them. Learn when to do battle and when to hold fast. Focus on your child's strengths. Remember that most importantly, you are all part of a family and love each other. When you're having trouble getting through some messy stuff, try working it out together. Ask your children how they would like to handle the situation. Their thoughts may give you new perspective.

Spend Time Together

Doing things together, from picnicking in the park to cleaning house, will help you and your children stay close and will most likely ease some of the tension.

Housecleaning

Yuck! Nobody wants to do it, much less alone! Say, "What do we need to do in here today?" Then tackle it together. Put a dance tune on the stereo or sing a favorite song together while you work. Ten minutes a day on the common areas should keep the house in reasonable shape and makes cleaning less of a big project.

A new chore

Explain why it needs to be done. Demonstrate how you want it completed, then let your children try it. Encourage them and point out the parts they did well. Work on improvements gradually.

Play

Dress up and put on a play or skit. Encourage your children to be creative. The skit can be about your family, an event, a favorite story. Invite friends to participate or watch. Don't forget to take pictures or videotape it to send to your spouse.

Your Name's Cafe

As you teach your pre-teens and teens to prepare meals, let them have some fun. Make the kitchen into their cafe. They choose the place mats, centerpiece, props, server's accent, and cuisine. Help them read recipes and teach them how to clean up after their guests.

Read together

For younger readers, use entertaining and dramatic voices. Take turns reading aloud. Fill in mispronounced

or unknown words without comment. Stop in the
middle and talk about how the book began, the setting,
and characters. How will the story end?

For teens, ask your library or church (or teen) to recommend
a book you can both read individually. Periodically check in with
each other to see what part of the book you're reading now. Talk
about the characters and what they're going through. Many stories will give you a common ground to talk about teen issues in a
non-threatening way.

Channel Emotions and Avoid Child Abuse

During a deployment, everyone in your family will have
heightened emotions. Feelings of hurt, anger, sadness, guilt, frustration, and joy are all normal. Channeling those emotions appropriately is the key to keeping everyone safe and comfortable.

"There are days when I'm really sensitive," Tonia Davis explains. "[My son] Hakeem will do something and I'll come down
hard on him and then I get mad at myself for being so hard on
this little kid. There are moments when he's looked at me and
said, 'Mom, do you miss Dad?' It's out of the clear blue sky. I'll say,
'Yes, I do.' And he'll say, 'Well, I do, too.' And we'll sit there and cry
together. He'll say, 'I know that's why you were really mad at me. It
isn't because of what I did.' It makes me feel like a real jerk."

The stress of deployment can lead to an increase in tempers
and a decrease in patience. Throw in children who need extra
love and attention and who are dealing with their own strong
emotions, and the mix can be trouble. When talking about their
deployment experience, many spouses confide that they often felt
the urge to hit, yell at, or ignore their children because they themselves were angry or upset at something or someone else. When
parents aren't careful about appropriately channeling their emotions, the result is often child abuse.

More than 800,000 children in the United States suffer from
child abuse each year and over 1,000 (most under age six) of these
abused children die, according to Health and Human Services

statistics released in 2001. For those who survive, the physical and emotional harm can last a lifetime. We all have an obligation to learn more about abuse and to do what we can to prevent it.

Abuse Defined

Child abuse is any mistreatment or neglect of a child that results in harm or injury. Child abuse, or maltreatment, includes:

physical injury:	purposely hitting, biting, shaking, kicking, burning, or throwing objects at a child
sexual abuse:	incest; inappropriate touching; sexual exposure not involving contact; using a child for sexual films, pictures, or prostitution
physical neglect:	failing to provide food, clothing, shelter, supervision, or medical attention
emotional cruelty:	verbal attacks; threats; humiliation; absence of affection, attention, or guidance

Abusers and Factors

Most child abusers are parents, relatives, or family friends who love the child they are abusing and who are having serious personal problems that they are taking out on the child. Common traits of abusers are low self-esteem and poor control over their emotions. Many were abused themselves earlier in life and grew up thinking abusive behavior is normal.

Stress is a major factor in child abuse. Too much stress can push even the strongest person to his or her emotional limits. Common sources of stress among military spouses include:

- deployments
- financial troubles
- perceived or real pressure to live a certain lifestyle
- frequent relocation (new job, friends, home, doctors, distance from family)
- social isolation
- marital problems
- lack of knowledge about parenting

- ❑ illness
- ❑ abuse of alcohol and other drugs

For some, everyday troubles build to high levels of stress, while for others, a single event triggers stress. Deployments intensify all of these factors. Many spouses talk of pressure from limited financial resources. Children add to the need for more money. One spouse may feel the other will be unfaithful. Some spouses feel they have few friends or relatives who know what they are going through during separations, and that lack of support builds up everyday problems.

Children of all ages can be demanding, and during a deployment when their own lives are disrupted, they may ask for more and more attention. Handling those demands is often difficult. At the same time, young or new parents sometimes expect too much from children and get angry when children don't meet their unrealistic expectations. Sick children have special needs that often place a greater financial and emotional burden on the family.

Factors That Can Lead to Child Abuse:

- ❑ immaturity
- ❑ lack of knowledge of children's needs or developmental stages
- ❑ overestimation of children's abilities
- ❑ parents' unmet emotional needs
- ❑ poor social skills
- ❑ poor childhood experiences
- ❑ isolation from families of origin and other potential sources of support
- ❑ substantial increase in stress without adequate stress management skills
- ❑ separation from spouse when spouse is usually target of abuse

And all too often, spouses turn to alcohol or drugs to get away from their problems, only to cultivate a bigger problem.

Solutions

The first step in preventing yourself from abusing a child is to learn how to control your feelings and channel your negative emotions. Ease the tension; don't try to handle everything yourself while your spouse is away.

- ❏ Talk to counselors about budgeting.
- ❏ Attend parenting skills classes.
- ❏ Use available day-care services, home-health visitors, school programs, and family counseling and support services.
- ❏ Volunteer at a crisis center or at least go into one and ask for information. Child abuse information cannot be kept confidential in military or civilian services. Unfortunately, the fear of causing a spouse/parent to lose career status stops some families from seeking help. If you're concerned about possible consequences of using military services, use private services. Most services are free in either case.
- ❏ Ask for help from your friends or neighbors. Sometimes trading favors to run errands or babysit can help to relieve tension.

How Spouse Abuse Fits in

If you were abused by your spouse who is now deployed, you probably feel temporary relief. It's important to get help and build support structures *now* because the problem will most likely reappear when your spouse returns. Reunion after a long deployment often means increased abuse in families where a military member has been a forceful, dominant figure. Once home, this authoritarian parent may use any means necessary, from threats to abusive physical force, to obtain compliance and reestablish authority. If this person was used to giving orders, it's hard to switch to a mutual-decision family arrangement. Alcohol dependency makes it even more difficult. Also, as you adjust to new ways of dealing with emotions, there's a danger that you may turn to abusing your children. Seek guidance from an experienced counselor or chaplain; these people have usually helped many other families in this situation.

If you abused your spouse who is now deployed, seek support immediately. You need help managing your stress and emotions. By getting the help you need, you'll save your children from abuse and help to build a better marriage.

In any case, take measures to support yourself. Whether you are abused, an abuser, or simply struggling with how to manage stress, you'll enjoy more success if you make personal friends outside your work and family and improve your communication skills. Adults who have more personal resources, nontraditional attitudes towards women's roles, and who have more friends outside of their family seem to have better support structures for combating abuse. Poor communication skills exacerbate the risk of violence. Ask a counselor about involving your spouse and children to help you make the change.

Reporting Abuse

Abused children need love and comfort. They need to know they are not at fault. And they need professional help. If a child talks about being abused, take it seriously. To report a case of abuse, contact the child's doctor, a counselor, police officer, teacher, or a child protective service worker at your local health department. Ask about crisis support help for the child and family.

You can also report the abuse to your state's child abuse hotline. Or call the National Child Abuse Hotline at 800-4-A-CHILD (800-422-4453). Hotlines offer emergency help, referral to area services, and information about reporting.

If you have questions or need help yourself (even if it's for prevention), contact your military Family Center or a community center. Look in the Yellow Pages under Family Services or

Social Services. Also, ask about Parents Anonymous, Parents Without Partners and other support groups for parents under stress.

Alternatives to Abuse

The National Committee to Prevent Child Abuse, a volunteer-based coalition, offers many alternatives to taking your stress, anger, and problems out on your children, including:

- ❏ Take a deep breath. And another. Then remember *you* are the adult.
- ❏ Close your eyes and imagine you are hearing what your child is about to hear.
- ❏ Press your lips together and count to 10. Or better yet, to 20.
- ❏ Put your child in a time-out chair (remember the rule: one time-out minute for each year of age).
- ❏ Put yourself in a time-out chair. Think about why you are angry. Is it your child, or is your child simply a convenient target for your anger?
- ❏ Phone a friend.
- ❏ If someone else can watch the children, go outside and jog or take a walk.
- ❏ Take a hot bath or splash cold water on your face.
- ❏ Hug a pillow.
- ❏ Turn on some music. Dance or sing along.
- ❏ Pick up a pencil and write down as many helpful words you can think of. Save the list.

For more ideas and information, contact your local child abuse prevention organization: check the phone book under county government listings. See if your military base has any programs or resources (start with the Family Center). You can also find useful information on the Web. Try the U.S. Department of Health and Human Services Children's Bureau at http://www.acf.dhhs.gov/programs/cb/ or Prevent Child Abuse America at http://www.preventchildabuse.org/.

Happy Reunions

You circle the return date on the calendar. You map out your "capture spouse" plans in great detail, arriving not-too-early and not-too-late. You throw a bag of family games in the van just in case of delay. And you all live happily ever after.

If only it were that simple! A happy reunion between your children and your deployed spouse has many factors, similar to your own reunion as a couple (see Chapter 9), including:

- ❑ how close the child was to the parent before the deployment
- ❑ how well the child understood the separation
- ❑ how the child reacted to events during the deployment
- ❑ how much and how well the child communicated with the deployed parent

A child's age affects many of the above factors. It's hard for younger children to cultivate a relationship with an absent parent because so much of their understanding is based on physical senses. Their concept of time is very different from adults'. They won't really understand why the parent left them. It's also hard for young children to maintain any real communication with the parent. You can help your children by using pictures, audio cassettes, and videos to keep a daily "presence" of the deployed parent. But even with the best of communication and relationship-building plans, children will react in ways you and your spouse should be prepared for.

Common Reactions and Preparation

Infants (birth to about 1 year old); toddlers (1 to 3 years old)

Six months is ½ of a 1-year-old's life, 1/3 of an 18-month-old's life, and 1/4 of a 2-year-old's life. What does "daddy" mean if the child's father has been deployed for the past six months? Perhaps it means a friend's dad, the picture she kisses goodnight, a voice on a tape recorder. Think of how your child reacts to strangers; it may be the reaction your deployed spouse gets at homecoming.

Put the picture and voice together a few days before home-coming and explain to your child that this person will be living at home with you just like [insert name of a father/mother figure similar to your spouse who lives at home with their child to help your child understand the relationship]. Remind your child for the next few days. Take your child around the house and answer questions like *where will daddy sleep?*

Infants may cry, fuss, or pull away from the returning parent and cling to the parent or caregiver they know. If they haven't been around deep, male voices, they may be frightened by a "new" male adult.

Toddlers may act shy and clingy or display a temper. Depending on communications during the deployment, they may not recognize the returning parent. They may return to behaviors they've outgrown such as asking to be fed at meals even though they've been using utensils and feeding themselves for a few months, or wetting their pants even if they've been potty trained.

Infants and toddlers both may be extremely jealous of the time you spend with your spouse. To help them ease into the relationship, spend some time hugging your spouse while holding your child and encouraging your child to join in the family hug.

Preschoolers (3 to 5 years old)

Preschoolers may feel guilty for making their parent go away. When a parent first returns, preschoolers may act out to get attention and to set limits with the new parent. They may demonstrate intense anger (too many changes) and seem very demanding. They need time to get comfortable with the parent again and may even poke or hit the parent to test the realness of his presence. Once they get to know the returning parent again, they may seek extra attention and cling to the parent for fear he'll go away again. Use defined reassurances such as "I have to go to work now, but *I'll see you at dinner time.*"

Prepare preschoolers by explaining the reunion in concrete terms. As with younger children, take them around the house. Use specific examples of the way things used to be as well as how they may be when the parent returns. For example, "This is where Mommy used to sit for dinner. Should we set the same place for her when she comes home?" or "See the clothes Daddy left in his closet/dresser? Let's wash a couple of his favorite shirts so they smell fresh when he comes home." Again, explain that your spouse will sleep in your room with you, that he'll have to go to work during the day, and so on. Help your preschooler understand common routines that involve your spouse.

Older children (5 to 12 years old)

Older children are often the most confused about their emotions over a returning parent. The relationship and communication between the child and parent before and during the deployment is crucial. Children this age may resent a parent for missing certain events. If they feel hurt by the parent's absence, they may try to say or do things that would return some of that hurt to the parent. For example, a child might point out how the other parent handled things differently—or better.

At the same time, this age group is the most likely to run down the pier to greet a returning parent. They want to please this parent and may feel guilty that they didn't do enough or weren't good enough while the parent was away. They might worry that the parent will discipline them for things that happened during the deployment. When given a chance, they'll also boast to friends about their parent's accomplishments and homecoming. You can expect these children to talk endlessly to update their parent on every detail of their life during the deployment (it begins with the question, "So, what did you do while I was gone?" and the answer, "Oh, nothing...").

Prepare your spouse by communicating beforehand the big and little ways in which your children have changed (clothes they wear, language, concerns, school activities, etc.). Your children won't like to be seen as they were six months ago.

Teens (13 to 18 years old)

They're moody. Irresponsible one minute, angels the next. Their hair and wardrobes change more frequently than the seasons. They want independence yet desperately need guidance. And boy can they "freak out" at a parent who doesn't know what is and isn't "cool." None of it will change just because a parent decided to come home.

Teens, in their careful attempt to gain independence from parents, may be unwilling to change their own plans to meet a returning parent at the homecoming site. Be cool. Give them plenty of advance notice of the scheduled homecoming time frame (even if it's a week-long window) and simply say they don't have to come but it would mean a lot to the family if they did. Happily make arrangements to celebrate as a family later if something comes up for your teen at the last minute and "everyone's going to be there." With any luck, your willingness to make the choice theirs will prompt them into choosing family over friends.

As much as they're trying to be adults, teens are much like children when it comes to their emotions at homecoming time. They'll probably be concerned about rules and responsibilities, especially if your parenting style changed during the deployment. At the same time, they'll be really excited about the return if their relationship with the deployed parent is a strong one.

When You Have a New Baby

Unfortunately, many dads are deployed during the birth of their child or for much of a baby's first year. Childbirth and caring for infants is a profound and special time for all parents. It's especially hard to be separated at this time. To help each other capture the magic:

- be considerate of each other's emotions
- share your feelings about parenthood
- share pure excitement, photos, special "firsts"
- share information about the baby's growth and development
- reaffirm your commitment to each other and your new family

Emotions

Both of you will experience the pride and happiness of announcing the birth to family and friends. It's a time of congratulations and wonderment at the miracle of life.

Along with all the joy is the reality of caring for an infant. For the parent at home, it can mean exhausting days, disrupted nights, and feelings of being very alone as you struggle to meet your needs along with your baby's.

The deployed parent is having emotions of his own. First-time fathers may be anxious about their new role and the challenges that lie ahead. Those who've been there for the birth of other children may reminisce and regret not being there (or, be very happy they're missing those first few months!).

Both parents will probably feel some guilt or anger, usually directed at the fact that one parent had to deploy at this time versus any other time. The key is to accept the separation and share the excitement through frequent communication.

Sharing Experiences and Information

What does the baby look like? Has she smiled? Does he have any hair? As the new parent witnessing the growth and development of your child, you want to tell the world all about every discovery. Your spouse wants to hear about it all. He wants to proudly show off pictures and feel a part of the first laugh, the first word, the first crawl, the first step.

Send pictures, videos, and written descriptions of all the little things that are a part of your new family member. Talk about what happens when you give the baby a bath, what the hardest part of being a parent to this child has been so far, what the baby smells like (the good and bad).

Sharing will help your spouse feel closer to your experiences with the baby and will also teach him a few of the things you are learning about caring for a baby.

Keeping Your Relationship Strong

Don't forget that you have a marriage to work on in addition to your new parenting roles. Keep some letters baby-free. To maintain the balance in your life you should be doing other things besides watching or thinking about your baby 24-hours a day. Tell your spouse about the other things. Ask questions about work and friends. Don't forget your spouse needs to feel loved too. When a new baby comes into the picture, it's easy to become consumed by it. It's also common to feel jealous (during the deployment, you're jealous your spouse doesn't have to deal with the baby; your spouse is jealous that you are focusing all your attention on this new person instead of him). At the same time, reaffirm how happy you are that you have a child and are looking forward to being parents together.

Introducing a New Family Member

To any child less than about 18 months old, your spouse will be a stranger. Your child will be a stranger to your spouse. *You* may even have a hard time picturing them together! Russ Moore had left for Desert Storm two days before his first son, Nathan, was born. He was gone the first seven months of Nathan's life. A few days before his return, Russ' wife, Stephanie, said, "Nathan will finally meet 'Daddy.' How funny! I can hardly believe he is *our* baby sometimes!" Even though she sent videos to Russ, the reunion was of two strangers. Russ had never been a dad before. He had only seen pictures and videos of a child he didn't witness the birth of but knew was his. Stephanie recalled the first few months of the reunion: "Nathan went right to his dad that first day. But he was still so attached to me; I know that hurt Russ sometimes. And it was almost easier to keep doing everything myself than to stop and teach Russ how to change a diaper, heat a bottle, etc., all the things it took me seven months to learn while he was away!"

Tips for Parents Returning to Infants:

- ❏ Before coming home, read a book about childbirth and caring for infants. Also learn about the development of children at different ages (helpful if you're coming home

to more than one child, too). You'll have a better understanding of what your spouse is going through, be more
aware of what to expect, and you'll have more confidence as an informed parent.

❑ Realize that your child won't recognize you because you
haven't been a physical presence in his life during the
deployment. Although pictures and voice tapes help,
they aren't the same as a living person; young children
need the whole package.

❑ Go slow. Watch for the child's comfort zone. If a baby
cries or a toddler pulls away when you approach, don't
force contact. Stand as close as possible and let the child
look at you, smell you, or reach out and touch you. Hug
your spouse while she holds the baby. Talk softly and
often so an infant gets used to hearing your voice. To
talk to toddlers, get down on the floor at their level.

❑ Play. If you can get your child to laugh at you, you'll
make a friend sooner. Be fun.

❑ While your spouse feeds, dresses, or plays with the baby,
changes a diaper, or gives the child a bath, stay close.
The child will probably watch you closely the first few
times to make sure you don't touch or come too close.
After a while, he'll get to use to having you there and
you can take over with your spouse nearby. Eventually,
your child will feel comfortable with you by yourself.

❑ Go with the flow. Take cues from your spouse. Offer to
take over as many responsibilities as you can; your
spouse probably needs a break. If you have other children, spend extra time with them. They may be feeling
left out because of the baby, too.

❑ Work on your relationship with your spouse. You and
your spouse will have plenty of non-baby things to work
out during your own reunion. Children of any age are
more comfortable with a parent when they know the

parents' relationship is strong. Any effort you put into your marriage will pay off for the whole family.

What Do the Kids Think?

Sometimes it's hard for adults to remember or understand what our children are going through. Observe and listen to your children. Try to view the deployment from their perspective.

Confusion and jealousy are common among young children when a parent returns. During one of Bob's six-month deployments, I became close friends with my next door neighbor, Kelly. I spent a lot of time with her and her 10-month-old son Mitchell. One night shortly after Bob returned home, I babysat Mitchell and Bob and I took him for a walk in a stroller. Mitchell kept turning around in his seat and watching Bob. If Bob tried to hold my hand or get too close, Mitchell screamed. He couldn't stand the sight of Bob touching me or kissing me. Children can be very possessive, at that age especially.

Children also have a different view of the world that's interesting for adults to hear about. Sometimes we're surprised by their innocent intelligence. Stacey West's 5-year-old son, Josh, hadn't said a word about his dad who had left for Somalia two days after Christmas. In mid-January, he looked thoughtfully at the TV (which wasn't on), then opened the pantry door and said, "Why don't we just send those people all the stuff in our cupboards. Then Dad can come home sooner."

It's also interesting to note what children remember about a deployment experience. These children answered the question: *What happened while your father/mother was deployed?*

"Everything bad happened. The dog threw up." —Kyle, age 6

"My older brothers were bossy; they thought they were men." —Gail, age 7

"At first we all fought a lot. Then we got used to doing everything without Dad. It was a lot of work." — Dan, age 8

"Mom was always busy with a million projects." —Heather, age 10

"I always looked for Dad on the TV whenever they mentioned the war. If the Middle East comes on the news, I get a little nervous that he might have to go back." —Josey, age 11

"My mom went to France to meet my dad who was on a ship for six months. One morning while she was gone, I was eating my Captain Crunch and I thought 'they're gone; they're never coming home.'" — Greg, age 14

"My best friend and I played with our [toy] combat men and pretended they were in Bosnia. We read my dad's letters about what he was doing there and pretended the combat men were saying and doing those things." —John, age 9

"We ate frozen dinners every night. Dad's not a very good cook. Sometimes we had hot dogs. I like those." —Chad, age 8

What is your child thinking today?

Chapter 8
Where Do I Go From Here?

I came home from work one day to find an unfamiliar truck in our driveway. As I walked up to the house, I saw my husband, Bob, helping a young Marine move boxes from the truck into our garage.

"Sergeant Snider is going to store his belongings here for a while," Bob explained. "I didn't think you'd mind since we aren't using this part of the garage for anything."

I smiled, nodded, and went inside to change my clothes, not wanting to know any more about it. As I walked into the living room, I heard the truck drive away and the garage door close. Bob walked in the door with an armload of flowers—a dozen red roses and bunches of daisies, gerberas, carnations, and snapdragons. They were beautiful.

"I love you," he began. Then he told me he would deploy to Somalia the following day.

I can't recall exactly what my first thoughts were. My mind was full of many questions, concerns, fears. One of my first requests was: "Can you get me a list of spouses' names and phone numbers?" In all the confusion and emotion of the moment, something told me I needed that list more than any other concrete thing before Bob left. I might not ever use it. I hadn't met anyone on the list. Yet, intuitively, I knew that if I ever needed to talk to someone who understood what I was going through, that someone would be on that list.

It was through this network that I learned about the wealth of other resources available in my military and local communities.

In a study by Marta Baker Garrett of the deployment experience
of Marine Corps spouses:
   89% were lonely
   71% sought help from a friend
   70% had disturbed eating or sleeping
   60% were tired or exhausted more than usual
   59% received help from family
   50% felt overwhelmed by responsibilities
   42% felt their spouse should write more often
   28% sought help from their spouse's unit
   16% sought help from the Family Service Center
   9% received private counseling

Resources include places, things, people, and organizations
that help you make more informed decisions. Resources give you
information, guidance, and support; sometimes, they simply help
you feel good about yourself and the decisions you've already
made.

Resources also provide you with necessary problem-solving
tools. Every individual, couple, and family has problems at some
point. The ones who make it through the easiest are those who
know how to find the solutions and aren't afraid to seek help when
they need it.

Your military and civilian communities work together to provide a variety of services.

You should get to know the military resources available to
you because most are free and you'll meet other people with similar military-life experiences. The starting point for finding and
using these military resources to help survive deployment is your
on-base family center. Family centers may go by different names,
but they all generally provide the same programs and services.

It's also important to become familiar with nonmilitary organizations because you may:

❏ be away from your home military base when you need information or assistance

❏ decide to live away from the base or post from which your spouse deploys

❏ live in a community that does not have a nearby military base or the military services you need (a common situation for reservists and their families)

❏ be referred to a local community organization after seeking assistance from your military family center

There are many sources of information to find the right resources for your needs or interests. Your base and community newspapers, phone book, chamber of commerce directory, library, and community Web sites are just a few places to find information about important local and national resources.

To Find a Resource in Your Community:

❏ Ask your local military family center to recommend a resource or to provide you with a list of commonly requested military and civilian resource numbers.

❏ Check the community service page listing in the front section of your local yellow page phone book.

❏ Look up an organization by topic in your local yellow pages.

❏ Check the national Web sites or phone numbers listed in this chapter (or call 1-800-555-1212 directory assistance to see if an organization has a national toll-free number), then check or ask for the number of a local office near you.

❏ Visit the reference desk at your local library.

❏ Use a Web search site, such as Google or Yahoo; either navigate to your county or city and then search for the organization or topic, or look for national organizations and then link to local chapters.

Often, especially in deployment situations, the best place to start gathering information is your military spouse.

Find out what support systems the deploying unit has to offer families. The command usually holds pre-deployment briefings and hands out information with other spouses' names and phone numbers, the name of a military contact person within the unit, and important information about special support groups and activities during the deployment. Some of the unit support groups and activities might include:

- ❏ key volunteer network, ombudsman program
- ❏ family support groups
- ❏ rear contact person
- ❏ hotline
- ❏ newsletter
- ❏ special communications options
- ❏ pre-deployment briefings
- ❏ unit Web page

Key Volunteer Network, Ombudsman Program

Key volunteers (Marine Corps), ombudsmen (Navy, Coast Guard), and support volunteers (all other branches) are spouses of military personnel of all grades who have taken on the mission of supporting unit families and helping solve problems that affect unit readiness. These volunteers serve as a link between spouses and the military command. They are trained in listening techniques; crisis, stress, and time management; and a variety of family readiness issues, including ways to keep in touch with long-distance families, dispel rumors, and refer families to appropriate resources.

The first thing my husband's unit did for the spouses was to set up a key volunteer network to help us communicate with and support each other and to provide a framework for passing along vital information.

During a deployment, volunteer networks provide information

Volunteer Network or Social Club -- Which is Right for You?

There is often some confusion about the difference between key volunteer networks/ ombudsman programs and social spouse clubs such as the Officers' Wives Club, Staff NCO Wives Club, and Enlisted Wives Club. Here are the basic differences:

Volunteer Networks:

- Unit, battalion, or squadron spouses only
- Primary contact by phone
- May be in place year-round, but most active during deployment

Social Spouse Clubs:

- All military spouses
- Primary contact in person
- Year-round; not related to deployment activity

Both provide information, friendship, and opportunities for volunteer service, but:

- Network information will be more specific to your unit. The friends you make will have spouses who work with your spouse and will be in a similar situation as you
- Main purpose is to support family readiness and accurately relay command messages
- Free

- Social club information will be more general to military life and the friends you make may have similar military experiences but not necessarily deployment experience
- Main purpose is information exchange and friendship in a social setting
- Dues

Both types of groups are open to both males and females; many invite "significant others" such as girlfriends or fiancés to participate.

about your spouse and the deploying unit, as well as referral information for various resources. Although social functions are not the primary focus of the networks, they are often held as a way for spouses to meet in person and feel more comfortable with each other.

Tips for Key Volunteers:

❑   Be a volunteer because you want to help others, not because you feel obligated.

❑   It is your job to pass along command messages. Do not interpret, speculate, or add your own opinion. Write down messages from the command word for word, and encourage everyone on your phone tree to do the same. This avoids misinterpretation.

❑   Keep rumors in check by asking "Where did you hear that?" Often, spouses will hear "news" on television or from a second- or third-hand source and will call you to verify.

❑   Introduce yourself by name, not as a key volunteer. Don't interrogate spouses on the first call. Get to know them gradually.

❑   Log your phone calls and make notes about what you talked about. This gives you a record to refer back to if needed.

❑   Set expectations about when you are available. Some people will take advantage of your kindness and generosity if you don't set limits. Remember, your own family needs your attention too.

❑   Don't gossip by telling your own family members, friends, or other spouses about the problems or personal issues a spouse has confided in you. Keep privileged information to yourself or with the appropriate counselor when necessary.

❑   When in doubt, ask for help. Don't feel as though you have to know the answers immediately. Find out the proper resource to refer a spouse to and then call back with the correct information.

Social clubs provide a year-round opportunity to meet other military spouses outside your spouse's unit. By forming these friendships, you develop a support system in addition to your volunteer network. By the nature of your contacts, you learn more general information about the military and base activities and get a better understanding of the military culture you're a part of.

There are many reasons to get involved in volunteer groups, social groups, or the various agencies and activities in the military community. Most spouses seek companionship or support. Younger spouses, especially, search for guidance and friendship. Other spouses want to offer their talents and experience to help others.

Mandy Blake explained that she probably wouldn't use a social group for support during a deployment. "I wouldn't get together and go bowling or out to dinner. But I would use the phone," she said. "I'm more of the nurturing type. It would help me to help younger wives with children. I'm not really one to seek out help as much as to help somebody else."

Lisa Palko needed someone just like Mandy to give her encouragement with her two toddlers and baby while her husband was in Okinawa, Japan, for a year. The two exchanged phone numbers and their conversations benefited both of them.

Even if you think you can survive your deployment without your volunteer network, perhaps you could share your strength with someone else.

Family Support Groups

Army and Air Force units often set up family support groups in place of the networks mentioned above. Although these groups are very similar to the key volunteer network (Marines) and ombudsman program (Navy and Coast Guard), there are differences worth recognizing.

The volunteer networks generally come together just before a deployment and focus on communication (phone trees) and deployment-related support. Often, only the spouses and sometimes children are involved. Participation usually fades after the deployment.

During a deployment, a family support group acts much in the same way, setting up pre-established calling lists (phone trees) to help disseminate information quickly. The main difference occurs during nondeployment time.

Family support groups generally involve the whole family and the community. Members include service members, spouses, children, parents, boyfriends/girlfriends, friends, relatives, retired service members, and members of the community who want to help military families. The purpose is to form a strong network of families during regular duty, including preparation for future deployments.

Each family support group organizes its own activities, such as family days, open houses, sponsor-a-new-family programs, trips, community projects, visits to training sites to learn more about the service members' job and surroundings, newsletters, and workshops such as car maintenance training.

Since these support groups are organized and directed by their own members, you can start one for your unit if there isn't already one in place. Commands recommend having either a network or family support group, not both. Ask your command for guidance.

Rear Contact Person

A *rear contact person,* or rear detachment commander, offers support in a variety of ways. Generally, this person is the primary military contact between families and the command. The lead key volunteer stays in constant contact with the rear contact person. In most instances, the first person you should call with a question about your spouse is your designated key volunteer. In certain situations, it would be appropriate for you to call your military rear contact person. Your spouse's unit should provide guidance for which procedure is more beneficial under which circumstances.

Some units may have a *family readiness officer* who is the direct link between key volunteer networks and the commander while the unit is stationed at home base; this person is not necessarily the person who stays behind during deployments as the rear contact person.

Tips for Units Selecting and Preparing a Rear Contact Person

Selection of rear contact/detachment personnel is very important. Units that boast the most successful family support programs have left behind one of their best service members during deployments.

❑ Select someone who is mature, able to accomplish rear detachment missions, and is sensitive to family matters.

❑ Select someone no more than two ranks below the unit commander, who can serve the duration of the deployment to maintain continuity.

❑ Identify a second, equally qualified person to assist.

❑ Designate early, before or immediately following deployment notification.

❑ Provide an outline of duties, including both unit and family support functions.

❑ Ensure the person knows how to respond to family issues and is familiar with appropriate support groups and agencies.

❑ Introduce to the lead key volunteer, ombudsman, or family support group leader.

❑ Solicit from each unit service member the name, address, and phone number of a "significant other" (spouse, child, care giver, parent, girl/boyfriend, or other). Send that person the name of the rear contact person, and outline the unit's preferred procedures for contact.

Hotline

Key volunteer networks have, from time to time, received a bad reputation for spreading false information and rumors. This happens in any chain of communication when *interpretation* is used by one or more people while passing along a message. Understand that this probably will happen during your separation. There are two ways to get the correct information if you think a message you received is misleading or untrue. The first is to call your lead key volunteer. This person gets the message directly from the command or the rear contact person. The next source of information is the ship, battalion, squadron, or unit *hotline*.

Once the deployment is underway, you may be given a hotline phone number you can call to hear the latest recorded deployment information. Often, the commanding officer of the deployed unit will record the message. Information usually includes the location of the unit, special promotions and awards given, child births, and a message to loved ones thanking them for support and telling them they are missed and loved. I listened to the message two or three times a week when my husband was deployed, even though the message was only updated once or twice a month. It was especially reassuring when mail was delayed.

Newsletters

Many units mail a *newsletter* or *family-gram* with deployment news and general communication guidelines. Family members who do not live close to the base from which the service member deploys sometimes feel left out; a newsletter can keep them in the information loop. It's important for service members to give names, phone numbers, and addresses of spouses, parents, or significant others—no matter where they live—to the key volunteer or ombudsman.

Phone Calls

Phone calls are often the most important tool families have to keep informed about the deployment and for them to keep the rear contact person informed as well. Often a unit will ask a volunteer to make occasional long distance phone calls to family members who live outside the area. Family members should also know how to contact a key volunteer or ombudsman in case of emergency or to receive additional information.

Special Communications Options

In addition to traditional communications methods available to you outside the military (postal service, telephone, etc.), you may have the option for unit-sponsored communications.

The Air Force Aid Society has offered prepaid phone cards under its "Phone Home" program for active-duty, Guard, and Reserve Air Force members of all ranks, single and married, who are deployed for more than 30 days.

In some instances, units offer Military Affiliate Radio System (MARS) communication options. Marsgrams are text messages of 50 words or less sent via radio, then delivered by phone or mail to the recipient. MARS facilities may also provide short (usually no more than five minutes) local phone patches free of charge between military personnel and their families and friends. Individual MARS facilities generally serve the primary areas of deployment for that base. All messages going outside the United States must have an APO/FPO zip code. Some MARS facilities can accommodate Marsgram requests over the Internet. A good place to start finding a facility is at the Army MARS headquarters Web site, at http://www.asc.army.mil/mars/ or Navy-Marine Corps MARS, at http://navymars.org/.

Another communication option to explore is sending care packages through the military. This option is usually offered during sudden and extended deployments. For example, many units offered to send care packages on military supply pallets during deployments to Somalia in 1992 and Haiti in 1994. There are size and weight restrictions and usually no guarantee of arrival date.

You can send packages to or from military addresses overseas through "space available mail (SAM)." For about the same price as sending a package at the surface mail rate, you can send it via air mail as space becomes available on a commercial or military aircraft. The Defense Department picks up the tab for the difference between the surface and air mail rates.

E-mail, when it's available, is a quick and inexpensive way to communicate. While most deployed units have computers, sometimes the phone lines and Internet connections are secured for classified and official information only and cannot be used for personal correspondence. When possible, most units offer at least a shared account or computer that can be used for this purpose. If available, you'll need access to a computer with an Internet connection, and you can set up a free e-mail account or monthly subscriber account. See Chapter 6: Communication.

Pre-deployment Briefings

These informational meetings are scheduled by units or family support groups. They are helpful even if you have been through a prior deployment. Information includes names and phone numbers of local resources to contact in various situations. Also, you'll receive legal advice, financial recommendations, tips for mailing packages overseas, information specific to this deployment, and a variety of other helpful hints. Just before a deployment, there are so many emotions to contend with that having someone remind you of key logistical concerns can ease your mind. If your unit did not hold a pre-deployment briefing, suggest that one be offered even after the deployment is underway.

Family Centers

The family center is the base commander's primary resource for coordinating family programs. In addition to services for active duty, reserve members on active duty, retired personnel, and all family members, programs are also available to next of kin of POW & MIA, widows, widowers, and next of kin of military personnel who were on active duty or retired at the time of death.

Most family centers are run by a combination of military and civilian employees and volunteers. These centers have slightly different names in each branch of service:

Army	Army Community Service Center
Air Force	Family Support Center
Navy	Fleet and Family Service Center
Marine Corps	Family Service Center
Coast Guard	Work-Life Center

Family center programs vary by installation and service. Common services include:

- relocation information
- hospitality kits
- pre/post-deployment programs
- money management counseling, including understanding the military pay system and preparing a budget
- premarital programs
- programs for foreign-born spouses
- individual, marriage, and family counseling
- spouse and child abuse counseling
- parenting classes
- child care resources
- benefits information
- exceptional family member services
- legal referrals
- agency referrals

One of the most important resources of any family center is the "information and referral" specialist who maintains a listing of personal, professional, and family support services in both the civilian and military communities. This is a good person to keep in touch with and to use to help you make and update your own list of contacts.

What you can expect if you seek information or assistance from a family center:

An *intake interview* to determine the assistance you want or need; it will probably include completing an "intake form." This may sound intimidating, but don't let it be. It's simply an informal meeting to let the center representative get to know you and your situation better. This will save both of you time and frustration later.

You will be given *phone numbers for services* available on base or in town for the assistance you need and any other information or resources you want to have for future reference.

The representative will give you a *referral* to the appropriate source to help you with your situation or question.

The center will *follow-up* with you to be sure your needs have been met. Don't be shy. The family centers are there to help you. If you don't get the help you need, tell them. They want to know how to best serve you. By helping families, they help the entire Armed Forces.

Senior deployment veterans may remember that family centers weren't around during conflicts such as Vietnam. In fact, many centers were established only in the 1990's, some as a response to Desert Storm. A few spouses have said they feel weak or stupid going to a family center for information or help. You shouldn't. The people who work at the centers recognize that you are intelligent, strong individuals who can handle a great deal. They also recognize that deployments are a lot to handle. It's okay, in fact it's smart, to know and use the resources available to you. Depending on the size of the center, they usually have lots of classes, workshops, and programs organized under several categories. Family centers may organize their programs in different ways, but most of them include the following:

Deployment and Readiness Support

This family center program provides training and coordination for key volunteer networks, family support officers, as well as families directly. The deployment program includes briefings, information, and assistance to families separated due to deployments and one-year unaccompanied tours. Many centers conduct tailored pre-deployment and pre-reunion programs, as well as family readiness and "kids and deployment" briefings.

The Readiness Support Center (it may go by different names) is an excellent resource for key volunteer coordinators. Usually, quarterly workshops and monthly meetings are offered for deployed unit coordinators. You can share ideas and concerns, including what is or is not working with your unit's families.

Family Support

Supporting families is one of the main missions of family centers, and most centers have licensed counselors to provide the initial counseling and assessments needed for referrals to appropriate civilian agencies and legal resources. They also offer scheduled classes and workshops such as:

- *Stress/anger management*—usually includes instruction on the cause and effect of stress and anger and how to deal with them on a day-to-day basis. Look for classes that also teach you stress management exercises that fit your lifestyle.
- *Parenting skills*—emphasizes practical and effective methods for raising responsible, confident children; encourages mutual respect and cooperation between all family members.
- *Couples communication*—teaches effective intimacy, communication, problem solving skills, and how to deal with conflict and manage anger.
- *Couples support group*—for couples who wish to work on communication and relationship issues in a supportive environment with other couples. This is a good class to take in a non-deployment setting.
- *Men's/women's support groups*—for men/women who wish to work on relationship issues in a supportive environment with other men/women.

- ❏ *Family Advocacy*—provides education, intervention, and counseling aimed at reducing child and spouse abuse.

Read the course or workshop descriptions carefully. Call the instructor and ask questions to be sure a particular class is right for you.

Exceptional Family Member Program (EFMP)

Families who have members with special medical, education, or therapeutic needs are supported through this program with referrals, advocacy, and relocation (for example, to a base with a medical facility that can treat a particular medical condition). Monthly support group meetings are available in some locations. This program is particularly helpful if you are stationed overseas.

Parent Support

Available on some bases, the parent support program is a great one to become involved in if you are a new parent or know someone who is. This group often provides monthly in-home support services to military members and spouses with a child under 2 years old. At your invitation, professionals will come to your home and observe how you manage your child(ren). They can help you with parenting skills, child abuse prevention skills, and issues related to moves and separations (e.g., during deployments) involving children.

Transition and Relocation Assistance

These family center programs assist family members who are moving from one installation to another, job hunting, or making the transition to civilian life.

The Relocation Assistance Center (again, the names may vary) provides a variety of resources for recently relocated families or those planning a relocation. Resources include:

- ❏ Welcome Aboard packets from many military installations worldwide
- ❏ move planning seminars including classes and literature about arranging a move, planning a relocation budget, pay and travel entitlements, and use of health benefits while traveling

❑ youth sponsorships such as pen pals in your new location

❑ foreign language tapes and study guides and world video tapes

The Defense Outplacement Referral Service (DORS) program is a national employment referral system that matches your employment qualifications and desired work location with the requirements of prospective employers. Employers then contact you directly for an interview or resume. Individual bases also offer employment assistance by providing local job listings, resource materials, and staff members who will teach you how to write a resume, interview, and find a job. Keep in mind, however, that this program is *not* a placement agency.

The Transition Assistance Program (TAP) provides services to active duty service members, their family members, and retiring military personnel to help make the transition to civilian life easier. This program also offers briefings to military members who are denied reenlistment or will be involuntarily discharged under other conditions. Information includes changes in medical care, housing, exchange and commissary privileges, and I.D. cards.

Welcome to Your New Duty Station

Welcome Aboard Orientations are offered at most bases to recently transferred members and their families to familiarize them with available base and community services. A Welcome Aboard packet is usually handed out with phone numbers and calendars of events, as well as local area maps and directories.

You can also make the adjustment to a new area easier by taking advantage of hospitality kits offered at family centers. These kits usually include place settings, pots, pans, dishware, utensils, and glasses. Car seats, futons, high chairs, portable cribs, playpens, and appliances are also available for a two-week checkout. At most centers, you can request to keep the items for up to 60 days.

Welcome Programs for New Spouses

If you are new to the military family or feel you haven't ever had a good introduction, you may want to attend a Welcome program. The Bride's School at Camp Lejeune, North Carolina, and Married to the Corps at Camp Pendleton, California were among the first programs created.

Pat Millish, program coordinator, started the Camp Lejeune's Bride School in February 1992, and it served as a model for other programs. Pat says it was a lot of work to set up the program but it was well worth it. In addition to helping new spouses become familiar with the military and how it works (pay, benefits, etc.) the program provided quite a bit of local information to help newcomers assimilate into the community. The program had the support of the Commanding General's office and advertised through marriage preparation classes, posters in the exchange and commissary, local grocery stores, and in the base and local newspapers. Most attendees were spouses of lance corporals, corporals, and second lieutenants, with an average age of 19 years. At first, the service members were reluctant to send their spouses to the program. They've since changed their minds. "I have not had one negative response to the class," Millish said. "In fact, I've had flowers sent to me by husbands as a thank you for all I did to help their wives out."

Call your family center for information about similar programs in your area. Although they may not be as extensive or specifically designed as the Bride's School, most family centers have excellent comparable classes and workshops.

Navy-Marine Corps Relief Society, Air Force Aid Society, Army Emergency Relief, Coast Guard Mutual Assistance

These nonprofit, private (but officially sanctioned and approved) relief societies help military members and families with *emergency* needs. Services include interest-free loans and grants, visiting nurses, and budget counseling.

Emergencies, by their nature, are not planned. For example,

you may find yourself suddenly needing to travel for a funeral. Perhaps an accident has left you with medical or dental bills that your insurance does not fully cover. Maybe the car needs to be repaired in order for you to go to work. Or perhaps there's been a delay or mistake in your paycheck, yet the rent and utility bills are due and you need to buy groceries. These relief societies can provide interest-free loans or grants for such emergencies. The money provided can *not* be used to pay nonessential bills, finance vacations, pay fines or legal expenses, or help you live beyond your means.

You can use this resource whether or not your spouse is deployed. However, the *service member* is expected to apply for assistance. If your spouse *is* deployed, the society will have to get his/her permission (usually by message) before providing financial assistance. A power of attorney authorizing you to borrow money in the service member's name (and commit the service member to repay the loan) may help speed the process. When you go to apply for assistance, bring a military ID card, current LES, and substantiating documents concerning the request, such as a car repair estimate, rental agreement, or utility bill.

Other services provided by the relief programs include a visiting nurse for mothers and newborns, pregnant women on bedrest, and those housebound for other reasons. Cindy Nelson was put on bedrest when four months pregnant with her first child. Her husband was deployed. She had to quit her job, which put an increased financial strain on their budget. She relied on friends to run errands and visit. On the advice of a friend, she approached Navy-Marine Corps Relief. A volunteer brought her groceries and called or visited her regularly.

The free budget counseling sessions, given by a trained budget counselor, focus on checkbook management, how to be a good consumer, and how to manage savings and credit accounts. This service is especially helpful if one spouse normally handles the checkbook/bills/spending. Learning the basics in this environment relieves some of the pressure of asking each other "simple" questions or teaching each other during an already stressful time.

A variety of other relief society services are offered at certain bases, including thrift shops where you can buy clothing, uniforms, and household items at reduced prices. Some offices offer layettes, also known as a "junior sea bag" or "bundles for babies," which include a bundle of clothing, diapers, and sundries. These bundles are worth approximately $70 but are given at no charge to families of service members (normally junior enlisted, E-5 and below). The only requirement is that the expectant mother attend a one-hour course on caring for and "Budgeting for Baby."

Find current programs and locations by contacting the organizations or visiting their Web sites:

Air Force Aid Society
1745 Jefferson Davis Hwy
Arlington, VA 22202
http://www.afas.org/

Army Emergency Relief
200 Stovall St.
Alexandria, VA 22332
703-428-0000
http://www.aerhq.org/

Coast Guard Mutual Assistance
4200 Wilson Blvd., Suite 610
Arlington, VA 22203-1804
 800-881-2462
http://www.cgmahq.org/

Navy-Marine Corps Relief Society
801 N. Randolph St., Suite. 1228
Arlington, VA 22203-1978
703-696-4904
http://www.nmcrs.org/

The relief societies work in close coordination with the family center, base financial and legal offices, American Red Cross, Veterans Administration, and other resources.

Consolidated (or Joint) Legal Assistance Office

This is the place to go to get free legal advice. On bases with several deploying units or large-group deployments, plan ahead to avoid the pre- and post-deployment crunch.

The legal office usually has specific hours set aside for certain types of appointments. It's safe to assume that for most issues, you need to make an appointment at least a week in advance. Other services are provided during walk-in hours, but the wait can be long. Check with your local office for times and scheduling procedures. Also, some offices require you to attend special classes before making an appointment. For example, a Dissolution (Divorce) Class is often required before you can schedule an appointment with an attorney concerning any matter involving divorce, legal separation, or annulment. Often, the class will answer many of your questions or give you a new perspective going into the meeting with your attorney. As with their civilian counterparts, military lawyers are obligated to respect clients' confidentiality.

Services usually provided during walk-in hours include:

- ❑ consumer law issues
- ❑ paternity actions
- ❑ contract reviews
- ❑ creditor problems
- ❑ credit purchasing advice
- ❑ contract disputes
- ❑ landlord/tenant disputes
- ❑ powers of attorney
- ❑ passport processing
- ❑ general information on immigration and naturalization
- ❑ notary public

- ❏ insurance policy reviews
- ❏ state motor vehicle laws
- ❏ residency matters

Services that normally require an appointment include:

- ❏ adoptions
- ❏ guardianships
- ❏ will preparation
- ❏ estate planning
- ❏ divorces
- ❏ name changes
- ❏ fitness report rebuttals
- ❏ state and federal taxation (usually certain hours set aside during tax season)
- ❏ consultation with an attorney concerning other legal matters

Services that are usually not provided by the base legal office include:

- ❏ bankruptcy action
- ❏ claims against the government
- ❏ court martial
- ❏ living trusts
- ❏ traffic violations
- ❏ driving under the influence (DUI) charges
- ❏ criminal matters

Chaplain

Base chaplains often have considerable military experience and are very willing to listen and offer advice. Also consider talking with a civilian priest, minister, or rabbi. All are obligated to hold in confidence any information you disclose to them.

MWR Events

Morale, Welfare, and Recreation (MWR) is an organization

on base that sponsors, organizes, or offers a wide variety of activities. MWR runs the base movie theaters, which often show recent movies at low prices, and base gyms and pools. The MWR ticket branch has discounted tickets for everything from civilian movie theaters in town, to local tourist attractions, to special events such as concerts and shows (on base and off). MWR often organizes tours and outings, and may run a sports and camping equipment rental office. In conjunction with the base gas station, rental trucks may be available. It's well worth your time to find out where the various MWR offices are, what they offer, and then stop by every so often. They can definitely help *your* morale, welfare, and recreation.

Armed Services YMCA

This social service agency is geared primarily toward young enlisted service members (E-5 and below, active duty or reserve) and their families. Typical programs include community centers, recreational centers and opportunities, child care, classes in English as a second language, and counseling for young families with financial trouble. Visit on the Web at http://www.asymca.org/.

United Service Organization

USO Centers and Canteens provide a "relaxing, homey, and wholesome alternative to daily stress." USO facilities specialize in helping service members cope with being away from home and helping families face the problems of a transient military life; for example, classes in cultural awareness help service members and their families assigned overseas. USO centers are not government funded. They rely on donations from individuals and organizations such as United Way and the Combined Federal Campaign. Funds are devoted to family outreach, assistance with pay and leave problems, recreational events, adult classes, job information, discount tickets, and more.

Worldwide, there are nearly 120 USO centers. Some are located in commercial and military airports, Navy Fleet Centers (resembling tourist offices with maps, bus routes, hotel information, and help with currency exchange and the local language), and family and community support centers. Visit on the Web at http://www.uso.org/

Social Spouse Clubs

Social spouse clubs provide an opportunity for military spouses to get involved in their communities and meet new friends. Most clubs plan social events and local tours in addition to volunteer service. A club's primary function varies with each installation. Though they are chartered and registered with an installation, clubs are not formal entities of the Department of Defense.

Most club members are women; however, a growing number of men are joining. Some bases have separate clubs for enlisted members' spouses and officers' spouses. Others grow out of specific units. Dues are common. By Department of Defense directive, you cannot be pressured to join or to donate time, nor does participation in club activities affect your spouse's career.

The contact person for each social club is often listed in the base newspaper. You can also get information about joining from your spouse's command or by calling the Officers' Club, Enlisted Club, or combined ranks club.

See earlier in this chapter for a description of the difference between key volunteer networks, family support groups, and social clubs.

Associations and Career Networks

The Naval Service FamilyLine (formerly the Navy Wifeline Association) is an educational organization for active duty Navy and Marine Corps personnel and their spouses. The association publishes a variety of pamphlets on financial planning, housing, medical benefits, and social customs and traditions of the Navy. One of their highlights is the COMPASS Program ("spouses mentoring spouses") to introduce Navy spouses to the Navy lifestyle. Visit on the Web at http://www.lifelines2000.org/familyline/home.asp.

Many military spouse clubs such as the Officer's Wives clubs, have Professional Clubs that attract spouses who would like to be involved but do not have much free time, cannot make events held during the work day, and share similar interests and concerns with other spouses in the professions.

Career networks focus on helping working military spouses deal with some of their unique pressures and struggles of career development. With so much relocation, it is more difficult for military spouses to maintain careers and advance in their chosen professions. Networks give you a contact in your new city and a colleague to turn to for advice. Of interest:

Military Spouse Business Network,
http://www.militaryspousebn.com/

Military Spouse's Career Network,
http://www.mscn.org/intro.html

American Red Cross

All Red Cross social services are provided free of charge and assistance is given without federal funding, 24 hours per day, 365 days per year. There are approximately 3,000 chapters including nearly 300 offices on military installations throughout the world. The Red Cross also communicates emergency messages and provides financial assistance. The Red Cross can be used in place of a military relief society if you can't reach a military installation. You should always contact the Red Cross office nearest your home or nearest the location of the emergency. If you need to send a message to your deployed spouse through the Red Cross, use the deployed unit's complete military mailing address, including the APO/FPO designation and any unit codes or numbers.

Some of the ways the Red Cross helps military personnel, veterans, and families:

Emergency Communication/Requests for Emergency Leave

In many cases, the quickest way to get a message to your loved one is through the unit. For example, late in my husband's deployment to Somalia, he had regular daily contact with his home base unit. If I called the rear contact person, I could get a message to Bob within a day. With many situations, however, such as front line combat, or when a unit does not have a formal rear contact, the Red Cross is the best emergency communication channel. It is also a formal means of communicating recognized by the Department of Defense that will give you copies of your messages.

Call the Red Cross in the event of critical accident, illness, or death in the service member's immediate family. The Red Cross will first verify the information. Then, if necessary, a *request* for emergency leave can be made to the proper military authorities. The Red Cross does *not grant* emergency leave. That is a military command decision. The Red Cross' responsibility is to verify the situation accurately with the proper authority (doctor, hospital, coroner) in the area of the emergency and to relay the message to the service member's command for action. Although the emergency leave may not always be granted, at least the message will get to the service member.

Emergency Financial Assistance

If the service member is granted emergency leave because an immediate family member is seriously ill or has died, the Red Cross can offer an interest-free loan or grant for travel expenses. Repayment is based on the member's ability to pay and is usually set up through an allotment. *With your service member's authorization*, the Red Cross will assist you in an emergency situation. As with a military relief society, check which authorizations are required of the service member before a deployment in order for a family/spouse to receive assistance during a deployment.

The Red Cross can also provide funds for food, clothing, and shelter, on a one-time basis, to see a family through an unanticipated financial emergency and offers free budget counseling.

Reassignment Requests

In extreme hardship cases, when emergency leave may not offer a complete answer to the problem, Red Cross staff can counsel your family on how to request a humanitarian reassignment closer to home or a hardship discharge. They will help you understand the procedures and documentation required. Again, the final decision is not made by and cannot be guaranteed by the Red Cross. It is granted or denied by the appropriate military authorities. Very few families have need for this. Hopefully you never will, but it's good to know where to get help or at least counsel when you think you might need it.

Communication

Regular communication with your spouse during a deployment takes time to get rolling. Sometimes you may not hear from each other for an extended time. The delay may be due to a change in the location of the deployed unit (e.g., ships generally receive mail in port and may experience no mail for a few days or even weeks in between ports). Whatever the reason for the lack of mail or phone calls, it can worry you. If you cannot get the information you want from your key volunteer or rear contact person, the Red Cross worldwide communication network can contact installations or ships and get a report (known as a "welfare report" or "welrep") on the welfare of your loved one to ease your mind. The service member can request the same information about you.

Information, Referral, and Advocacy

If you feel uncomfortable contacting the family center, you can often get similar information from the Red Cross. It is another source of confidential guidance for non-urgent problems.

Education

The Red Cross offers classes such as swimming lessons, lifeguard instruction, CPR, First Aid, and babysitting courses, sometimes at no charge. Some require pre-registration and most count toward a specific certification. CPR and First Aid classes cover adult, child, and infant; choking and rescue breathing; and first aid. It's a good idea for spouses and parents to take this class together, regardless of deployment status.

You can find the Red Cross in your local phone book, and many military bases have a branch Red Cross office.

Visit on the Web at http://www.redcross.org/; see especially the link to "Armed Forces Emergency Services."

Other Community Resources

There are numerous civic and government organizations that offer service, counseling, advice, assistance, skills, information, training, crisis intervention, food, cash, shelter, clothing, and so on. Your family center on base can usually provide local points of contact, but you may have to find and contact an organization on your own, especially if you are not near a military base.

Below are more than two dozen organizations that may meet your particular needs. Many function at both the national and local level. Listed here is the national contact information; in most cases, the national organization will refer you to local chapters and send you literature at your request.

Many local chapters have Web sites. Or you can usually find local chapters listed in the business/organizational section of the white pages of your local phone directory and sometimes in the yellow pages, under Counseling Services. You may want to browse—both on the Internet and in your local phone directory—before you actually need an organization to discover the wide array of services and opportunities available. You may even decide to volunteer or work part-time for one of them.

Alcoholics Anonymous

A fellowship group in which men and women share their experiences and help each other overcome alcoholism. Usually no fees or dues. Books, pamphlets, and audiovisual materials that describe the 12-step program of recovery. Focus is on frequent meetings and mutual support.

212-870-3400 and your local phone directory

http://www.alcoholics-anonymous.org/

Al-Anon and Alateen

Two fellowship programs similar to Alcoholics Anonymous. Al-Anon is for family members of alcoholics. Alateen is a fellowship of young Al-Anon members, usually teenagers, whose lives have been affected by someone else's drinking.

888-4AL-ANON and your local phone directory

http://www.al-anon.alateen.org/

American Consumer Credit Counseling (ACCC)

ACCC is a nonprofit organization that provides budget, credit, and debt counseling free of charge. It is not a collection agency nor a lending institution. A local ACCC organization will help you find a way to pay your bills using the money you have. Many times you'll be able to take their recommended solution and apply it by yourself. If necessary, and if you request it, the counselor can try to negotiate with creditors for regular monthly payments that will be administered by the local ACCC office—in which case you'll be assessed a small servicing fee, equal to a percentage of the money disbursed to creditors each month, for this debt repayment plan.

When you meet with an ACCC counselor, you will be asked to fill out an application, so you should bring your most recent LES or pay stub, a list of the bills you owe, and your most recent credit card statements. The counselor can also look at your budget (See Chapter 3) and make sure it is in line with your income.

Most communities have an ACCC organization.

800-769-3571 and your local phone directory

http://www.consumercredit.com/

Association for Retarded Children

Teaches vocational skills, offers individual living training programs and other educational programs, and services for people with disabilities.

Check your local phone directory.

http://thearc.org/   Many local chapters have Web sites.

Baby Nutrition

Several major manufacturers of baby food and products provide hotlines and Web sites for questions about your baby's nutrition and care. Many have useful information, such as "sleep strategies for Moms-to-be," "What to look for in a Childbirth class," discussions of childhood development stages, and so forth. At some sites, you'll also find coupons and rewards programs. A few examples:

Beech-Nut Nutrition	800-BEECH-NUT
	http://www.beechnut.com/
Gerber Products	800-433-7237
	http://www.gerber.com/
Johnson & Johnson Baby Products	866-565-2229
	http://www.johnsonsbaby.com/
Pampers	800-726-7377
	http://www.pampers.com/

Other parenting sites include:

ABC's of Parenting	http://www.abcparenting.com/
BabyCenter	http://www.babycenter.com/
Parenting Magazine	http://www.parenting.com/
Parents Place	http://www.parentsplace.com/
Parent Soup	http://www.parentsoup.com/
The National Parenting Center	http://www.tnpc.com/

Or type "parenting" into your favorite Web search engine.

Better Business Bureau (BBB)

The BBB is a good resource if you are considering purchasing an item from or entering a contract with a business you don't know much about. This is also the place to go if you have a complaint against a business. The BBB can tell you how long a company has been in business, if the company has had any complaints registered against it, and if those complaints were resolved. You can also research companies at some BBB Web sites. Many local BBB Web sites include information on scam alerts and useful stories for consumers (what to know about auto auctions, is the scanned price always right?, area codes you should never dial).

Check your local phone directory.

http://www.bbb.org/ (includes a locator for your local BBB)

Camps (Youth, Family, Summer)

For information on choosing a camp and a complete listing of American Camping Association accredited camps contact ACA:

800-428-CAMP

http://www.acacamps.org/

Classes

Many organizations on base and in the civilian community offer a wide variety of classes, ranging from budgeting, yoga, resume writing, repairing your car, cooking, and plumbing, to first aid, photography, and ceramics. Many community colleges mail periodic bulletins; also check announcements in your local base newspaper, on commissary and exchange bulletin boards, MWR, your local YMCA, and, of course, your family center.

Consumer Information Catalog

This free catalog from the federal government lists more than 200 free or low-cost booklets on topics such as careers, education, child care, health, nutrition, money management, federal programs, parenting, and more. The Web site also links to Kids.gov, which has an extensive collection of links to kid-friendly Web sites in categories from Arts to Transportation.

Consumer Information Catalog

Pueblo CO 81009

800-FED-INFO

http://www.pueblo.gsa.gov/ (you can order the catalog here)

Crisis and Counseling services

Shelter and counseling services for abused spouses, runaway

or pregnant teenagers, rape victims, and others. Operated by government (federal, state, county, city) and civic organizations.

Check your local phone directory.

To find a local chapter Web site, try a Web search program using keywords such as Crisis Counseling, the specific crisis you are seeking help for, and your state or city.

Death of a Child; Compassionate Friends

Compassionate Friends is a nationwide self-help group of individuals who have experienced the death of a child, brother, or sister. There are almost 600 local chapters.

Compassionate Friends National Office
PO 3696
Oak Brook IL 60522-3696
877-696-0010 and your local phone directory
http://www.compassionatefriends.org/

Disabilities Hotline

The National Information Center for Children and Youth with Disabilities is maintained to help professionals, teachers, and parents of children with disabilities to learn about the disabilities, and how to educate children with disabilities.

800-695-0285
http://www.nichcy.org/

Domestic Violence Hotline

The National Domestic Violence Hotline was created through the U.S. Department of Health and Human Services and maintains a nationwide, 24-hour hotline. The hotline provides immediate crisis intervention assistance to those in need. Callers can receive counseling and be connected directly to help in their communities, including emergency services and shelters. Also, operators can offer information and referrals, counseling and assistance in reporting abuse to survivors of domestic violence, family members, neighbors, and the general public. Help is available to callers in Spanish and to other non-English speakers, and the hearing impaired.

800-799-SAFE

http://www.ndvh.org/

Drug Abuse

The National Clearinghouse on Drug Abuse and Alcohol provides treatment information and referral.

800-729-6686

PREVLINE (Prevention Online)

http://www.health.org/

Narcotics Anonymous

818-773-9999 and your local phone directory

http://www.na.org/

Lamaze Childbirth

Lamaze (often called "natural") childbirth programs are sponsored by the American Society for Psycho-prophylaxis in Obstetrics and focus on childbirth preparation and family-centered maternity care. You may find sources under Lamaze or APSO.

800-368-4404 and your local phone directory

http://www.lamaze-childbirth.com/

Many local chapters have Web sites.

Parents Without Partners

This international, nonprofit, membership, self-help organization is devoted to the welfare and interests of single parents and their children.

561-391-8833 and your local phone directory

http://www.parentswithoutpartners.org/

Pregnancy and Infant Loss Center

This support organization is for parents who have suffered a miscarriage, stillbirth, or infant death, and provides literature on pregnancy loss and grief.

Pregnancy and Infant Loss Center

1415 E. Wayzata Blvd.,

Wayzata MN 55391

952-473-9372

http://www.pilc.org/ Also try searching "Pregnancy and Infant Loss Center" in your favorite Search engine to find local loss organizations.

Product Safety

The Consumer Products Safety Commission (CPSC) serves as a central contact for reporting product-related injuries. Find out what products have been recalled, including toys and child nursery items. The CSPC offers free booklets on crib, toy, and baby safety.

U.S. Consumer Products Safety Commission
Washington DC 20207-0001
800-638-2772
http://www.cpsc.gov/

Runaway Hotlines

Runaway Hotline

This national, 24-hour hotline promotes communication between parents and runaways who do not want to divulge their location. It also provides referrals to shelters, counseling, transportation, and legal and medical services.

800-231-6946

National Runaway Switchboard and Suicide Hotline for youth
800-621-4000
http://www.nrscrisisline.org/

Salvation Army

Provides food, shelter, bus passes, and clothing to qualified families.

Check your local phone directory.
http://www.salvationarmy.org/

Social Services Department

Operated by your local state, county, or city government, most social services departments provide cash aid, public assistance, and food stamps to qualifying families.

Check your local phone directory white pages in the government section, usually under social services, human services, or welfare.

Suicide Hotlines

National Hope Line Network
800-SUICIDE (800-784-2433)
http://suicidehotlines.com/national.html

Youth Crisis

The National Youth Crisis Hotline provides help for suicide, child abuse, depression, pregnancy, sexual abuse, and other crisis situations.

800-448-4663 and check your local phone directory.
http://www.1800hithome.com/

Youth Organizations

There are many national and local organizations that provide developmental, recreational, and educational opportunities for young people. Prominent ones include:

4H
Conducted by the Cooperative Extension System and the U.S. Department of Agriculture, these programs help young people develop life skills and form attitudes that enable them to become self-directing, contributing members of society.

202-447-5853
http://www.fourhcouncil.edu/

Big Brothers/Big Sisters of America
Match at-risk youth on a one-to-one basis with adult volunteers who serve as mentors and role models.

215-567-7000
http://www.bbbsa.org/

Girl Scouts of the U.S.A.
Helps girls expand their personal interests, learn new skills, and explore career possibilities. Includes programs for most age groups, including Daisies and Brownies for younger girls.

800-GSUSA44 (800-478-7248)

http://www.girlscouts.org/

Boy Scouts of America

Geared toward character development, citizenship training, and mental and physical fitness. Includes programs for most age groups, including Cub Scouts for younger boys.

214-580-2000, and your local phone book

http://www.scouting.org/ Most local councils have Web sites

Women, Infants & Children (WIC)

WIC provides nutrition education and supplemental foods for qualifying women, infants, and children under age five. To participate, women must be pregnant, breastfeeding, or have recently delivered a baby. Participants must also be identified as at-nutrition-risk by a health care professional, receive regular medical check-ups, meet certain income guidelines, and reside in a local agency's service area.

WIC provides vouchers to be used like checks for supplemental foods such as milk, cheese, eggs, peanut butter, juice, cereal, and iron-fortified infant formula.

WIC is usually administered under county health services departments.

Check your local phone directory white pages in the government section.

http://www.fns.usda.gov/wic/

Women's Resource Centers

Dedicated to helping individuals who may be threatened or victimized by domestic violence, homelessness, or sexual assault, these centers offer supportive services, shelter, food, clothing, and counseling.

Check your local phone directory.

Check on the Web using a Search engine to look for "women resource center" and the name of your city.

Reunion

Experience is not what happens to a man. It is what a man does with what happens to him.

—*Aldous Huxley*

HOMECOMING

Photo by Chris Taraschke

We're Looking for a Few Good Men: Capt Luke · Fightin' Bob · Sgt Ski

Crystal Marsden, Karen Price, and Chris Taraschke planned a quiet yet dramatic homecoming for their Marines. The men returned from Iraq after a one-month delay, missing the homecoming parades given by enthusiastic Persian Gulf War supporters. The families stood beside this homemade sign on the Fort Macon State Park beach waiting for the ship to emerge from the early morning fog and cruise into Morehead City Port, North Carolina. The two happy groups watched each other through binoculars as the captain sounded the horn and tears of joy flowed freely over broad smiles.

Chapter 9
Homecoming

There are as many different types of homecomings as there are people who experience them. If you ask my Marine husband what homecoming means to him, he'd say, "real toilets, real food, and privacy." To Army spouse Jim Spade it means having someone in the house who can braid his daughter's hair. To Navy fiancée Julie Evans, homecoming is touching and smelling her best friend again (and then marrying him!).

Even the media presents its own homecoming story. To the public eye, a homecoming is the picture-perfect embrace, a happy series of parades, parties and celebrations. When a soldier comes home, the stress of war is magically relieved and the people on the TV screen or on the front page of the newspaper go home to live happily ever after. For those of us still waiting, we believe our own homecoming will be as perfect.

Dreaming of homecoming is a coping mechanism most spouses use to get through the last few months or weeks of the deployment. As the big day approaches, we find ourselves wallowing in dreamland with sprigs of anxiety, self-doubt, and frantic preparation.

Nancy McKenzie's experience with her husband, Mac's, homecoming from Somalia has many typical elements of a homecoming experience. She describes:

> *When we found out he was coming home, we got*
> *extremely excited and starting making plans. [My son]*
> *Ryan and I decided that the first night we would go out to*

dinner with his father. He loves to go out to eat. We were going to have everything planned so we wouldn't have to clean anything that day. And we were all going to stay home from school. Since Mac didn't have showers in Somalia, we wanted to make sure he had the right soap. All the details were going to be just right. You want it all to be perfect so when they come home everything is just the way it should be.... but there's always something that doesn't go right.

We went to bed early. We didn't have to be on base until 10 a.m. so I planned to get up at eight and vacuum one last time. At about 6 a.m. Carol [the lead key volunteer] called me and said they were coming in early, at eight. When we got there at eight, the guard said that they wouldn't be in until nine now. We went back to our van. All the [official] white vans came driving up. I said to Ryan, 'No, your father will be coming in on a regular bus. Only higher ranking officers will be on the vans.' Then we decided that we'd get out and walk up and at least see everyone else getting excited and being reunited. We got there and there's my husband standing there. He's been waiting for half an hour. He had been invited to join them on those vans and we weren't expecting it. So he'd been watching everyone else get excited for that half hour while we were sitting in our van. It was sad because we were waiting in separate spots and no one knew.

That day, we sat around and talked to each other all day. Every once in a while Mac would come out and in a stream of consciousness tell me little things. We went out for dinner. Mac got a couple days off, which was nice. Ryan was at school and I was at work so it gave him some time to himself to regroup. It gave him a chance to get used to the house and the routine. Ryan came home first so he had some time alone with his father. And then I'd come home for dinner.

adjustments

It took us two weeks after Mac came back to get together again. I was working. That's part of my routine that he was used to, but at the same time, you only have so much time in the evening. There never was enough time with all the things that had to be done. It took us over two weeks to adjust to each other and then we planned a vacation. That was when we had the time together freely and that's when we really clicked again.

Mac's very quiet when he comes back. I ask twenty million questions. He doesn't answer all my questions. I accept that. If I get some answers, fine. If not, I ask again. We have to draw it out of him. Once he feels comfortable and he's adjusted, it flows out easier. But initially, it takes a while. You're so excited you want to hear about it. I have to get it all out, too.

Anticipation

At home, you find you can focus on little else but daydreaming about your spouse *finally coming home*. In addition to staying "busy" (cleaning the house, buying groceries, and finishing all those projects), here are a few things you may find yourself thinking and feeling:

I want the first moment to be just right.

Will my spouse like the way I look (weight changes, physical condition, new hairdo)? What should I wear to greet him/her?

Although I knew Bob would love me just as much if I showed up in sweats, on the advice of a male friend, I wore a casual miniskirt. On the way to the car, Bob told me I looked *great*. I smiled and whispered into his ear, "I'm not wearing any underwear." Poor guy had the whole ride home to think about that.

I made it!

Some spouses look back at lists of projects and goals or reread journal entries. Give yourself a pat on the back. Even if you didn't make all your goals (most people don't), you accomplished a lot. Many spouses like to reflect on how they've changed and grown personally during this time.

Oh, yeah, those other goals.

After looking at all you've learned, you might still feel a sense of having failed to meet some personal goals such as weight loss or saving money. Don't worry about it. This is your chance to meet those goals *with* your spouse!

Will we accept the changes?

Whether the changes in your life are big or small, and no matter how well you've communicated with your spouse, you'll still feel a little uncertainty about how those changes will be accepted. Have you found new interests? How does your spouse fit into the picture? Will you give up something new or is there another solution?

How has your spouse changed? What kind of situations (e.g., seeing combat, famine; experiencing lack of privacy, regimentation) have changed your spouse's outlook? Many people reread letters from their spouse and their own journal entries to help them notice how both of their thoughts and interests have changed.

You may also wonder what unplanned changes will take place after your reunion. Will friendships you developed in your spouse's absence survive once you have your spouse to spend time with again?

How strong is our relationship?

Maybe he learned from his time in the desert to put the cap on the toothpaste because if he didn't he brushed with sand the next day. Then again, maybe he didn't! Starting to remember previous irritations? It will take time to adjust to living with each other again.

If your relationship was troubled before the deployment or if you had a hard time communicating during the deployment, you're probably wondering how you'll make that bond stronger this time. Previous problems most likely did not go away during your separation. Commit to working at your relationship. Pick one aspect most important to you and write it down. Remind yourself every day to work on that part of the relationship.

Have I made good decisions?

Believe in yourself. Don't get defensive if your spouse or others question your decisions. Simply explain why you decided what you did. Making decisions during a deployment can be stressful; your spouse knows this from military work. The decisions you made were the best under your own circumstances. Don't second guess yourself. If you have confidence you did the right thing, so will those around you.

Sex...

It's normal to feel excited but also a little anxious about resuming sexual relations. On the one hand, it's like riding a bike. On the other hand, it's like two people who haven't seen each other in months getting on the same bike and trying not to fall off while pedaling. It takes a few tries and communication to get in sync. Some people find it difficult to talk about sex. Take your time.

Our reunion will be perfect.

Euphoric homecomings are the stuff military dreams are made of. We all need those dreams. Think about what you would like to happen. While every spouse who's gone through this before will tell you your homecoming dreams don't ever come true *exactly*, the important parts do.

What is my spouse thinking about?

While you are dreaming at home, your spouse is having thoughts of his own from somewhere else in the world. He also wants the first moment to be right, wonders how you've changed, hopes your relationship will be strong, prays his children will be happy to have him home again, and fantasizes about making love to you. Your spouse probably also:

- ❑ wonders what you meant in some of your letters (from your not-so-clear-communication days)
- ❑ hopes you are aware of how demanding his schedule has been (fatigue is common among deployed personnel from working 12-, 14-, and sometimes 24-hour workdays)
- ❑ worries that young children won't recognize him or that teens won't need him anymore; wonders how well they dealt with the separation and what they think of him for leaving them; hopes they'll still think he's cool even though he doesn't know the latest phrases and hasn't seen the new hit movies
- ❑ has tried to convince himself that just because you coped well without him doesn't mean you want to be without him
- ❑ knows it will be hard not to feel like a stranger in his own home
- ❑ wants to understand and accept all the decisions you made during the deployment
- ❑ feels guilty for missing important family milestones (e.g., birth of a child, an anniversary, a special day)
- ❑ wonders what cultural things he's missed; starts remembering how things work in America
- ❑ thinks about finances (especially if there have been major changes in the family such as a newborn or a change in spouse employment)

How will our children react?

Children react differently to the homecoming and reunion depending on their age, their relationship with the deployed parent, and how you react and prepare. Talk with your children. They have at least as many questions as you do about the reunion. (See Chapter 7.) In general, children:

- ❑ hope the deployed parent will be glad to see them

- wonder if the parent will be mad about a report card or will yell at them for not completing a chore like they were supposed to
- may feel like the deployment had something to do with their behavior or that the parent *wanted* to be away from them
- feel anxious about how long the parent will stay home; may be worried about the parent leaving again soon
- wonder if the rules and lifestyle at home will change
- may worry about their parents' relationship if they sensed a troubled or abusive relationship before the deployment

They may just be really, really excited, too—for themselves and for you two. When Bob returned home after five days away, our 2-year-old son Alexander was so excited, he tried to tell him everything all at once. And he giggled as gibberish came out—he couldn't decide what words to put together first. Then he put his hand on our two faces and said, "Daddy you kiss Mommy!" He beamed with a big, big smile when we kissed!

Expectations

No matter what you, your spouse, and your children are wondering and dreaming about, the happy scene of the family running down the pier with open arms is not as sure as some other things you should expect:

You'll all have mixed feelings.
- You'll be excited to be together.
- You'll feel apprehensive about adjustments to the changes that have taken place.
- You'll hope for a perfect, reunited family.

Everyone has changed.
- You and your spouse will both be more independent.
- Your children will be more self-reliant and mature;

they'll have new interests (e.g., girls who played with toys now like boys!).

Everyone needs reassurance that they are loved, wanted, and needed.

- ❑ Hugs will go a long way.
- ❑ Everyone in the family wants to feel like their contributions are worthwhile.

Your parenting and decision-making relationship will be strained.

- ❑ The family wants the service member to get involved again but not "take over."
- ❑ Children need time to adjust to a parent who hasn't been around.
- ❑ Parents need time to adjust to making decisions together.

You and your spouse need to "court."

- ❑ One or both of you will want romance and pampering.
- ❑ You're two people who've lived separate lives; get to know each other again.

You'll all be tired.

- ❑ You'll be tired from added responsibilities at home.
- ❑ Your spouse will be tired from the deployment.
- ❑ Your children will be tired from feeling too grown up.
- ❑ Emotions tire everyone.

It will take several weeks to adjust.

- ❑ Your family is adjusting to having your spouse back in their lives; your spouse is adjusting to a more complex lifestyle again that involves family intimacy. It simply takes time.

Communicate your concerns, expectations, and feelings about homecoming. The more you communicate with each family member, the fewer misunderstandings or disappointments.

Homecoming Day

Who gets the first hug? *You do!*

Counselors tell service members to hug their spouse and then each child; it signals a good relationship between the parents and makes children feel comfortable.

Homecoming day is a wonderful, stressful day.

Tips for making yours "perfect":

❑ Decide with your spouse what you want the day to be like. Then talk over the options with your children.

❑ Fit children into the homecoming day plans. Expect them to be excited and possibly act out because they don't know how to channel their energy and feelings. They can prepare banners and balloons, help prepare dinner, or decide on a place to go out for dinner.

❑ Plan the "pick-up." Who will go or will your spouse be dropped off? What will you do to keep busy in case of delay? Will you come straight home? What condition will your spouse be in (often, in need of a shower immediately!)?

❑ Be flexible. Arrival times and sometimes arrival days change. Keep in contact with your key volunteer/ ombudsman or unit contact person. Update children, parents, and friends.

❑ Go with the flow. Sometimes plans work, sometimes they don't. The important thing is that you're together. You can figure it out as a family from here.

The Honeymoon

Let the fun begin!

Plan time as a couple and a family. Which you do first is a personal choice. Many counselors suggest spending time your family first and then planning a second honeymoon with your spouse later. Julie LaBelle disagrees. She and her husband Ed

planned a week-long honeymoon together in London before coming home together to their three children and dog. She learned
that they needed at least 24 hours together before seeing the
children. They got in at midnight and were bombarded with all
the realities: "the toilet, microwave, and washer had all broken
down, the taxes were due, and the kids each had their own issues
to deal with," Julie recalls.

Most couples agree that it's a good idea to hold off on gather-
ings with friends and relatives. Answering machines or voice mail
are your friends. You need at least a few days with each other and
your children first. Some spouses want to hold big parties to "show
off" and welcome home their proud service members. But most
service members say they'd rather wait. I usually felt like I needed
a break away from work and the house, so Bob and I would plan
a 2- to 3-day getaway right after his return. It gave us quality time

Courting Ideas:

- ❏ Say, "I'm glad I married you" or "I'm happy I'm in this relationship with you."
- ❏ Hold hands as you walk.
- ❏ Give your spouse a back rub or a foot massage.
- ❏ Write a poem for your spouse.
- ❏ Hug your spouse from behind; kiss the back of his/her neck.
- ❏ Ride bikes together. Watch the sunset. Build a snowman.
- ❏ Sit on the same side of a restaurant booth.
- ❏ Share a milkshake with two straws.
- ❏ Plant a tree together in honor of your relationship.
- ❏ Look into one another's eyes as you talk.
- ❏ Play board games.
- ❏ Take on a fun challenge together, such as hiking up a mountain or learning to surf.
- ❏ Say "I love you" every time you think it.

together with few distractions and ensured him the privacy (no calls from friends, neighbors, or work) he found so important during reunion.

Sex

What would a honeymoon be without (desirous, awkward, tentative, satisfying) sex, right? Sex is such a powerful, beautiful, instinctive way for couples to express love and intimacy, it tends to be the focal point of both partners' homecoming fantasy. Sometimes riding that bike is easy, honest, and better than you ever dreamed. But, just as with other aspects of your reunion, if your sexual expectations differ and you haven't communicated your desires, you can expect disappointment or misunderstandings.

The best time to talk about reunion and sex expectations is before the departure, especially if you've experienced previous deployments/reunions, or as far in advance of the homecoming as possible. Jeff and Renee Portal started talking about differing expectations close to the homecoming, and Renee misinterpreted it as a change in Jeff's feelings for her. She warns, "When you've already set the fantasy in your mind, it's hard to change it at the last minute. You start to think the other person changed his mind, when really that's what he thought all along. It would have been so much easier to build a plan together from the beginning." Throughout the deployment, be as open as possible about your sex and intimacy concerns and desires.

Couples often find general intimacy topics easy to write about in a letter. Sentences like "I miss being with you at night," "I can't wait to hold you in my arms again," or "I'm imagining sending you a long, warm, wet kiss... you decide where!" are easy for most people to think up. These sentiments are generally non-threatening and are difficult to misinterpret. It becomes more difficult to communicate feelings about how you want to approach sex and intimacy upon return.

Like all private matters, each couple handles "sex talk" differently. You'll have to draw on your knowledge of your partner and listen to what your partner tries to express. For example, saying "I'd like to get to know you again before we have sex" is probably not really what you mean. Hopefully you're writing regularly and still "know each other." What you mean is that you feel a little awkward and want to take it slow; you want it to be "right." The mechanics of sex is not the hard part; it can resume immediately (if you want to). Intimacy, however, is what takes time. If you're nervous about it, try writing something less threatening like, "I'm looking forward to our love making. It's been so long, we'll probably want to take it slow and help each other remember what we like. I'm a little nervous; it's sort of like our honeymoon all over again!" You've told your partner how you feel, proposed a solution (taking it slow and helping each other), and have made a subtle invitation for your partner to agree.

Or, if you simply want to confirm interest, try "I know what you mean; I'm really horny, too. Can't wait! I have been working out, but I don't think I'm in good enough condition for 10 times a day! Why don't we hop in the sack a few times the first day to lighten that load; then I'll help you be a little more creative!"

The "final approach" before landing is also important. One wife said she was "disgusted and disappointed" by a package of black and red lace lingerie her husband ordered and had delivered a week before his homecoming. The card said: "One for each day the first week I'm home." The wife said she suddenly felt self-conscious about her body and worried that she wouldn't live up to her husband's desires. She wanted to talk and laugh and be romanced, not be on display. Her husband just meant for her to have something special and to let her know he still thinks she's sexy. They worked it out by sharing their feelings their first night together. Both said they wished they had talked about it sooner to avoid hurt feelings.

Tips for reestablishing intimacy and great sex with your spouse:

- ❏ Plan private time together without children, parents, friends, or relatives.

- ❏ Limit alcohol intake; too much reduces sex drive and performance.
- ❏ Resolve intimacy reducers, such as anger, resentment, distrust, jealously, and anxiety.
- ❏ Remember that fatigue is common during initial re-union. If your partner is too tired for sex, it's not a sign of rejection. Sleep in each other's arms or use some other form of intimate touch to connect.
- ❏ Expect and don't worry about awkward moments, especially the first few times you are back together. You'll probably be operating at quite different speeds. Focus on re-establishing intimacy. Great sex will follow.
- ❏ Tune in to your partner. Talk, cuddle, be playful. Realize it's normal to feel strange together, especially after long separations. Be patient and gentle. You don't need sex in order to be intimate. Hugs, kisses, caresses, and whispers express love, too.
- ❏ Communicate your sexual desires. You want to please each other—say how. Don't rush into new positions. Negotiate any experimentation. Build trust and comfort (sex the first time may be painful for some women).
- ❏ Take precautions against pregnancy unless you've planned a pregnancy together.
- ❏ Sex is more than just intercourse and orgasm. Have fun and enjoy being with one another.

Adjustments/Reunion

For a young child, the day after Christmas can be sort of a let down, even when every wish was granted and is sitting under a still-lit tree. Some couples experience this same let down the day after the honeymoon. Whether the honeymoon lasted an hour at the pier, a day or two, or several days, at some point the excitement and wonder turns into everyday life and real decisions.

- ❏ "I mowed the lawn for six months. I wanted my husband

to do it for the next six months! For two weeks, the lawn didn't get mowed. So what."

❏ Carol was both mother and father to her 5th grade son for six months. "Suddenly, he was asking my husband for advice; it was hard to give up that role."

❏ "We changed our thoughts on what was important and what wasn't important. After all those months of me worrying about Jeff, about his health, other problems seem so small. The only thing that really matters is that he came home healthy."

❏ "Our marriage is even stronger now. We really like each other. We really know for sure that we want to be around each other."

For many, reunion is more difficult than separation. For some, the experience builds an even stronger lifelong bond. On average, couples say it takes 4-6 weeks to readjust. These reunion tips will get you started on the right track:

Welcome your spouse, with time to adjust.

Returning service members often experience culture shock when they come home. They may have trouble communicating, eating, sleeping, or being intimate. After months of living, eating, and working with the same military coworkers, being home with a family is a different world. Those deployed outside the United States have the added adjustment of getting back to an often chaotic American lifestyle.

They usually look forward to fewer demands and a looser schedule, yet are comfortable with routine. During the first few days, there are physical adjustments to time zone differences, jet lag, and a completely new schedule. The intensity of the deployment (especially for those in combat zones, humanitarian efforts, or dangerous situations) is suddenly replaced with the routine of life at home. Their entire surroundings have changed, from a sleeping bag on the ground or a cramped bunk to a comfortable bed and quiet house at night, from taking orders to answering family questions. Privacy, convenience, soft toilet paper. Whatever food they want to eat. Hot showers. In the first few days of bliss, they think what else could anyone want?

Karen Robinson recalls an embarrassing post-deployment moment when their son forgot to set Dad's place at the dinner table. Oops. A sense of humor and confident love is a critical welcome mat.

Appreciate that roles and people have changed.

Interests may have changed, such as preferences in food, clothing, or recreation, and thoughts about money or careers. Find out what new skills each person has learned or what new interests they have. This is a good starting place to build new relationships. Spend time alone with each family member.

Reestablish family relationships and negotiate comfortable new roles.

Stay involved in children's activities and interests. Let your spouse know about upcoming schedules and which activities are most important to the children. Make room for your spouse to take on special roles with your children.

Be sensitive to combat experiences.

When the deployed spouse is in combat, or a similar situation marked by human disaster, there will be tremendous *additional* stress on top of the stress and anxiety of regular separation. Fear of loss is greatly intensified. Some returning troops will have witnessed killing, wounding, and disfigurement of enemy soldiers, civilians, their own comrades, and in some cases close friends. They may have lived under the awful uncertainty of chemical, biological, or SCUD missile attack (as in the Gulf War), or of unmarked mines (Afghanistan). Female soldiers may have had an added strain of fighting to defend a culture that does not fully accept them.

Your spouse may or may not want to talk about "the horrible things." Give him or her time, and don't press. But be receptive. The best thing you can do is *listen* attentively and let him know

you are grateful for the sharing. You may have to be extra atten-
tive to notice the moment in which your returned spouse wants
to share something troubling.

Combat is also a tremendous strain on your family at home.
The media provides graphic, up to the minute updates, usually
emphasizing tragedy and disaster, often giving the impression that
it is happening everywhere in the deployment area. Rumors, mis-
information, and speculation about the welfare of loved ones
amidst all the news only serves to heighten family stress.

The returning spouse should also understand that the stress
the family has undergone, of not knowing anything for sure, having seen (sometimes more than the deployed spouse) combat up
close on TV, and fearing the worst, was a terrible trauma that also
needs to be shared.

Stick to your budget.

Your spouse may not remember how much money your family needs. Spending money you don't have will create more trouble
later. Also, you may need to rethink your budget. The end of a
deployment means changes in pay and allowances once again.
Perhaps you family's financial needs have changed during the
deployment due to a new baby or a change in employment.

Learn to talk face-to-face again.

Your spouse may have had some deployment experiences he
doesn't know how to explain to you. Some things he may want to
forget. Let him know you are ready to listen when he is ready to
talk about it.

Separations don't usually solve problems. This includes household habits as mundane as leaving the toilet seat up, or as serious
as substance abuse or violent tendencies. Commit to working on
your relationship together.

Reaffirm your love and the fact you want your spouse to be a
part of your life. Your spouse may feel a little hurt by your success.
Avoid the "I had it worse" game. Respect each other and the job
each did.

Some couples who have been apart for a long time experience awkwardness in trying to find the right words for what they mean to say in person. Perhaps you were successful communicating by letter during the deployment because you could think through the way you wanted to say something before sending the message. If so, try writing a few letters when you're first together again. Read each other's letter in the presence of the other as a way to start the conversation, especially if the subject at hand is a hard one to begin discussing. It won't be long before your letters become short notes or you're back to talking freely face-to-face.

Expect children to test limits.

Discuss changes in discipline procedures away from children and implement them over a period of weeks. Also see Chapter 7 for ideas for including children in certain decisions.

Reconcile infidelity.

If you suspect your spouse has been unfaithful to you, don't snoop around looking for clues. Trust your spouse. Ask your chaplain (or civilian pastor, priest, or rabbi) for support, not your friends or relatives (don't start rumors).

If you chose to have an affair or sexual encounter during the deployment, your conscience may be asking, "Should I tell my spouse?" Consider why you want to tell. Does it benefit your relationship with your spouse? Or are you telling to relieve your guilt? Will your spouse find out from someone else if you don't tell first? What are the risks of not telling? Is there a chance you may infect your spouse with a sexually transmitted disease?

If you are struggling with this issue, don't try to tackle the situation yourself. Talk with a chaplain. Get guidance before you bring out the truth and then involve your spouse in the support to help you both work through the emotions and trust issues together. Infidelity does not necessarily mean that love is gone from your marriage. It does, however, mean your relationship needs work. Recognize it will take time to rebuild a relationship damaged by infidelity.

Recognize and address unhealthy adjustments.

Most couples and families adjust positively within a matter of weeks. However, it's important to recognize signs that you are not getting back in sync or that you're doing so in a negative way. Danger signs include depression, social isolation, substance abuse, excessive anger, violence. If you or your spouse thinks you may need help individually or as a couple, don't hesitate to ask for it.

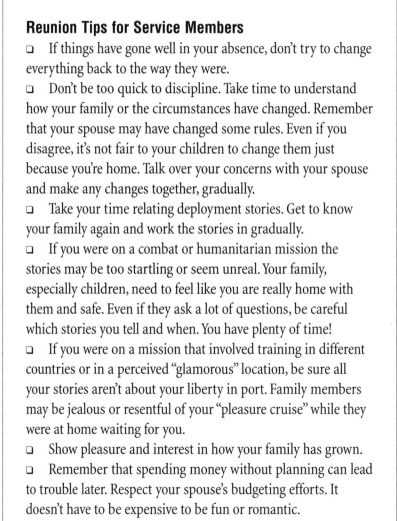

Reunion Tips for Service Members

❑   If things have gone well in your absence, don't try to change everything back to the way they were.

❑   Don't be too quick to discipline. Take time to understand how your family or the circumstances have changed. Remember that your spouse may have changed some rules. Even if you disagree, it's not fair to your children to change them just because you're home. Talk over your concerns with your spouse and make any changes together, gradually.

❑   Take your time relating deployment stories. Get to know your family again and work the stories in gradually.

❑   If you were on a combat or humanitarian mission the stories may be too startling or seem unreal. Your family, especially children, need to feel like you are really home with them and safe. Even if they ask a lot of questions, be careful which stories you tell and when. You have plenty of time!

❑   If you were on a mission that involved training in different countries or in a perceived "glamorous" location, be sure all your stories aren't about your liberty in port. Family members may be jealous or resentful of your "pleasure cruise" while they were at home waiting for you.

❑   Show pleasure and interest in how your family has grown.

❑   Remember that spending money without planning can lead to trouble later. Respect your spouse's budgeting efforts. It doesn't have to be expensive to be fun or romantic.

Sometimes when too much time elapses before a family seeks help they need, they start to attribute the problems to something else other than the deployment separation/reunion. For example, if a couple has trouble communicating or reestablishing intimacy after the deployment, they may gradually grow apart. One spouse may overindulge in work or a hobby. The other may become depressed. If the marriage falls apart, they may blame compulsive work habits or depression for the divorce rather than the long separation and lack of proper reunion.

Take fifteen minutes each day.

When you get back together, you'll eventually fall into a daily living routine. How you structure that routine is important. Don't go by old habits. Listen to each other and discover your current needs. While all the time you spend together is important, there are fifteen very important minutes each day that can set the groundwork for reconnecting and building your relationship. What do you and your spouse (together or individually) do:

❑ during the first five minutes when you wake up in the morning?

❑ during the first five minutes together at the end of the work day?

❑ during the last five minutes before you go to sleep?

Is saying "I love you" part of that routine?

In the morning

Some people like to receive a kiss first thing in the morning. Others like to sleep in and just get a kiss goodbye when a spouse leaves for work. Others like to eat breakfast together. What would your spouse like to do in the morning?

After work

During the first five minutes after a long day at work, few people enjoy being grilled, criticized, given a list of problems, or hearing everyone's complaints about the day. Some people do like to spend a few minutes by themselves, changing clothes and men-

Happy Reunions

Couples who've enjoyed many happy reunions share these tips:

❑   Communicate openly and honestly.

Communicating in person doesn't mean you have to do away with letters or notes. If you're having trouble finding the right words or still feel in the habit of having written warning before a discussion, try exchanging notes. Useful openings include:

> "While we were apart I..." (tell about one special thing you did or thought about or discovered)

> "In the next few days/weeks, I'd like you to..." (here's your chance to say what you need, whether it's time alone or romance)

> "Some things in our relationship I'd like to consider renegotiating are..." (be reasonable and choose the things most important to you)

❑   Accept each other and the changes that have taken place. Approach each other as equals. Express pride in your spouse's accomplishments. Appreciate and encourage further growth.

❑   Make changes slowly. Don't be too quick to take over or give up a responsibility. The old way is not necessarily the best.

❑   Be patient and flexible. Stay confident and optimistic. People may look or act differently, but they are the same people you know and love.

❑   Stay in good physical shape. Bike, run, lift weights, or play sports together. The combination of physical activity and doing something you enjoy together helps relieve stress.

❑   Limit criticism. When needed, keep it constructive. To resolve conflicts, stay on the subject. Don't accuse, blame, confront, or bring up the past. Rather than say, "You always...", use the formula, "I feel...when you... ."

❑   Reaffirm your love and commitment. Jealousy is often caused by insecurity, especially in young relationships.

tally making a transition from work life to home life. Others like to be greeted at the door (by a spouse, child, dog) and welcomed into their home. Some like to retreat to their own special place for a while; others need a few minutes of sharing (not necessarily problem solving!). Find a way to include both preferences. Who gets home first? What would you like? What would your spouse like? What happens after the time alone or the greeting? Most couples like to start the evening off with a positive conversation; some families use the dinner table to relate the day's events and connect with each other. Whatever time and environment you choose, make sure you give each other at least five minutes of your full attention.

Before bed

Every family has a different routine just before bed. Some couples go to bed at different times. Others make love before going to sleep. Some people like to read in bed while others like to go to sleep right away. Most people have a hygiene ritual; make sure yours doesn't infringe on your spouse's. The last few minutes before you go to sleep should be pleasant ones. A good feeling helps you sleep better and puts you in a better state of mind for tomorrow. What does your spouse like?

Here It Comes Again

Some homecomings don't get to the adjustment stage before the couple or family is back to preparing for another deployment. This happens most often with frequent or extended field exercises, or longer unaccompanied tours when the service member comes home for a 2-week to 30-day break.

Heather Langley's husband came home for 20 days in the middle of a one-year tour. "We fought the whole time," she said. With two young children, the couple had hardly any time to themselves. "Between kids in the house and a million things on his 'to do' list, we just couldn't connect. It definitely was not romantic at all." Their 3-year-old son had adjusted to daddy being a picture on the wall and occasionally a voice on the phone. "He was confused at first; but after about a week with dad in person, they were having a great time together," Heather explained. "We had to go through the whole adjustment thing again when daddy left. Our daughter (8 months old) didn't know him at all. She was afraid of him and glad to see him leave!" Despite the difficulty of the short reunion, Heather (like most spouses) says she's glad for the opportunity. "It's really, really hard on us. But when he's gone, I miss him so much. It's worth the extra effort to spend even a few days together." Heather and her husband said next time will be much easier, now that they know what to expect. And they plan to better communicate their own expectations to each other before the reunion.

The Rest of Your Life

Your new life together may or may not include more military deployments. Chances are good that you'll have some form of separation, even if only for a short time. Hopefully, what you've learned from each other during this deployment and reunion will carry you through other challenges you face as a couple and family. If you think about a deployment in the context of your whole life together, it's a relatively short amount of time. The following relationship tips are adapted from Dr. Anne Goshen's research with couples who reached their Golden Anniversary:

- ❏ *Pick your fights.* Constant battles over small issues are emotionally taxing and tend to blunt the impact when you really need to make an important point.
- ❏ *Be a friend to each other.* Show your partner the same trust and loyalty you give and expect from your best friend.
- ❏ *Communicate.* Don't expect your partner to be a mind reader. If something is important to you, talk about it.
- ❏ *Say "I love you."*
- ❏ *Be romantic.* Just because you've been married for a

while doesn't mean you can't hold hands or plan a special evening together.

❑ *Have a life outside the marriage.* Find time for at least one outside activity. A little bit of independence can enhance your relationship.

❑ *Resolve disagreements.* Disagreements that are left unfinished can fester and lead to deep resentment. Never go to bed angry.

❑ *Show you care with your actions.* Do something nice for each other without having to be asked.

❑ *Share.* Make time to share projects, ideas, concerns, dreams.

❑ *Take care of yourself.* Take pride in your appearance and health.

❑ *Hang in there.* All couples go through rough times, emotionally and financially, but for some these crises make the relationship stronger. Keep in mind what brought you together in the first place.

❑ *Enjoy every homecoming.* Whether it's eight months or eight hours, be glad each time you have one more opportunity to be together again.

Epilogue

Once upon a time there was a Marine and his family. The Marine traveled around the world helping people who were suffering, defending people who wanted freedom, and practicing how to use his equipment so he would be ready when called to duty again. His family prayed for his safety, cared for each other and the families around them, and wrote lots of letters about how quickly they seemed to be growing up in his absence.

I spent a few years writing this book. I read hundreds of articles and research reports, listened to families talk about their experience, read old letters and journals, and often cried without realizing it. I became lost in that world of deployment and survival all over again—the amazing rescue missions, the pride, the deep love and perseverance. I held workshops for military—and civilian—families and shared the tips in this book with them. In each story, each workshop, a familiar theme arose: plan, communicate, use resources, and go through the experience together. I hope this book helps you be more prepared for and better understand deployments and gives you ideas for ways to make the experience a positive one for you and your family.

My military deployment experiences taught me many things.

I gained a close Marine Corps family.

There were a few deployments during which I was so caught up in what I was going through personally that I took for granted or simply didn't recognize I had something people outside the military didn't have. I had a community of friends, some of whom I may not have chosen on my own, who experienced intense life lessons with me and became my best friends. A close circle of people I could trust, who had seen me and shared themselves with me at our weakest and strongest moments. We are still close friends after many years and many moves.

I grew to know myself and my husband in a different way.

I could say the Marine Corps took away from me—took my time with my husband, upset our holidays, our routines, made us worry. But in reality, deployments gave us both the opportunity to discover more about ourselves and each other as individuals and as a couple. I had time to explore interests I may not have otherwise invested time in. Bob learned incredible lessons about human suffering that matured him and helped us both put priorities in perspective. Sometimes, our only communication for months was by letter; we shared intimate thoughts that strengthened our friendship and love as we grew to know each other in a different way.

I made a choice to be positive.

Marriage by itself changes the way you view the world; it changes your priorities. Being married to the military adds a bit of chaos to that relationship. But what comes out of it is up to you. If you get to know yourself, allow yourself and your spouse to grow, and communicate how much you care for each other even amidst the chaos, the life-changing experience of a deployment will be a positive one. You'll be happier and your marriage will be stronger. Since my outlook was one of the few things I actually had a say in, I made a choice to make my experience positive.

There is always something to be thankful for.

There is so much to be thankful for when you've survived a deployment. I thank God for bringing Bob home safely from many dangerous situations, including two helicopter crashes. I thank

Bob for working so hard at building our relationship. I thank my family and friends for being there when I needed a laugh. ...And, I am thankful for lessons that will carry me and Bob through other life experiences outside the military.

I make a difference.

One of my proudest moments was when Bob received the Navy Achievement Medal. His commanding officer thanked *me* for making it possible. He thanked *me* for loving Bob and for supporting him as he served his country. Bob told me several times that I made it easier for him to feel good about doing his job while away. Other Marines thanked me for helping their spouses have a positive experience. Don't take your job as a military spouse lightly. You do make a difference!

One day, the Marine came home. He gave each person in his family a big hug and smiled a lot. He and his family talked about their experiences and helped each other get comfortable living together again. They were honest and loving. They thanked each other for their support and for making the experience a positive one. ...And they lived happily ever after.

Index